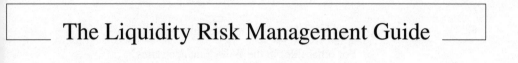

The Liquidity Risk Management Guide

For other titles in the Wiley Finance series,
please see www.wiley.com/finance

The Liquidity Risk Management Guide

From Policy to Pitfalls

Gudni Adalsteinsson

This edition first published 2014
© 2014 Gudni Adalsteinsson

Registered office
John Wiley & Sons Ltd, The Atrium, Southern Gate, Chichester, West Sussex, PO19 8SQ, United Kingdom

For details of our global editorial offices, for customer services and for information about how to apply for
permission to reuse the copyright material in this book please see our website at www.wiley.com.

Library of Congress Cataloging-in-Publication Data

Adalsteinsson, Gudni, 1967–
  The liquidity management guide : from policy to pitfalls / Gudni Adalsteinsson.
    pages cm. – (Wiley finance series)
  Includes bibliographical references and index.
  ISBN 978-1-118-85800-4 (hardback)
  1. Bank liquidity.   2. Bank management.   3. Risk management.   4. Asset-liability management.   I. Title.
  HG1656.A3A33 2014
  332.1068′1–dc23
                                                                                    2014007145

A catalogue record for this book is available from the British Library.

ISBN 978-1-118-85800-4 (hardback) ISBN 978-1-118-85802-8 (ebk)
ISBN 978-1-118-85801-1 (ebk)   ISBN 978-1-118-85803-5 (obk)

Cover design by Jim Wilkie. Front cover image © iStock.

Set in 10/12pt Times by Aptara, Inc., New Delhi, India
Printed in Great Britain by CPI Group (UK) Ltd, Croydon, CR0 4YY

To my family

Contents

Preface

For the past few years liquidity problems have taken centre stage for banking and economic policy. The first wave of the tsunami almost paralysed the funding markets and exposed considerable vulnerabilities within the banking liquidity management. In the absence of suitable solutions and improvements, banks started hoarding cash, which in turn has yet created other kinds of imbalances and liquidity complications. This response was in many cases orchestrated by the regulators.

Part of the problem with liquidity risk lies in its abstract nature. Unlike other types of risk embedded in banking, some of which banks deal with every day, liquidity risk losses are few and far between. Due to the dire consequences of running out of liquidity, both to the bank itself and the wider economy, liquidity failure or losses cannot be assumed to be part of the risk/reward business of banking. Therefore, liquidity risk management can become a world of hypothesis where risk professionals can go happily through their whole career of being the 'liquidity fire-brigade', without ever seeing fire or smelling smoke.

The initial idea for this book came after I worked for one of the Icelandic banks during the last financial crises. After spending years in the United Kingdom and Germany helping banks and funds investing and providing liquidity, I was now on the other side of the equation sourcing funds and liquidity. Having a first-hand experience of how the liquidity fire can go from a distant story on the news to an inferno in your own backyard makes one review and question the framework being used and assumptions applied. What previously were far-fetched scenarios and unlikely assumptions turned out to be the way reality played out. After a brief period at the UK Financial Services Authority, where I had the opportunity to analyse a variety of bank liquidity frameworks across a number of jurisdictions, I noticed how difficult it seemed for some banks to approach this 'hypothetical' problem of liquidity risk in an organized manner. Most banks use the individual ingredients of a liquidity management framework, such as liquidity stress testing or a Contingency Funding Plan (CFP), but in far too many cases this is done separately from each other. Fewer seem to have put the individual pieces of the puzzle together into an integrated framework where the results of one part are used in the other.

All of this made me want to create an approach that puts all the various areas of liquidity risk management into a single overarching framework. After much deliberation a framework skeleton was born where the focus was on creating a general approach that could both alert and mitigate various kinds of liquidity risk, keeping in the back of my mind the lessons learnt from the past. The framework includes all the familiar pieces but the approach, which is of crucial importance, is different and new. The outcome and quality of a liquidity framework is largely dependent on how it is being built up and in which order. Liquidity risk management is to a certain extent based around a set of assumptions on which the outcome is reliant and thus the framework needs to be built up in a step-by-step approach. By doing so the methodology – and its shortcomings – are better known by stakeholders. Being able to recognize and understand the limitations of each of the parts as well as the framework as a whole is of vital importance. The only way to accomplish such a review properly is through an integrated framework. This method is in contrast to lining up all the individual parts in a 'to-do list' and referring to them as a methodology.

Liquidity risk management is a continually evolving field, where past mistakes are used to shape future methods. However, rather than trying to come up with a solution that would only have helped in the special circumstances during the last crises, the framework put forward in the book is focused on the general principles and underlying characteristics of liquidity risk. Recognizing that liquidity risk is not dead and that it is not known how or where it will present itself next time, the aim is to find the source of the problem instead of trying to cure the symptoms.

List of Figures

1

Introduction

Much has been written about what went wrong in banking prior to and during the financial crises. These are, however, in many cases two distinct elements, which both contributed to the unprecedented financial crises.

From the start of the new millennium banks and capital markets enjoyed almost extraordinary times of prosperity where almost every factor both external and internal helped to fuel the growth. Macroeconomic conditions were generally good in the Western world and globalization became more than a buzz word with the influx of Asia and the Eastern bloc. Banks and in fact many other industries were reaping the benefits of deregulation, which had taken place simultaneously in various corners of the world. Apart from a short breather around the dotcom bubble the markets were moving forward at a great pace.

Credit spreads dropped, which helped to fuel the real economy and mid-sized corporates were financing themselves at yields only available to quality sovereigns a few years earlier. The other side of the coin was the search for sufficient yields on investments, which became more and more challenging as time passed with the ever increasing inflows of cash. Technological advances both within actual systems and the field of financial engineering meant that banks met investor demand for 'unchanged' yields with increasingly complex derivatives products. There is no reward without risk and in spite of the strong ratings that most of these products were granted, a higher reward was gained by additional risk. Leverage became a key ingredient in the returns offered. The 'plain vanilla' fixed income instruments were replaced by structured products and the emphasis of investment banks shifted accordingly. The team in which I had started in one of the investment banks shifted within a couple of years from being the distribution platform for new bond issuance from various companies to structuring and marketing different kinds of collateralized obligations and structured investments to the same investor base.

All pictures have cracks if looked at closely enough and the one painted above was no exception. The increased leverage in the overall system made it vulnerable to any market adjustments or even changes in assumptions on credit quality. The story of how effectively one product in one country (subprime housing loans in the United States) triggered global turmoil has been well covered.

This is the first part that went wrong. The second part was the inadequacy of banks and banking systems to withstand the external shocks, which led to the full-blown financial crises. The wave that hit the systems was of unprecedented magnitude but the walls and blocks in place to prevent the risk were in many cases inadequate. The biggest shortcomings were the lack of adequate liquidity systems, which is the area this book focuses on.

Much changed in the aftermath of the crises. The first response of regulators and supervisors was to apply measurements to prevent the same mistakes being repeated with the aim of restoring the banking system and promoting a more stable economy. Some of the risk measurements that have been put into law and are now being implemented, such as the Basel III framework, are a direct response to the specific factors that went astray. This holds especially true for the new inaugural liquidity ratios, the liquidity coverage ratio (LCR), which will come into effect in 2015, and the net stable funding ratio (NSFR), which is destined to be met with more resistance and may well take a new decade before it becomes a standard. When the criterion for meeting the two ratios is assessed it becomes clear that their purpose is to prevent history from repeating itself, that is avoiding longer-dated assets being financed with short-term liabilities. Once the standards are being met, it will be difficult if not impossible to imagine the scenario from 2007 happening again, which is something all stakeholders will welcome. However, will it avoid other liquidity problems happening? The short answer is no. No single measurement can capture and control all aspects of liquidity risk, however useful it may be.

It is important to realize that there will be liquidity problems again in the future. The only certainty is that as long as liquidity risk is embedded in the banking systems, there is always a possibility that the risk will go out of control. The problem is we do not know what will go wrong, where or which type of risk it might be; the only thing we know is that it will happen again. This is not a 'the end is near' apocalypse forecast and neither is it implying that the magnitude of future problems will be equal to the last one. It is only a fair reminder that liquidity risk is not dead. On the contrary, liquidity problems are more common than most of us realize. As an example, during the savings and loan crises in the United States in the 1980s and 1990s some 1,200 savings and loan associations failed, costing the US taxpayer about $150bn.[1] This shows that liquidity risk is not just something that has been happening over the last ten years.

> If you do not expect the unexpected, you will not find it; for it is hard to be sought out and difficult.

Not knowing where the risk comes from or when it will happen, what is there to do? To make things even worse the liquidity risk cannot easily be identified. It is not listed on any exchange. Nor can it be found on any financial institution's balance sheet. Nonetheless, we have established above that liquidity is a critical factor to the well-being and viability of every financial institution.

The approach in this book can be captured in the above 'expect the unexpected' phrase, which is believed to originate from the Greek philosopher Heraclitus of Ephesus.[2] Though not likely to have been discerning himself about liquidity risk management, Heraclitus did however make a point, which is still valid some 2,500 years later. Rather than trying to avoid the last mistakes from happening, which are well known, it is a better approach to prepare for the unexpected. That can be done by developing a system that can identify various unknown threats from different sources and mitigate them.

In the absence of having a sound methodology some regulators adopted the 'shot gun approach' during the last crises. Not knowing where to aim the best solution was to open fire on anything that moved and hoping the future threats would be amongst the victims. No deaths were reported but many banks have struggled to come to terms with the cost of the burden of maintaining large liquidity buffers, which in some instances do not reflect the risk profile of the firm. For the lack of a better solution, this might be called a pragmatic approach.

However, in the long run the solution is not simply to ask banks to increase their liquidity buffer. Just as investors' most common reaction to increased risk is a 'flight to quality' the regulatory and management approach response to risk failures is sometimes to do more of the same, sometimes much more. This goes on until participants feel the threat has passed or is forgotten. Then these risk measures fall out of favour and are considered as an unnecessary burden for a healthy business. The situation is similar to one we all know while driving. After being through something we felt was a close call we slow down and become more cautious. Nevertheless, it is not long until the experience has worn off and we are back to our usual speed as if nothing had happened. This happens in risk management as well. We are even seeing the same supervisors easing their liquidity requirement again but without a risk justification, effectively admitting to being too conservative the first time around. This does not send the right message to businesses, which need to accept that the liquidity requirements set by the regulators are adequate and for their own good. A lack of support to the regime is not good for anyone. Therefore, the solution is not simply to lock everything down that will be abandoned sooner or later, knowingly or unknowingly, but to introduce tangible improvements.

1.1 THE IMPORTANCE OF AN OVERARCHING LIQUIDITY RISK MANAGEMENT FRAMEWORK

1995	Mexican crises
1998	Russia default
2001	Argentina sovereign default and banking crises
2008	Global financial crises
2012	Greece banking and sovereign crises

Above is a list of a few selected liquidity crises that have taken place over the past two decades. In reviewing them it is difficult to find one single common thread apart from the fact that financial institutions and sovereigns had problems servicing their liabilities when they fell due and payable, which is the very definition of liquidity risk. The history does, however, help in a more general manner as it provides a good understanding of the correlation between liquidity sources and their interplay. An example could be the asset-backed commercial paper (ABCP) (the CP issued by special purpose vehicles with collateralized obligations as its sole assets). ABCP might not cause problems again, but the wider experience of asset contagion is something that has been added to the toolbox of every risk specialist.

In the aftermath of the financial crises, liquidity risk management became the centre of attention. The emphasis on improved liquidity risk management did not only come from the individual bank level and their stakeholders. It was even to a larger extent an ultimatum from central banks and governments on behalf of the taxpayers, to demand that banks should recognize the large implications to the economy should they fail to control liquidity risk properly.

However, there are additional reasons for liquidity risk becoming critical to modern banking. The following fundamental but interlinked reasons can be named: a change in the traditional banking intermediation model and amplified competition. Historically, banks relied on stable and low-cost core deposits (demand, savings and time deposits) as the primary source of funding to generate a portfolio of (rather illiquid) loans held to maturity. This is a fundamental risk, as banks are in general structurally illiquid. However, as long as there was an easy access to stable core deposits banks would in normal circumstances be fine. More recently the availability of alternative investments and savings products offered by a wider variety of financial institutions has resulted in a decline in traditional deposit markets from which banks had funded themselves. Secondly, the technological advancement of customer benefits, where depositors can instantly chose between multiple banks, has changed the competitive landscape of traditional banking and decreased what can be generally called 'core deposits'. Both of these factors call for an improved liquidity management framework, which can be aligned to changing external conditions.

The question then is how well banks are doing in having an adequate liquidity framework in place. Surveys indicate that apart from holding more liquidity than before, liquidity risk frameworks and governance are still not as well developed as other parts of their risk structure and can still be seen as the weakest link.

1.2   THE '6 STEP FRAMEWORK'

The book proposes a new risk management framework to deal with fundamentals of liquidity risk, in any shape or form in which they may arise. Rather than trying to aim at the symptoms of liquidity risk, which are always changing, the focus is set on the fundamental causes, which do not change over time or are different between banks or banking systems.

The book is not a magic pill against all diseases but emphasizes the elements all banks have in common, which can be seen as the core to risk management. By applying a top-down approach when orchestrating the framework the bank will build up a system that is suited to its individual needs and characteristics, rather than trying to mix together various solutions to individual problems. Only by applying the top-down method can the bank be sure that all the risk elements are accounted for and that they come together as individual wheels in a larger machine.

The '6 Step Framework' provides the step-by-step guide to build up the necessary framework and the essential details of each of the subpieces. Most of the mistakes in the past were due to changes in assumptions or the assumptions generally agreed upon simply turned out to be wrong or outdated. Without the adequate assumptions and the way to arrive at the adequate assumptions, even the best models can fail or build up a false confidence. Consequently, the focus within the '6 Step Framework' is on the assumptions and on interlinking each of the pieces together with the others rather than trying to play out each scenario.

Liquidity management is a vast subject and the more complex and sophisticated banks will have to expand on the depth of each of the 6 Steps. The book sets out the critical pieces each part needs to have, such as the layout for liquidity scenario stress testing and the adequate approach. It does, however, leave it up to the risk managers to build up more details if needed for the specific risk to that individual bank. The '6 Step Framework' is a framework into which other methods can be linked as they meet the necessary criteria and comply with the other parts of the framework. The framework is therefore applicable to both small and large banks.

There are a few rules that need to be observed when applying the '6 Step Framework'. The first one is to acknowledge that the framework is not like a recipe book. Every step in the '6 Step Framework' builds on the previous one, which in the end leads to a thought-through system. Starting with the desserts first and then moving to the appetizers will not give the desired results and the risk management chef will find that some of the necessary ingredients will be missing.

Secondly, financial institutions should be aware that liquidity risk management is and should remain a cost centre – but a vital cost centre for the bank's operation and continuity as a going concern. The chapter on the various functions of the ALM (asset–liability management) covers the increased mandate they and the treasury can have and how it can sometimes cross over into capital markets and trading, but the fundamental function of ALM needs to be clearly segregated from profit taking activity, even though they take place close to each other.

Last but not least, the approach is intended to be practical and fill the void in the market place between general high-level policies and some of the advanced technics. As mentioned above, there is a space in the framework for advanced technics as every bank sees fit, but the models should not replace the assumption stage and have a life of their own. The book therefore does not attempt to describe or promote the various detailed methods currently applied but provides the necessary fundamentals they all need to be based on.

1.3   THE STRUCTURE OF THE BOOK

This book makes no special distinction in application to banks or bank holding companies and unless explicitly noted the term 'bank' generally refers to the regulated entity that has both the strategic and operational responsibilities for management of assets and liabilities.

Leading organizations view liquidity risk management as an integral part of the long-term enterprise strategy, not simply a short-term operational undertaking. The '6 Step Framework' can be used to set out the high-level needs of the banks and is not prescriptive in nature. On the contrary, it realizes that the design of liquidity risk management should be tailored to the size, degree of internationalization and the strategy and complexity of the institution's business model.

The book's presentation of liquidity management follows a top-down approach. To make sure liquidity management fits into the overall risk structure the book starts at the very basic elements of banking and sets out the fundamental roles that banks play in the real economy and how this role is one of risk taking, which is embedded in the fabric of banking. When the essential factors of risk versus returns have been explained the book takes a look at the role of the unit that deals with liquidity risk, the asset–liability management unit and the ALCO (Asset–Liability Committee).

As the ALCO is a critical organization for the build-up of a liquidity management framework, the book puts this responsibility into perspective along with the other duties of the committee, which should help in understanding the governance and policy part of the framework better.

After the stage has been set with the overall risk chapters, the book continues narrowing its focus, concentrating on liquidity risk management. The illustration in Figure 1.1, which shows the '6 Step Framework', is also a guide though the liquidity management chapter of the book.

The starting point of the '6 Step Framework' is the bank's analysis of its Sources of Liquidity Risk. This step is an essential prerequisite for the higher steps and jumping steps will increase the risk of falling. It realizes that no two banks have the same Sources of Liquidity Risk. A traditional retail bank funded with client deposit accounts has a materially different funding profile to a securities trading house. The step sets out a mechanism to identify the material sources and gives a list of ten different risk factors banks can assess for their franchise. The

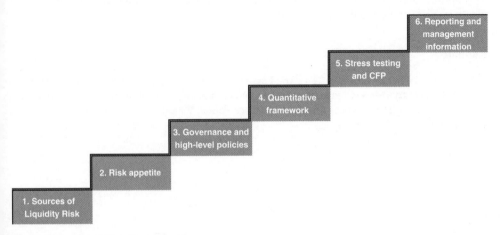

Figure 1.1   The '6 Step Framework'

outcome of the source of liquidity risk assessment is used in various parts of the '6 Step Framework', including stress testing and contingency funding planning.

After analysing the various risk factors the framework starts to build up. Starting by defining and setting out the risk appetite the bank shows that it is willing to accept it as part of its business and decides how that risk can be most appropriately defined and expressed.

The third step of the framework is dedicated to the governance structure the bank needs to have in place to manage its liquidity risk, including defining roles and responsibilities of the various parties and the chain of command and information. This step includes a guide to set out two of the most important policies within the overall framework, the liquidity policy and the funding policy. It also includes the arrangement of fund transfer pricing – a very hot topic within the field, as banks are required to have a system in place to allocate funding cost appropriately to businesses. This item is now commonly on the top of the to-do lists in the banking community.

Under the policy and governance level of the framework lies the quantitative framework, which is the fourth step. This step provides the necessary framework to measure and project the bank's balance sheet. It provides the necessary understanding of the difference between the balance sheet approach and cash flow projections and sets out the different yardsticks used under the various methods.

The fifth step of the framework is dedicated to stress testing and contingency funding planning, both of which are vital parts of the risk mechanism. As this is the penultimate step it builds on the findings of all the previous steps, which all contribute to the bank having an appropriate stress testing based on the bank's risk profile and the contingency plans reflect the individuality of the operations.

The sixth and final step sets out how the information and findings of the previous steps are best communicated within the organization in order to create the best understanding possible at each level within the firm to facilitate better decision making.

Basel III is the topic of the final chapter of the book. This new set of global standards will shape liquidity risk management for years to come and banks across the globe are currently preparing to meet its first measurement deadline. The chapter looks at how to access the Basel III liquidity requirements and what adjustments banks need to make on their suite of assumptions to align them with the global standard. This should help banks access their need to adopt the Basel lens on seeing the universe or whether two separate but parallel systems would be better suited to the bank's needs.

Endnotes

1. See Eisenbeis, R. and Kaufman, G. (2009) Lessons from the demise of the UK's Northern Rock and the US's Countrywide and Indymac, from The failure of Northern Rock, A Multi-dimensional Case Study, SUERF – The European Money and Finance Forum, Vienna, 2009, p. 87.
2. Heraclitus (c.535 BC–475 BC).

2

Primer in Banking

Although this book focuses on liquidity management and liquidity risk it is useful before embarking on that tour to take a top-down look at the role banks play in the real economy and the risk associated with being a service provider of funds. This will provide a better understanding of the embedded risk in banking.

The central role of a bank is one of being a financial intermediary. As other intermediaries it buys goods and services from producers and sells them to the final user (consumer). This analogy might seem alien to banking, but a clear example would be the trading and brokering services banks provide and where their role is one of being the middleman. As further expanded later, a retail bank is also an intermediary when it takes deposits from depositors and lends onwards. Here the flow of services or products might be the opposite from the usual definitions; that is in retail banking we have the consumer providing the products (deposits) and the final user or beneficiary can be a producer (a firm).

Why does the economy need a middleman? The answer has certainly changed over the centuries as banks have evolved from a place of safekeeping to more active business partners and risk takers. In today's technologically advanced economy, there are surely markets that could link the fund provider with the user, but apart from the obvious transaction cost and the difficulty of matching the two interested parties, there are other fundamental reasons why banking exists and where liquidity risk plays an important role.[1] Freixas and Rochet, amongst others, have pointed to the economies of scope and scale as the main contributors to the existence of banking.[2] An example of economies of scope is where an intermediary (with limited liability) is needed to match providers with a low-risk appetite to a user with a high-risk appetite. They also point out the role information asymmetries play in making the middlemen take a role in the business. The most obvious reason in the eyes of the layman is the economies of scale, which make banking a useful service provider, and of course the maturity transformation service, which we will discuss in detail later in the book.

Figure 2.1 is a simple diagram of the intermediary role of a bank, which is both a deposit taker and a lender. The focus of this book is the relationship between the assets and liabilities and the risk it creates. This is where banks get their rewards from underwriting and managing the risk.

2.1 RISK IN BANKING

The 'risk and reward' square in the following illustration is the function of risk management, dealing with all the various elements of risk involved in transposing deposits into loans. The risk in banking is multidimensional and intercorrelated but can be simplified into credit risk, interest rate risk/market risk and liquidity risk. Embracing these three categories of business risk is the operational risk that is embedded into every process and action the bank conducts. Figure 2.2 is a high-level risk overview for a bank.

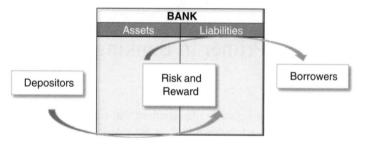

Figure 2.1   The role of banks as intermediaries

The four categories differ in the way they impact the bank, some through the capital, others through the profit and loss accounts and yet others affect both. Figure 2.2 is a way to demonstrate an effective risk framework within a banking organization. At the centre there are three types of core business risk within banking: credit risk, interest rate/market risk and liquidity risk. The next layer of risk is operational risk, which stems from 'inadequate processes, people and systems', as defined by the Basel Committee for Banking Supervision (BCBS) and encompasses the whole of the bank.[3] To capture the risk the bank has an overall risk infrastructure, which should be based around the principle of people, processes, systems and technology and reporting. These are only the primary categories of risk in banking and there are other risk factors at play. The *Comptroller's Handbook* (OCC) defines seven categories of risk that are in addition to liquidity risk, credit, interest rate, price, operational, compliance, strategic and reputation risk, and various other lists have been created.[4] The following subcategories of the major four are:

- Credit risk
  - Retail and corporate credit risk (lending risk)
  - Counterparty risk

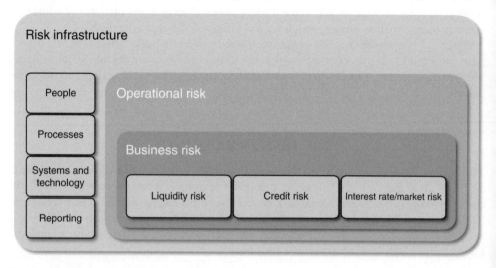

Figure 2.2   Overview of risk in banking

- o Settlement risk
- o Country risk
- Market risk
  - o Interest rate risk
  - o Foreign exchange risk
  - o Equities
  - o Commodities
- Liquidity risk
- Operational risk
  - o Execution risk
  - o Model risk
  - o Fraud
  - o Legal risk
  - o Regulatory risk

Interest rate risk is categorically a subcategory of market risk but is highlighted here as it is one of two major responsibilities assigned to the ALCO and ALM units.

2.1.1 Managing the Risk

From a top-down view we can conclude that the role and function of banks is to manage risk for a fee. As straightforward as this may sound, this is what makes banks different from other industries and in fact what banks have even been criticized for doing. Banks can be called risk machines and managing risk is their core competence, just as flying aircraft is the heart of an airline. The difference is that the airline tries to avoid risk as much as is conceivable and aims to be as risk free as possible. Luckily, taking risks is not within their business model. Banks, however, take risks for a living and are all to some extent risky. This is one of the reasons we get paid interest on our deposits as we are getting paid for the risk of the bank not being able to honour the obligation at the expiry date. Continuing with the airline comparison, the business model the airline operates looks at an incident where risk has materialized as a failure of their risk controls or processes. Banks, on the other hand, realize that taking risk for a living means that sometimes the risk will reveal itself and create losses. This is understood by bankers and the reason why banks make provisions for this, but sometimes this is forgotten by observers who believe something must have gone wrong in a bank that reports delinquencies or bad loans. Needless to say, banks should not simply underwrite the risk, fasten their seatbelts and hope nothing will go wrong, but operate systems, processes, controls and hedging strategies to mitigate some of the risk. Not all of the risk can be protected, as they would most likely put themselves out of business by doing that, but generally they aim to hedge or mitigate the possible impact of significant risk factors that would have a material impact on their earnings or viability. This is why the field is called risk management and not risk prevention. Consequently, the approach to risk is also materially different from other industries where risk monitoring is associated with ensuring the operations meet certain external (often regulatory) minimum standards. Banks working efficiently with risk is a way for them to enhance their profitability as well as decreasing risk levels. Even within banks themselves there is not a full understanding of the concept that sometimes associates risk with compliance, especially for risk that has a low probability. This has made banks vulnerable to low probability but high severity events, as we saw in the last financial crises.

The example above describes different ways to respond to risk and can be set out in a more formal method which places risk in one of four categories, depending on how it should be responded to:

Avoid:	Some types of risk need to be avoided all together. This is clearly applicable to risk or risk events that would have a material negative impact on the financial viability of the firm, liquidity shortfall being one of them.
Mitigate:	Another response is to mitigate the risk if possible. This applies more often to items that are not great in size or impact and hence can easily be mitigated without much cost. A stable funding profile is an example of a mitigation of liquidity risk.
Transfer:	Hedging or transferring risk is another way of decreasing the overall riskiness of the balance sheet. As hedging comes at some cost, this is only defensible for risk of some importance (such as interest rate risk) that justifies the cost. As explained further below, the problem with liquidity risk is that it can only be remedied with more liquidity, which makes risk transfer a difficult exercise.
Accept and manage:	Factors that are too expensive to transfer (hedge) or mitigate need to be managed and this is where most of the liquidity risk factors end up.

What falls into each category depends on the business model and the industry the firm is within.

If banking is mainly about accepting and managing risk, it does indicate that being wrong some of the time seems to be unavoidable. This is, however, where liquidity risk sets itself apart from other factors like credit risk. Banks cannot run assuming they will from time to time suffer some losses due to lack of liquidity. In terms of credit risk, they know that no matter how good their lending practices are they will experience loan losses (again this is why banks charge us for the loans they provide). For mainly two reasons this is not possible for funding and liquidity risk.

Firstly, liquidity can only be amended with more liquidity. This might sound ambiguous but is a vital cornerstone in the building of liquidity frameworks. We will look at the example of lending again. By putting reserves aside, the bank can prepare itself for unexpected loan losses. Both general and specific provisions make the bank able to withstand losses and the bank's capital is there to act as a buffer and absorb losses. A liquidity event, that is an event where the bank cannot meet its obligations when due, cannot be rectified with provisions. Nor can the problem be remedied with the capital buffer, as the assets the capital is invested in may not be sufficiently liquid to provide cash should the need arise. As a side note, we therefore understand that a bank can be solvent but not liquid.

The only remedy is more liquidity, which is either cash or assets that can be turned into cash. This is one reason why a liquidity shortfall is not a 'business-as-usual' event and why banks try to avoid event-driven liquidity risk. However, banks do underwrite and take on liquidity risk as part of their business and this is probably the biggest service they provide to the real economy, which we will discuss later, but liquidity event risk or shortfalls are not part of that risk taking.

Unpredictability is another major factor why banks do not run the risk of running out of funds. Liquidity events are by their nature low probability events but sometimes with severe impacts and consequences. The problem here is the probability of a liquidity risk happening that cannot be measured or calculated. With credit risk, even a simple assumption about the risk makes it quantifiable. If we assume, let us say, 1% of the total loan balance defaults each year we have an estimate of the probability. We can build that and the severity of empirical

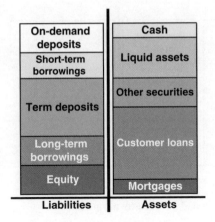

Figure 2.3   A simplified balance sheet for a commercial bank

data and models. Liquidity risk is stochastic in its behaviour, which, along with the uncertain severity, makes it impossible for banks simply to 'run with it'. One of the factors in liquidity risk is the level of confidence in the intuition. Only by breaching their obligation to the bank can a borrower not pay on his loan, whereas in many instances a liquidity risk can arise simply because the depositor, or rather depositors, decide all at the same time to take out their money from the bank, something they have the right to do. This example of lack of confidence shows how different and unpredictable liquidity risk is. No one can forecast a 'level of confidence' into the future or assign a probability for it to decrease or fall.

This uncertainty results in banks maintaining liquid assets to an amount that is far higher than their historical need for liquidity and (hopefully) much more than they will ever need to use. This uncertainty and 'waste' of resources makes proper liquidity management an instrument both to mitigate risk and increase earnings.

2.1.2   The Bank's Balance Sheet

When narrowing the focus liquidity risk it is useful to draw up a high-level balance sheet for a conventional bank (see Figure 2.3). This will further extract the origin of the liquidity risk. On the liability side the bank has deposits and borrowing, which are either short dated or for a longer period of time. These along with the equity are used to fund the bank's assets, which are mainly customer loans and securities. These are the basic categories and the size of each bucket is determined by the type of financial institution. A securities house will usually have a high reliance on short-term funding, especially secured funding, and very little if any deposits. Its asset base will mainly contain securities and other tradable instruments and a limited amount of customer loans. Due to the liquidity risk discussed earlier, that bank will not only hold cash sufficient to bridge the timing gap for payments but also a buffer of liquid assets to a level we would only expect to see in banks that serve the purpose of mitigating liquidity risk. To understand liquidity risk better, it is helpful not to think of the balance sheet as a static amount of assets and liabilities as they appear in financial statements. Instead, we should think of the assets and liabilities as streams of payment going in and out of the bank, some within a few days and others further out in the future. Every asset (let us say a loan) starts as a payment going out of the bank, which then gets repaid over time with principal

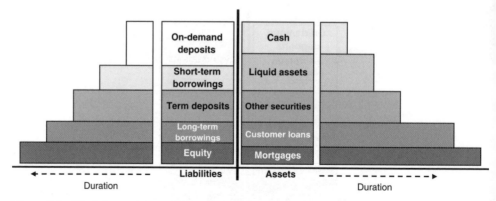

Figure 2.4　The balance sheet and the maturity mismatch

and interest rate repayments. Analysing the balance sheet through this lens we see that this static picture is not very helpful in understanding the risk at hand. Even though the items of the balance sheet add up and we have sufficient funding to finance the assets, we cannot see if the funds are available at the point in time when they are needed. The critical time element is missing and it is the timing of cash flows that is the core of liquidity risk. To complicate things, it is not only the mismatch of the cash flow streams that is the risk (cash flow mismatch is a key concept in liquidity risk) but the general imbalances between the cash flows for the assets versus those for the liabilities. The main characteristic of a bank's balance sheet and for the banking system as whole, for that matter, is its short-dated cash flows on the liability side but long-dated flows on the assets side. This is the main service banks provide to the real economy when they turn short-dated liabilities into long-dated loans,which is referred to as maturity transformation risk. When the balance sheet shown in Figure 2.3 is drawn up again, this time with the maturities of each balance sheet item next to it, we see the embedded risk (see Figure 2.4). The liquidity balance sheet looks different from the usual financial statement as it adds the timing aspect to the illustration of quantum.

Figure 2.4 shows the duration of the assets and liabilities as well as their quantum. We can see that even for a bank that has a well-balanced and diversified liability base, the asset side has a longer duration than the liabilities, creating the transformation risk.

This inherent or embedded risk in banking is one of major reasons why liquidity risk management is of importance.

Endnotes

1. Technological advances and changes in customer behaviour have resulted in interesting developments on how fund providers can reach the fund users without formal intermediaries. Portals specializing in pooling of savings and matching have become popular and such concepts as crowd funding have emerged.
2. Freixas, X. and Rochet, J.C. (2008) *Microeconomics of Banking*, The MIT Press, Cambridge, Massachusetts.
3. Bank of International Settlements (2008) *Principles for Sound Liquidity Risk Management and Supervision*, September 2008.
4. Office of the Comptroller of the Currency (OCC) (2012) *Comptroller's Handbook*, Washington, DC, June 2012.

3
The ALM Function – The Framework on Top of Liquidity Management

Even though this book focuses on liquidity management and policy and as such is not a book about ALM, it is important to understand how liquidity management fits into the overall framework of asset–liability management. In this chapter we will therefore discuss the various tasks ALM is responsible for.

The term Asset–Liability Management (ALM) is a loosely defined term by market participants but for the purposes of this book ALM will be viewed *as the strategic and tactical management of a bank's assets and liabilities*, rather than execution or tactical allocation only. ALM is therefore the practice of managing risk that rises due to mismatches between the assets and liabilities of a firm and can be defined as a strategic management tool to manage interest rate risk and liquidity risk. As such ALM is part of the risk management framework of a bank, but does not limit its scope to one type of risk but rather all risk factors that come into play when a mismatch is between assets and liabilities. This makes the ALM approach to risk management different from other risk bodies in three major ways.

Firstly, as opposed to other committees or divisions within a firm that have their mandate specified by the type of risks, such as a credit risk committee, ALM looks at various different risk factors.

Secondly, the ALM is empowered to focus on strategic decisions as well as tactical implementation. Thus, whereas a credit committee makes specific (tactical) decisions about certain lending proposals, the ALM or specifically the ALCO (Asset–Liability Committee) is rather focused on setting the strategy and making sure the firm operates within the overall objectives and policies. ALM is therefore a decision channel from objectives into actions. However, most ALM functions have differentiated between the strategic element, which is usually set by the ALCO, and the tactical duties, which can include implementation of the strategy.

The third characteristic of the ALM is that its mandate spans the entire legal entity of the firm or even a group. The ALM function should be conducted centrally at a sufficiently high level to have a complete overview of all the activities of the bank.

The scope of the ALM role does vary, depending on the size and the complexity of the organization, but the core functions are liquidity and interest rate risk. In addition to these main responsibilities, ALM or its governing body can also be charged with powers over market risk, capital management and even overall credit risk. Some banks also have their management accounting and monitoring of forecasts and planning within ALM.

Financial institutions were the first to start ALM operations but corporates now also apply ALM strategies and techniques. An airline hedging its fuel cost or a manufacturing company hedging the price of steel for its production can be seen as ALM practices.

3.1   ALM WITHIN RISK, FINANCE AND THE BUSINESSES

In the traditional organization a bank had a clear distinction between the businesses, that is the risk taking unit and the finance unit, which provided the support functions including risk monitoring. As banks expanded the need for firm-wide but still centralized risk functions became apparent, which took over the monitoring and supervision of all risk factors. To be able to quantify the risk, banks needed to be able to aggregate each risk type from the different businesses. It also became evident that some types of risk were best managed centrally for the whole firm. This created the need for a centralized ALM function, which took on the role of risk monitoring, measuring and managing. The ALM function is different from the risk division as it does not only measure and watch over the risk but also actively manages it, and is as such a risk taking unit. An example would be a bank that manages its interest rate risk. The bank's ALM function is responsible for the interest rate risk identification, monitoring and managing, whereas the risk function does not manage risk. ALM is therefore both a front line operation and a second line of risk defence. This deviation from the rule of separating risk taking from risk monitoring is due to the nature of the risk ALM is responsible for and within most banks the risk division is responsible for all risk factors apart from the interest rate risk and liquidity risk. This can create a gap in the possibility of the risk officer having a complete view of all risk factors. This is usually mitigated by aligning the ALM into the overall risk framework by having the risk unit assuming the role of a controller and by having the risk committee approving the ALM's methodology and policies.

There is, however, not a single mould for an ALM function and it varies a lot where banks draw the line between ALM and risk. In some banks, ALM acts solely as a passive risk unit providing the only monitoring and measurement functions, whereas elsewhere ALM makes 'business' decisions on funding strategy, deposit pricing and interest rate management. ALM methods are still being developed and the focus is increasing on the forward looking business partner role of ALM and how it can actively contribute to increased profitability. This reflects the new tools available, such as fund transfer pricing (FTP) methodology. The way banks split the tasks between risk and ALM is usually a clear indication of how advanced they are in using the tools ALM has to offer.

3.1.1   Centralization versus Decentralization

The degree of centralization of the ALM function is yet another issue of various approaches. Banks have adopted a variety of structures to manage liquidity risk, reaching from highly decentralized to highly centralized. There is no 'one-size-fits-all' approach but the reason for the decentralized approach, which in many ways goes against one of the best practice principles of doing liquidity management at the highest level in the firm, is either historical or a result of its funding franchise. Banks located in one market usually follow the centralized approach as it is the most simple and yet effective way for them to manage their risk. Financial groups, which in some cases have been created by mergers of banks operating in different markets, can have a different approach. In some instances the units have little in common and are run independently. As will be discussed later in Chapter 6 under the Sources of Liquidity Risk, it is still important for groups to have a degree of centralization, if for nothing else than to avoid the contagion should one part of the group suffer.

The reasons behind the choice of model are various. When the Swedish banks entered the Baltic States and set up their subsidiaries there, they followed the centralized model. Factors like the size and stability of the Baltic countries versus their home market, the use of the same currency and economies of scale all contributed to the subsidiaries being largely financed through intercompany funding. Whether the problems that occurred later on in the Baltic region could have been more easily managed under a decentralized model is a difficult call to make, but the sharing of the burden would have been different.[1] In general the level of centralization can be described as:

- Fully centralized. For banks to be able to run a fully centralized liquidity management function, there has to be no limitation of movements of funds between different parts of the banks. This is usually not fully applicable for banks that operate across different jurisdictions but is common amongst smaller banks. This is also the model of choice for firms that usually have more challenging funding profiles, such as security firms, where they need to be able to source money through a centralized issuing desk and utilize various areas of the bank.
- Centralized with exceptions. Most banks of a critical size and sophistication fall into this category. The aim and strategy is towards centralization to embrace the benefits of a single overview and approach but at the same time there can be areas where the business model or sometimes even systems do not justify or support the centralized approach.
- High decentralization. Banks operating in various markets with little but the name in common are an example of this sort. If entities are self-funded or attract most of their funding from the local markets (especially if they deal in various currencies) then the decentralized approach is appropriate. This does not suggest, however, that no centralized functions should operate. At the bare minimum, there need to be group-wide policies and minimum standards for liquidity management and a centralized platform to analyse each unit's performance, strategy and risk profile. Some of the well-known banking collapses were due to lack of central support and oversight over satellite offices away from the bank's headquarters.

The section on funding strategy (Section 8.5) discusses in more detail the relationship between the funding strategy and liquidity management.

3.1.2   Accounting and ALM

The role of asset–liability management has developed over time and is linked to the development of accounting methods. Traditionally and in its simplest form, banks used accrual accounting for most of their operations. On the liability side they would take deposits and at later stages also borrow money from the capital markets. They would then invest those proceeds in assets by granting loans or other types of investments. Both the liabilities and assets were predominately held at book value. This opened up the risk of assets and liabilities developing in a different manner over time due to the different structures of those instruments. The most obvious risk is the interest gap risk, where the assets and liabilities of the bank have different interest resetting frequencies, usually with the liability side being more short dated than the assets. Should the interest rate increase the bank would need to refinance a loan at a higher yield than before. The shortcoming of the accrual accounting method in this case is that it does not respond to this change in economic conditions soon enough, though eventually a higher funding cost will be visible once the refinancing has taken place. We will come back to different types of interest rate risk later but a simple example should explain this problem.

A bank takes deposits from the public at the annual rate of 2% with a 2 year maturity and grants a 5 year loan at 2.5%. The bank appears to be profitable at the outset, earning 0.5% in interest income per annum. However, the bank now has a gap risk as the deposit is only for 2 years but the loan granted is for 5 years (the assumption here is that the interest rate is fixed once and for all for the loan and the deposits). After one year the interest rate has changed, the public is demanding 3% rates for deposits and the 4 year prevailing lending rate is now 4% (the observed lending rate is now for 4 years as 1 year has already passed). The bank is now faced with a problem. Their own funding cost has risen so they are soon to become unprofitable and, secondly, the loan they granted is below the prevailing market rate. The accrual accounting will not realize this problem at year 1 and will show a profit in year 1 equal to 0.5% net interest income, not realizing the change in the environment, which can jeopardize the going concern of the bank.[2] Mark-to-market or market value accounting will show different results after 1 year, taking into account the higher refinancing cost and the cost of lending below market rates. Therefore, the accrual method is not applicable to reflect the interest income risk the bank is now faced with while the market value method highlights the risk. As banks are required to follow the accrual accounting method and can only use market value for a limited part of their assets, the use of ALM methods was seen as a substitute for market value accounting. Today the role of ALM is wider but the origin derives from accounting and how to best manage the risk on the banking book.

3.2   THE ASSET–LIABILITY COMMITTEE (ALCO)

We will begin by taking a 'top-down' view of asset liability management, starting with the committee empowered to make the high-level decisions on the composition of assets and liabilities, namely the Asset–Liability Committee (ALCO). The role of the ALCO can be seen as the same as the role of the ALM unit, with the former being the decision-making authority and the latter the department that executes the ALCO's decisions.

The overall role of the ALCO committee is to set the strategic direction in asset and liability risk management by focusing on the balance sheet as a whole for either a legal entity or a group, whichever is appropriate. These main objectives can be further laid out as:

- To provide a transparent aggregated overview of the quality of earnings and assets and assess the impact of changes in risk drivers.
- To ensure that all risks under its control are proactively controlled and managed and that risk levels are within the limits and risk appetites set by the Board.
- To provide a forward looking strategy on how to manage its risk drivers and incorporate those into the business decisions and product pricing.

These overall goals or objectives are supported by the appropriate governance, policies and risk framework for each of the risk categories it is responsible for. As the first step is one of setting the proper governance, it is a good practice to set the ALCO defined terms of reference or mandate letter. These should include the following:

- Where the ALCO gets its power and to whom it reports. This can be the Board, Executive Committee (Exco) or a subcommittee of the Exco.
- Who the members of the ALCO are and how the committee reaches its decision (voting, quorum). As the ALCO has a broad authority it is considered important that the members are from the ranks of senior management, including the CEO. Some banks have a hierarchy of ALCOs within the group but as a rule the most senior committee is attended by senior staff. It is important to include the business heads in the ALCO to ensure it is empowered to be a service partner to the businesses and its decisions are balanced between the needs

of risk and business. The ALCO usually consists of the following members: CEO, CFO, CRO, Treasurer, Head of ALM and the relevant business heads.
- Duties of the ALCO. The terms of reference should set out all the duties of the ALCO, starting with a list of risk types that fall under its power. They will include:
  - Liquidity and funding risk, including liquidity stress tests, contingency funding plans and funding strategy.
  - Interest rate risk, both in the banking book and trading and other drivers of net interest income sensitivity.
  - Structural nondiscretionary interest rate risk in the banking book and other potential noninterest rate drivers of income volatility.
  - Review and analysis of business and operating plans and how they impact the asset and liability mix.
  - Capital management and adequacy.
  - Fund transfer pricing (FTP) mechanism.
  - Funding pricing decisions and strategy.
  - Foreign exchange risk.

The duties and role of the ALCO are further discussed in the next chapter.

The ALCO would be expected to compose, maintain and update the detailed policies and framework by which the above risk factors are being managed. In its letter of January 2011, the UK regulator justly pointed out the importance of the ALCO being forward looking in its approach, as '*risk and return cannot be managed by looking in the rear view mirror*'.[3] This is an important piece of the mandate the ALCO receives and the one that makes a good ALCO have a material impact on the on-going business and profitability of the bank. This is also the biggest pitfall of ALCOs. Though monitoring and compliance are of importance in risk management and can be done without a formal meeting, freeing up the time necessary to focus on proactive management of assets and liabilities.

The above-mentioned wake-up call does not appear out of the blue. There is a strong need for greater strategic planning and better utilization of assets and liabilities, not only from a risk perspective but also from a business standpoint. This agenda also falls back to the point of ALCO membership. For the ALCO to have the necessary authority to determine strategy it needs to be composed of senior management. For most banks, this means the Exco members. Without them, the ALCO will fail to reach its goals.

It is vital to set the ALCO the appropriate governance to ensure its alignment with the bank's overall risk framework. This will further help to avoid silos or risk being built up, as happens in a decentralized approach.

Within the organization chart, the ALM unit is usually shown as the entity dedicated to working for the ALCO and executing its decisions. This is not always the case. In many banks the ALM unit forms a part of the treasury and reports to the treasurer, who can assign interest rate and liquidity management to the ALM function but capital management and F/X risk management to other teams. There are also banks that prioritize the risk aspect of ALM and assign the responsibility to the CRO.

3.3   AREAS COVERED BY ALCO

The traditional areas of activities of the ALCO and ALM are set out in Figure 3.1. The scope of mandate of the ALCO varies between banks but almost without exception includes interest rate risk and liquidity risk. In many cases the ALCO is also charged with the power to oversee

Figure 3.1   Areas covered by the ALCO

foreign exchange (F/X) risk and capital management. A balance sheet management survey in 2009 indicated that three-quarters of international banks have assigned the primary oversight of F/X and capital management to the ALCO though the team responsible for the day-to-day management is not always the ALM unit.[4]

3.3.1   Interest Rate Risk Management

Interest rate risk arises due to the timing differences in repricing of assets and liabilities on the bank's balance sheet. It refers to the exposure the bank has to adverse movements of interest rates.

One of the major decisions for the ALCO is in deciding whether the bank should take a relatively neutral approach to interest rate risk or be prepared to pursue a more directional approach with the aim of higher earnings. The overall interest rate policy is set by the ALCO, which gives the management a mandate to use the ALM unit. As explained earlier, all banks carry some level of interest rate risk, which can be seen as a normal part of financial interme-diation, but the ALCO sets the policy on how much should be hedged in the market and what risk limits for interest rate risk the ALM unit has for positioning. As previously described, the ALM measures and monitors the interest rate risk embedded in the banking book of the bank, performs sensitivity analysis and projections on NII (net interest income), taking into account various factors such as gap risk, yield curve shifts, basis risk (frequency of interest rate resetting), etc. Notwithstanding which strategy the bank decides to pursue it needs to have the appropriate processes, systems and resources in place and a market neutral approach should not lead to the focus being taken off interest rate management.

Many banks put the market risk under the same hat as the interest rate risk since the risk drivers are of a similar nature. Market risk describes the sensitivity of the value of positions to changes in market prices. This is similar to interest rate risk where the sensitivity of the positions was to 'rates' instead of 'prices'. The main goal in managing market risk is to avoid the impact of negative price movements as well as keeping the income stream or valuations with as little volatility as possible. The appropriate risk management tool depends on whether the market risk is traded or nontraded. Usually the traded market risk has been modelled and monitored with VaR (value at risk) methodology, but the structural shifts that happened during the financial crises have put a question mark on its usefulness to manage illiquid assets or assets that can become illiquid during turmoil.

3.3.2   Liquidity Risk Management

The foundation for liquidity risk management is the risk a bank, for various reasons, will not be able to refinance its assets as the liabilities come due or to fund asset growth. A further liquidity risk element can be added that is more relevant under normal business conditions, which can be described as the bank being only able to refinance its obligations at higher rates, which can jeopardize the bank's profitability and even its future as a going concern.

Normal banking business will create asset liability mismatch or a funding gap, an excess cash surplus in some maturity buckets and a shortfall in others. In both cases the mismatch needs to be managed. The ALM unit will calculate and report the liquidity gaps (asset–liability mismatch in different maturity buckets) and run a sensitivity analysis on both the assets and liabilities. For a full picture of the situation this will include off balance sheet items as well as on balance sheet items. ALM will calculate the funding needs of the banks and manage the surplus cash and cash-like instruments the bank is required to hold (liquidity buffer). Just as with interest rate risk, liquidity risk is a major component in banking and the two are also connected as the future funding cost is related to the interest rate environment. Liquidity management also influences the net interest margin through the size of the liquidity buffer and the return it provides. As will be discussed later, the gap risk cannot and should not be eliminated but appropriately managed. The actual management of the liquidity portfolio can sit within different parts of the bank, being within the treasury or the ALM team, but more importantly the output of the portfolio, such as the size, quality, limits, etc., should be set by ALM and approved by the ALCO.

As part of the liquidity management mandate the ALCO also is responsible for setting the appropriate liquidity stress testing methodology, reviewing its results and using the findings to incorporate them into the bank's funding strategy.

3.3.3   Capital Reporting and Management

The ALCO's involvement with capital is twofold, around issues of actual capital levels and forward looking. Part of the task is to report on capital usage of different business units and propose capital allocation and charges. The ALCO will also oversee the capital planning of the firm, including the capital forecast and capital generation. This is important in order to provide an insight into how the future balance sheet might look under different scenarios and the financial health of the company.

3.3.4   Setting or Recommending Risk Limits

The ALCO is responsible for setting the appropriate risk limits in the areas of interest, the rate risk and liquidity risk. The setting of major limits should be determined at a higher level within the organization, the Board setting the ultimate risk appetite and the major limits supporting that statement. As the ALCO is closer to the risk factors and their appropriate readings it usually makes its recommendations to the Exco or Board on what metrics are of importance. If the power to set risk limits is delegated to the ALCO then it must be ensured and noted that the limit is within the overall risk appetite statement set by the Board and the appropriate control mechanism needs to be honoured. As ALM is responsible for monitoring compliance with the limits it is important to make sure that there is a distinction between supervision and management; that is those doing the monitoring cannot have the power to change the limits. Setting the limits could just as well be included under the three areas mentioned above and as such is not looked at as a separate area or function of the ALCO. However, it is not unusual to give this role of the ALCO special consideration as it is of a different nature from the other parts the ALCO plays in the liquidity framework. In its limit setting as a delegated authority from the Board, the ALCO is taking the role of supervisor, which needs to be kept separate from the strategic and tactical tasks it performs.

3.4   ENHANCED ROLE OF THE ALM UNIT

The above-mentioned areas of responsibility are the cornerstone of asset and liability management. As they are of great importance to the bank, it is apparent that a well-functioning ALCO and ALM unit are of critical importance, both strategically and operationally.

Banks have increased the mandate of the ALM unit and at the same time a much richer framework has been developed. The ALM unit can have the task of focusing solely on the core functions, interest rate risk and liquidity risk, and act purely as a cost centre. This role of ALM as a simplistic support function is more common in emerging markets where external constraints may limit the scope of the ALM unit as hedging and other tools might not be available. As the markets become more developed the opportunities for a more active ALM function open up and the mandate can broaden. It can still be in the form that ALM only provides a passive asset–liability management service even though it is more advanced than before. Another philosophy is to set up ALM as a profit centre and allow the ALM unit to make a profit out of their interest rate management versus a predefined alternative base case. This is usually done via cooperation between ALM and the treasury, sometimes referred to as 'integrated treasury operations', where the bank keeps directional trades separate from the market making role of the treasury or the money market desk. The market making role of the treasury is sometimes included in units that are more customer focused, such as the capital market division maintaining the 'internal service' role within the treasury. The integrated treasury operations are profit making from their directional trading activity but at the same time provide hedging and other risk mitigation actions. There are understandable challenges in having the same team as a profit and cost unit and banks have tried to keep the mandates somewhat separate.

The most active role is when the ALM unit is provided with a wider mandate by making them involved in the larger balance sheet allocations, also taking capital usage and regulatory capital into account, where the ALM unit is contributing directly to the profit of the bank. This is usually in the form of projects around balance sheet reshuffling or reorganization.

The importance of a strong ALM function has become more pronounced after the events of recent years. Banks have placed their risk into silos, credit risk, liquidity risk, market risk, operational risk, etc., which in order to be more easily managed are viewed separately and independently from each other. This is understandable from a management and process perspective but it is a dangerous pitfall to assume that it is a sufficient method and the various types of risks can be analysed in complete isolation. Recent financial crises showed that one type of risk can transform itself into another and the transformation can happen quickly. What started out as a credit risk problem – or rather a fear of credit problems – soon manifested itself in serious liquidity risk events. This took many banks by surprise as 'credit risk' was not on the 'top 10' list of sources for liquidity crises.[5] This drives the need to develop an integrated view on risk across all types, where the ALCO and risk have the necessary top-down viewpoint to see the firm-wide connections of risk factors (sometimes referred to as enterprise-wide risk management). Such an approach could have alerted banks early enough to avoid the spiral of the financial crises. Moreover, this leads to the argument that an ALM risk framework needs to be built around the distinct characteristics of the bank's operations and to be tailor-made to its functions. No two banks are the same and standardized risk procedures are not sufficient or appropriate, even though the risk analysis and management can be standardized.

The power and scope of the ALCO is usually reasonably clear and easy to define and does not overlap with other parts of the bank's risk framework. The largest exception can be credit risk, where some organizations, usually the smaller ones, have assigned part of credit risk responsibility to the ALCO. In that setup, even though ALM does not manage credit exposure, the setting of risk limits, including overall credit limits, is by the ALCO. This is not to say that ALM is taking over from the Credit Risk Committee and in reality there is limited overlap. The Credit Risk Committee sets the credit risk policy, what type of lending the banking should be doing, what type or credit risk is acceptable and so on. The individual business segments then manage their credit risk within those parameters. The reason that the overall credit risk appetite is discussed at the ALCO is to improve the overview of the assets side of the balance sheet and to make sure that features such as impact liquidity, funding and profitability are aligned.

Endnotes

1. See Committee on the Global Financial System (CGFS), CGFS Papers No. 39, *Funding Patterns and Liquidity Management of Internationally Active Banks*, Bank for International Settlements, May 2010.
2. The conclusions of the accrual accounting method are by no means wrong. It calculates the true cost that has occurred and been realized and will ultimately recognize a similar loss. As the cost has not yet occurred it is not recognized. The interest rate could change again in favour of the bank so this risk does not necessarily have to materialize.
3. See Financial Services Authority (FSA), *Dear CEO Letter – Asset and Liability Management*, FSA, January 2011.
4. See PWC, *Balance Sheet Management Benchmark Survey, Status of Balance Sheet Management Practices among International Banks – 2009*, 2009.
5. This is not to say that bank runs due to (perceived) credit problems are new phenomena. More information flows, increased transparency and increased leverage amongst investors are all things contributing to risks, transforming them much faster than before.

4

Liquidity – Background and Key Concepts

After having set out the main responsibilities of asset–liability management, the time has come to focus on the liquidity part of the mandate. In this chapter the concepts of liquidity and liquidity risk will be brought into the picture and an overview given of the various liquidity concepts. Rather than listing them one by one, it is more useful to introduce them in stages and through examples.

4.1 DEFINITIONS AND MORE DEFINITIONS

In order for something to be measured it first needs to be defined. Liquidity risk is not a new concept; a more fitting portrayal would be to call it an old one. As far back as the late 18th century economists understood the significance of the gap between the cash flows of assets and liabilities.[1] One of the fundamental economic functions that banks provide is 'maturity transformation' by accepting short-term deposits and granting long-term loans. Maturity transformation is fundamentally a part of the liquidity concept, so it can be said that the notion of liquidity is as old as banking and embedded in their role.

As the oldest and most fundamental role of banks is to be an institution for maturity transformation one would expect a general acceptance and understanding of the function they provide. However, as we touched upon in Chapter 1, this seems from time to time to get forgotten and banks have been criticized and even stamped 'reckless' by borrowing short and lending long. As will be discussed in more detail in later chapters, not all short-term funding can be seen as the most risky funding available and there are multiple other factors at play.

4.1.1 Liquidity – Definition

There is a lack of general consensus on how to identify liquidity and no generally accepted, single definition of the term 'liquidity' is to be found. The simplest form of definition would be to define liquidity *as the ability to obtain cash when needed*.[2] Consequently, liquidity can be created by borrowing or converting assets to cash.

Defining liquidity only as a 'stock' of funds does not fully capture all of its attributes. One can also define liquidity as a way to buy time, focusing on the time value of liquidity. This indicates that liquidity is not only a one-dimensional concept solely determined by quantity (an amount) but as importantly is a function of time; that is it matters to have the liquidity *when needed*, as stated above. As every liability and asset on the balance sheet is not only a 'stock' amount but rather a bundle of incoming and outgoing cash flows, we need to define liquidity in terms of time. This is usually the way liquidity is expressed in a bank. For instance, a financial institution is commonly said to hold a number of days of liquidity, meaning the institution has enough liquidity sources to cover a certain number of days of scheduled outflows. This

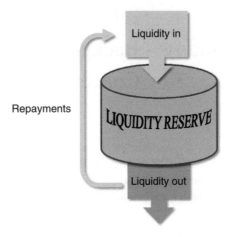

Figure 4.1   Sources of liquidity[3]

expression is useful to the reader as it provides information about liquidity in measures of time, whereas a statement asserting a bank has $100m of liquidity is not a meaningful measurement.

This leads us to the conclusion that liquidity has a quantity as well as a time aspect – both equally important. Figure 4.1 helps to further understand the liquidity concept.

Liquidity can be seen as a tank of money, which increases when money comes in and decreases when funds exit the tank. A bank has a liquidity reserve (a quantity) to meet its outflows (liquidity out), which can either be repayment of outstanding liabilities or the provision of loans. The liquidity reserve builds up by adding new liquidity (liquidity in), which could be in the form of deposits placed with the bank, bond issuance or repayment from its loan portfolio. The quantity in the tank gives a good indication of the liquidity of the bank, but the amount and timing of inflows and outflows are equally important. A small amount of outflow means the tank can support the bank for a long period of time whereas large outflows will make the bank quickly run out of funds. However, it is not only the amount of outflows that is the determining factor. The amount and timing of inflows add to the amount in the tank. We therefore determine liquidity as a combination of the stock (i.e. the liquidity reserve) and the net cash flows.

A bank can identify various sources of liquidity that contribute to the 'liquidity in' stream of funds. These inflows have three possible origins:

1. They can be money borrowed from the market or customers. Increasing its liabilities is the fundamental source of inflows for banks.
2. Money can come in from repayments. When loans made to customers are repaid they turn into a cash inflow for the bank. The same applies to interest rate payments.
3. Asset sales. A bank can create inflows by selling its assets, both liquid and if possible illiquid.

In a nutshell, all funds coming into a bank belong to one of the three above-mentioned categories and only through them can a bank increase its liquidity position. As cash coming in from the businesses (money coming in from repayments) is not really manageable in the short or medium term, liquidity management is mainly focused on the other two, that is how to manage the borrowings and create liquidity with assets.

4.1.2   Liquidity Risk

Having better understood the term liquidity we move to defining liquidity risk. Again, Figure 4.1 can help. Liquidity risk can be explained diagrammatically as the risk related to the previously mentioned inflows and outflows.

A bank can have sources of new liquidity dry up; for instance the bank may not be able to issue new bonds or a lesser amount of new deposits are placed with the bank. On the outflow tap the risk could develop when higher than expected loan growth occurs or higher amounts of deposits are withdrawn than expected. Note that the cash flow risk can come from both sides of the balance sheet. Liquidity risk is therefore not only a function of liabilities but assets as well.

When attempting to formalize the definition of liquidity risk, we again find ourselves in a universe of limited standards, but the most common definition of liquidity risk is: *Liquidity risk is the inability to meet obligations as they become due and payable.* This we can agree is the primary and most rudimentary definition of liquidity risk, that is the risk of default and insolvency. Some authors have expanded on the definition by adding *in the currency required* at the end of the definition and even pointing out the market risk element by adding *expected and unexpected obligations*. Both of these additions are examples of certain specific sources or types of liquidity risk but as there are many other types of liquidity risk, this book does not attempt to incorporate them into the general definition of liquidity risk. Then there are others who define liquidity risk as *the inability to meet obligations as they become due and payable or only being able to do so at an unsustainable cost.*

The definition above is the one generally used for funding liquidity risk. The BCBS definition of funding liquidity risk does include the cost aspect and sees the risk as being that future obligations can only be refinanced at a higher cost or in the worst case scenario as not at all.[4] While the primary liquidity risk definition was an 'either–or' binominal concept of solvency, that is a firm can or cannot settle an obligation at maturity, this extended definition is forward looking and measured over a specific period and can have multiple outcomes, depending on price and time. One of the outcomes, and the most severe one, is default, making this definition in that instance equal to our primary liquidity risk definition. No one wants to pick a fight with the boys from Basel, but the introduction of the cost concept is a double-edged sword. This definition has become more popular as banks have, through technological advancement, enlarged their market place for liabilities and assume that the main problem is not getting the liabilities but rather the price needed to attract them. This is a valid observation and definition, as often the first sign of a liquidity risk is that the bank starts to refinance itself at interest rates that jeopardize its viability. Furthermore, one can argue that this definition reflects more appropriately the liquidity management function. Liquidity risk management is not limited to avoiding default and is rather focused on managing liquidity as efficiently as possible (which is what day-to-day liquidity management is mostly about).

However, there is an argument for not mixing liquidity risk with the price of liquidity. By doing so we are adding the earnings impact to the default risk. The issue with higher costs of supplies for a firm (and we can call liquidity an ingredient for a bank) is not truly a liquidity risk but a general cost issue, which applies to various factors within the firm and to some extent dilutes the purpose of the definition.

Figure 4.2   Definition of liquidity risk

The difference between these two definitions should, however, not cause any complications to the practitioner but it is beneficial to be aware of the different points of view. Even though the former definition is still more accepted this book will promote the latter and conclude that liquidity risk or funding liquidity risk *is the inability to meet obligations as they become due and payable or only being able to do so at an unsustainable cost.*

For the dedicated reader who cannot get enough of definitions, there is more to come. The reason for placing the word 'funding' in front of liquidity risk in the definition above is to differentiate it from another widely used term – market liquidity risk – and the risk literature distinguishes between these two.

Market liquidity risk *relates to the inability to realize assets due to inadequate market depth, or market disruption.*[5] There is an obvious difference between these two concepts but both of them can be the cause of liquidity problems for a bank.[6] The funding liquidity risk happens when the bank cannot refinance its liabilities (which could be due to internal and market-wide problems) whereas market liquidity risk is solely focused on asset value, which is purely an external risk. Therefore, liquidity risk can be further split into funding risk and market risk as demonstrated in Figure 4.2. Some have taken this a step further and broken market liquidity risk into three subcategories but for our purposes the general definition is sufficient.[7]

To make it easier to understand this ocean of definitions it can be helpful to think about funding liquidity risk as the refinancing risk on the liability side of the balance sheet and the market liquidity risk as the liquidity risk associated with the asset side. Even though the literature defines market risk and funding risk as two separate concepts, they are in reality very connected. For a bank that relies on secured funding, market risk and funding risk are very dependent on each other and are in practice two sides of the same coin. For the purpose of this book, however, it is useful to differentiate between the two as it will make the hunt for Sources of Liquidity Risk easier and add to general understanding of the liquidity risk framework. This also helps us to understand the drivers behind liquidity events and consequently take them into consideration when building stress test scenarios and contingency plans.

4.2   THE LIQUIDITY GAP

We have now established that liquidity risk is the risk of being unable to meet obligations as they become due and payable or only being able to do so at an unsustainable cost. One can easily imagine that there can be multiple causes for this risk and various ways for it to crystallize. Chapter 6 reviews the different major Sources of Liquidity Risk, but it is useful to understand the fundamentals behind how they impact on the bank.

In a hypothetical world of no liquidity risk, every asset would be funded with a corresponding matched funding. One can argue that as long as this relationship is true the bank has hardly any liquidity risk. The asset will mature at the same time as the funding and so if the funding is not available (or is too costly) the bank can decide not to renew the loan or make other loans. As the world is far from being ideal, there is, however, an unavoidable funding risk in banking. This is due to the so-called liquidity gap. Liquidity gap *is the maturity mismatch between assets and liabilities in each maturity segment*. The maturity transformation discussed in the introduction is an example of a liquidity gap.

The liquidity gap makes the banks also vulnerable to market liquidity risk (remember that market risk is the risk that a bank cannot easily transfer marketable assets into cash). This is especially valid if the liabilities mature earlier than the assets. In Figure 4.3 we can see the maturity mismatch report from Lloyds 2012 Annual Report. Even though the maturity buckets are only five it gives a clear overview of a profile of a commercial bank.

From the report we see that the bank has a considerably higher amount of short-dated liabilities than assets and this mismatch continues up to the last period (over 5 years), where the amount of assets finally exceeds the liabilities. As the bank's equity is also a source of funds, the total amount of liabilities is lower than the assets. Figure 4.3 helps to identify the gap or the difference between the assets and liabilities in each time period. This brings up the next concept, the cumulative gap. For liquidity risk management purposes we are not only concerned about each gap but how they cumulate over time. This will tell us when assets exceed liabilities and determine the maturity transformation the bank is taking on. Having a good understanding of what constitutes maturity transformation is a vital point in fund management, as we will discuss later.

We have mentioned that equity has not been reported with the liabilities. There are other items not appearing in the liquidity gap table, such as undrawn credit lines or possible margin calls, and in the example intangible assets are excluded.

After observing the report it is essential to query whether the balance sheet actually behaves as set out in the liquidity gap table. This is largely determined by two factors, the predictability of the cash amount and the predictability of the timing of the cash. Each line within the balance sheet can be viewed with this in mind. A fixed rate bond is a good example where the amount and timing is clear. Then we could look at on-demand deposits or current accounts, where it is not possible to determine either the timing or amount. A margin call (European) could be a liability where the amount is unclear but the timing is clear and a callable bond is an example of a product where the amount is clear but the timing is not. The maturity mismatch concept will be dealt with further within the reporting step, Step VI in Chapter 11, and it plays a pivotal role in the scenario stress test analysis.

In that chapter we also look at other ways to analyse and slice up the balance sheet, such as splitting the balance sheet according to the (market) liquidity of each instrument and matching liquid funding with liquid assets, etc., but at this stage the liquidity gap approach is first and foremost introduced to highlight the importance of the timing of cash flows.

4.3 THE TIMING FACTOR OF LIQUIDITY RISK: TACTICAL, STRUCTURAL AND CONTINGENT

As if things were not complicated enough, there is yet another way to map the universe of liquidity risk. Luckily this matches quite well with the former definitions. In the previous chapter we stated that liquidity was related to time as well as quantity, that is liquidity as a

Maturities of assets and liabilities	Up to 1 month £m	1–3 months £m	3–12 months £m	1–5 years £m	Over 5 years £m	Total £m
At 31 Dec 2012						
Assets						
Cash and balances at central banks	80,035	259	4			80,298
Trading and other financial assets at fair val	7,949	9,813	5,479	7,116	123,633	153,990
Derivative financial instruments	2,450	938	2,744	17,743	32,675	56,550
Derivative financial instruments	14,827	6,513	3,674	3,728	675	29,417
Loans and advances to customers	44,781	8,718	31,052	91,821	340,853	517,225
Debt securities held as loans and receiveable	153		22	439	4,659	5,273
Available-for-sale financial assets	565	130	764	4,409	25,506	31,374
Other assets	5,394	463	2,057	519	41,992	50,425
Total assets	156,154	26,834	45,796	125,775	569,993	924,552
Liabilities						
Deposits from banks	14,131	3,212	11,296	8,435	1,331	38,405
Customer deposits	322,788	14,159	37,857	50,589	1,519	426,912
Derivative financial instruments	12,818	5,556	12,843	20,164	33,256	84,637
Debt securities in issue	13,912	10,505	12,167	46,374	34,411	117,369
Liabilities arising from insurance and invest	27,230	1,469	5,270	20,676	82,947	137,592
Other liabilities	10,171	298	1,571	1,363	27,458	40,861
Subordinated liabilities	402	1,541	294	8,298	23,557	34,092
Total liabilities	401,452	36,740	81,298	155,899	204,479	879,868

Figure 4.3 Maturity mismatch report for Lloyds Bank 2012[8]

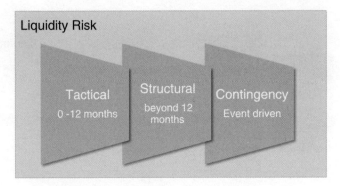

Figure 4.4   The three time dimensions of liquidity risk

way to buy time. We can now introduce the time element further into the risk definitions and the management of liquidity.

The starting point is the origin of the risk. The liquidity risk arising from day-to-day activities is viewed and handled differently from the structural liquidity risk originating from the overall asset–liability profile of the bank. Both of these are business-as-usual types of risk, of which the bank should have a good overview, but what differentiates them is the timing aspect, the first being tactical and the second structural. In addition to these two there is also a third origin capturing external unforeseen events – something outside the usual planned operations.

The three categories can be viewed as three 'time' segments and are named tactical, structural and contingency depending on the timeframe they appear in. This is set out in Figure 4.4.

The tactical liquidity risk, sometimes called the operational liquidity risk, is for the shorter term liquidity risk facing the bank. These are the short-term cash flows coming from all short-term instruments, both on the liability and asset sides. This could be the risk associated with money market funding and deposits issuance, intraday liquidity management (cash and collateral), securities borrowing and lending, repo (repurchase agreement), etc. The tactical liquidity risk is usually up to 12 months and includes all the possible liquidity shocks that can occur.

The structural liquidity risk refers to the liquidity risk built in the bank's current balance sheet structure due to asset–liability mismatch and is therefore also sometimes called the mismatch liquidity risk. Long-term bond issuance, Euro Medium Term Note (EMTN), etc., would fall into this category and the risk is associated with the larger funding profile of the bank. These structural features are more difficult to change than the shorter tactical ones.

The contingency liquidity risk is the risk that future events may require considerably more cash than the bank's projections allow and expect. This could be due to unexpected delays in repayments of a loan granted (term risk) or drawdown on a loan facility or deposit withdrawal (call risk). To deal with this type of unforeseen shocks the bank cannot use proper liquidity management and planning as in the first two boxes, but can only try to prepare by measuring their impact (via stress testing, scenario and sensitivity analyses) and develop contingency plans to cover these abnormalities and ensure its continued operations. This could also be called an event risk.

In Figure 4.5, the segmentation method has been merged into the market and funding liquidity risk concept mentioned earlier, as these two schools of thought fit well together.[9] The definition of funding liquidity risk and market liquidity risk concerns the sources of risk

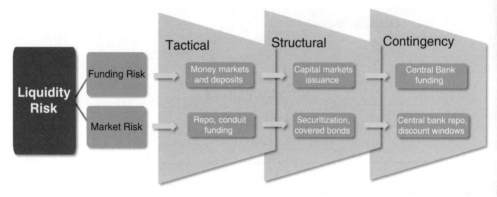

Figure 4.5   The combined view of liquidity risk

whereas the previous definition focused on the aspect of timing and how each time period had a different profile. We can build this into one overall description and definition of liquidity risk.

4.4 IT'S ALL ABOUT THE 'L' WORD

With the liquidity risk definition part over, the next step is to introduce the overall liquidity management framework, the '6 Step Framework'. However, before diving into the policy and processes it is useful to take a high altitude overview on how liquidity risk is perceived, what makes it different from other risk factors and at the same time understand how it ties into the broader systemic risk.

Just like the other 'L word', liquidity risk is invisible but important. The first thing we notice about liquidity risk is that it cannot easily be seen in corporate accounts and public statements. A bank, or any firm for that matter, can demonstrate strong earnings and a healthy looking solid balance sheet but still be heavily exposed to a looming liquidity risk. The two US investment banks that ran – or almost ran – out of steam in 2008 both showed profits and were well-capitalized businesses in the last quarter prior to their liquidity problems, which put a stop to their plans. This shows how liquidity risk can pass unnoticed.

General accounting methods do not grasp liquidity risk, which can be understandable as Sources of Liquidity Risk can be completely exogenous and hence do not manifest themselves in company statements. Firms have addressed this by adding a cash flow statement to their account so the flow of cash can be reviewed along with the profit or loss numbers. Banks have also included liquidity measures in the notes section of their accounts, usually showing at least the mismatch gap report and even some ratio metrics. Unfortunately, this does not give a full insight into the liquidity health of the organization and much work is still needed to bring reporting into company accounts.

4.5 LIQUIDITY, SOLVENCY AND CAPITAL

Liquidity risk has been called a secondary or consequential risk in the way it usually materializes after some other risk events or triggers have occurred. Though not universally true, in most cases the stress trigger event can be found endogenously or exogenously in sudden market, credit or operational risks. This is different from, for example, the origin of credit risk, which (even though it is market wide) can be found in the loan stock of the bank itself. This difference is more pronounced when we look at how banks allow for risk.

Banks hold capital as a buffer against losses. These losses arise from damages from the businesses (business risk), asset provisioning (market and credit risks) as well as losses resulting from operational risk. As long as the bank has capital to absorb the losses it stays solvent, but being solvent does not mean that the bank is liquid as there is no certainty that sufficient capital can be turned into cash quickly enough to meet obligations due. However, an insolvent bank cannot stay liquid (at least not for long). Therefore solvency is a necessary but not sufficient condition for being liquid.[10] The reverse also holds true – lack of liquidity or illiquidity can force a solvent bank into insolvency. We can think of a bank that is so cash strapped that it needs to sell assets at a considerable discount to settle obligations. If the size of the losses exceeds the bank's capital then the bank is insolvent.

As liquidity risk is a secondary risk there can be multiple sources for the risk, making it difficult to have a uniform set of rules to cover all the different risk factors. Again to draw a comparison with capital, there are standardized rules for capitalization (including the so-called Basel rules) to hold capital against potential future losses. As described above, the sources of risk that can crystallize in losses and use up the capital buffer are known, though the risk profiles of banks are different. Therefore a more or less standardized method can be used to absorb those losses (the Basel I minimum capital adequacy). A similar approach to liquidity risk is not possible. Banks can be asked to keep a certain amount as a buffer, such as cash or cash-like instruments, in order to offset the liquidity mismatch and other Sources of Liquidity Risk. This is, however, not a sufficient risk measure as every bank's situation is different and dynamic and not only endogenous but also a function of the market. Consequently a more advanced approach is needed for liquidity risk. This also signifies that it is not possible to compare buffer levels between banks, as can be done with capitalization, and so all comparisons or rankings are difficult and somewhat meaningless. Any attempt to have a uniform set of minimum liquidity quantum can build up false comfort in the system as it will effectively not be able to take into account the quality and availability of the secondary liquidity. For instance, take a bank with a medium mismatch asset–liability profile but a large proportion of its assets in highly liquid and sellable assets. To require the bank to hold a large buffer when it can easily transform its assets to cash would be the wrong requirement. It could even have the opposite effect, at least when implemented, as the action of one bank to conserve or increase liquidity can collectively have the effect of reducing liquidity in the market as a whole.

This does not mean that standardization is of no avail, as discussed further in Chapter 12, which deals with Basel III. There is scope for some sort of standardized methodology to measure liquidity risk or at least the parts of it that all banks have in common. This could be the mismatch gap and eligibility criteria of assets in the liquidity buffer.[11] The Basel III liquidity coverage ratio (LCR) is an example of such a minimum criterion where scope is the asset–liability mismatch for the first 30 days, which is then to be covered by predefined liquid assets.

4.6 LIQUIDITY FROM A MACROECONOMIC PERSPECTIVE – THE SINGULAR CASE OF CONTAGION RISK AND ASYMMETRIC INFORMATION

Analysing banks from a microeconomic perspective gives a very different outcome from viewing banks through the lens of macroeconomics, which takes into account the implications on the wider real economy.

When looking at liquidity risk on an individual firm level, the risk for banks is not essentially different from that of any other type of firm. Storing liquidity can be seen as inventory management, where the aim is to have sufficient stock when needed and be able to meet fluctuations in demand. The severity of the situation of being 'sold out' is, however, not compatible either on a single firm basis or even on a system level, which is where the similarities end. As is well known, a banking collapse can have a different and a wider repercussion than a default of a manufacturing firm, but does not necessarily lead to the conclusion that banks should always be treated differently under times of stress and without exception be bailed out. In the United States, bank failures are not uncommon, both from a current and historical perspective. It is only when the liquidity problems of a bank start to affect other banking institutions, directly or indirectly, that we are faced with a macroeconomic problem and so-called systemic risk. To address these problems central banks have measurements that ease the liquidity shortage by allowing banks to borrow either secured or unsecured from them. Ultimately, it is the central bank or government that has the mandate to rescue a bank from bankruptcy and it is usually the macroeconomic importance of the bank that is the deciding factor for government or central bank intervention.[12]

In terms of economic theory arguments for special treatment for banks need to be based on the existence of a market failure and the creation of externalities via contagion to other institutions. Asymmetric information (one type of market failure) on one bank's solvency can create a liquidity problem for the bank that a market mechanism has difficulty in correcting. All firms have liquidity risk in their operations but banks differ from other corporations in a fundamental way as their idiosyncratic risk can turn into a systemic risk with wider implications, whereas in other sectors a failure of one firm does not necessary impact on another. On the contrary, the failure of a competitor could benefit other firms within the industry. When banks address their liquidity risk it can actually affect other banks in a negative way, again making liquidity risk different from other types of risk. By simply following a conservative liquidity strategy a bank can contribute to a continuation and escalation of a liquidity crisis. This is for sure one of the reasons for the liquidity crises starting in 2008, where hoarding of liquidity led to an overall liquidity shortage.

To stop this vicious cycle governments/central banks attempt to have a mechanism to stop the build-up and extension of the contagion risk. The largest of those is the concept of lender of last resort (LLR), where they have the responsibility to provide market liquidity through market crises, deposit insurance and minimum liquidity reserve requirements (this was even noted as early as 1873 by one of the founders of financial and banking risk Walter Bagehot[13]).

Another argument for a strong liquidity framework is the social cost that lies in the existence of a lender of last resort. Firstly, the cost for the public when banks turn to the LLR can be very high and, secondly, the existence of the LLR can also induce moral hazard behaviour and agency problems (see, for example, Jensen and Meckling[14]) as well as raise the question of fair competition when the 'too big to fail' principle is applied and some institutions are helped and others not. Therefore, there are ample macroeconomic and social reasons for forcing banks to have measures in place to prevent them running into liquidity problems. This of course is the reason why banking is a heavily regulated industry. Apart from the optimal size of the liquidity buffer, the guidance from the regulator should generally go hand in hand with the bank's business incentives. Banks are incentivized to hold as little liquidity as they can get away with, as opportunity cost is a prevailing factor. Davies and Green[15] pointed out the counter-cyclicality of liquidity in banks, meaning that banks hold less liquidity in upturns than downturns, and Diamond and Rajan[16] show that there is a correlation between rate level expectations and the size of the buffer. We can therefore draw the conclusion that the optimal liquidity level set at individual bank levels is lower than the macroeconomic risk would require.

The question is then how is it possible to provide more protection to taxpayers since banks are not incentivized to do so. There is no single agreed way or mechanism to tackle this problem and not everyone agrees that simply raising the amount of liquidity buffer required is sufficient or the best solution. Regulators have taken a different view. Some, like the UK Prudential Regulation Authority (PRA), are forcing banks to hold more liquid assets whereas other regulators have not done so but rather emphasize the quantitative measurements of liquidity management (i.e. that banks pay closer attention to their own liquidity risk[17]). The different points of view are crystallized by the fact that BCBS had not, prior to the creation of Basel III, emphasized higher liquidity levels across the European banking sector.

Endnotes

1. See, for example, Knies, K. (1876), *Geld und Credit II, Abteilung Der Credit*, Leipzig, 1876.
2. Matz, L. and Neu, P. (editors) (2007), *Liquidity Risk Measures and Management, A Practitioner's Guide to Global Best Practises*, John Wiley & Sons, Ltd, p. 3.
3. Adapted from Financial Services Authority (FSA), *Liquidity Reporting Workshop: Basic and Advanced Product*. Available at: www.fsa.gov.uk.
4. In the publication *Principles for Sound Liquidity Risk Management and Supervision*, September 2008, the BCBS defined funding liquidity risk as follows: '*Funding liquidity risk is the risk that the firm will not be able to meet efficiently both expected and unexpected current and future cash flow and collateral needs without affecting either daily operations or the financial condition of the firm.*'
5. See Basel Committee for Banking Supervision (2008), *Principles for Sound Liquidity Risk Management and Supervision*, September 2008, p. 1.
6. See, for example, Nikolaou, K. (2009), *Liquidity (Risk) Concepts, Definitions and Interactions*, European Central Bank, Working Paper Series No. 1008, February 2009, p. 24.
7. The three subcategories are: the bid–ask spread, market depth in terms of the price (i.e. elasticity to a given volume of security sales) and, finally, market resiliency (how quickly the price bounces back).
8. See Lloyds Banking Group, *Annual Report and Accounts 2012*, p. 336. Available at: www.lloydsbankinggroup.com.
9. Adapted and expanded from D'Haese, W., *Liquidity Risk Management Comes in Three Loops*. Presentation made at the Conference on Liquidity Risk Management as Part of Centralized Asset and Liability Management, Cairo, Egypt, 2009.
10. Take Northern Rock as an example. Northern Rock was legally solvent but could not fund its operations in the market and was dependent for Bank of England for funding, making it solvent but not liquid.
11. See, for example, Davies, H. and Green, D. (2010), *Banking on the Future, the Fall and Rise of Central Banking*, Princeton University Press.
12. The size is not the only deciding factor for intervention and other factors are surely taken into consideration. Northern Rock was only the seventh largest bank in the United Kingdom but still was rescued, most likely due to the contagion effect of a bank default in the United Kingdom.
13. See Bagehot, W., *Lombard Street: A Description of the Money Market*, Henry S. King & Co, London, 1873. Available at: www.gutenberg.org.
14. See Jensen, M. and Meckling, W (1976). Theory of the Firm: Managerial Behaviour, Agency Costs and Ownership Structure, *Journal of Financial Economics*, October, **3** (4), 305–360.

15. See Davies, H. and Green, D. (2010), *Banking on the Future, the Fall and Rise of Central Banking*, Princeton University Press.
16. See Diamond, W. and Rajan, R. (1999), *Liquidity Risk, Liquidity Creation and Financial Fragility: A Theory of Banking*, NBER Working Paper No. 7430, December 1999.
17. In 2013 the Financial Services Authority (FSA) was dissolved and the prudential regulation part of it became the Prudential Regulation Authority (PRA), which is a part of the Bank of England.

5

The Appropriate Liquidity
Framework – Introduction to the
'6 Step Framework'

After discussing liquidity on a rather theoretical note we arrive at the heart of the book, which is to be the practitioner's guide to liquidity management in banks. This chapter, and the following ones, focus solely on the application of liquidity management and the different tools applicable. It is possible to apply the methods laid out in this chapter without having piled through the previous chapters, but a good practitioner should have a fundamental understanding of the various shapes of liquidity risk and how it can manifest itself. By going directly into the application and trying to follow 'if A happens, then do B', one is at risk of not having fully understood the risk presented within the bank.

All risk mitigants rely on assumptions and it is only by applying a top-down approach with a wider set of information that one can accept the assumptions to be the most adequate. This is not just a general health warning but has been a major source of some of the larger liquidity scares. The most recent financial crises demonstrated how the different approaches and assumptions resulted in failure of some banks and the survival of others.

5.1 SETTING THE STAGE – FROM POLICY TO A PRACTICAL FRAMEWORK

It is key to pick the appropriate starting point when building a liquidity risk framework. It can be tempting to take a short-cut and simply pull up some widely known metrics and apply them to a bank balance sheet and risk profile and then analyse and report the outcome. As described earlier, liquidity risk takes many forms and sizes, all depending on the risk profile for each firm, and no two firms are identical in business strategy or profile. The 'one-size-fits-all' approach might leave important risk not observed and still hidden within the organization even though the measurements and metrics draw up an acceptable picture. Furthermore, by focusing merely on tactical risk management the risk management structure of the bank is not dynamic in its nature and is open to the risk that the business strategy changes but the measurements remain the same. What one can perceive as fundamental, like the types of funding products used, can change relatively quickly and history has shown that not all banks managed to make their risk framework reflect those changes. The increased use of securitizations and other types of secured funding were examples of a case where not all banks managed to identify the risk embedded in those products and its markets. Another example, from my own experience, was the introduction of 'putable CDs', otherwise called extendables (see endnote 1 and Box 5.1.[1]

Box 5.1   Extendables

An extendable is not a complex product. A bank issues a CD (Certificate of Deposit) to buyers. When a CD is extended, the coupon steps up and if things go as planned a rather short-term funding (1 year would not be uncommon) can be extended into a longer-dated one (3–5 years). For the issuer, looking at the 5 years as a whole, the cost would be lower than issuing a 5 year bullet bond. The attractiveness for the buyer is getting paid a higher coupon than normally received on a short-dated instrument. This description of the product highlights both the attractiveness and its major faults. One can perceive this correctly as a 1 year product whereas the issuer can be tempted to focus on the possible extended maturity of let us say 5 years, and on that basis will find the product appealing. It is a prudent management to view the expected maturity as only the next extension date, not giving the scenario of extension any weight. However, the markets believed the risk of no-extension to be limited and even unheard of. In the beginning, it was seen as unlikely that a large block of the issue, not to mention the whole issue, would get put back. Usually the CD was sold to multiple investors, which gave the assumption that the risk of a put was not in the hands of one buyer bur rather distributed and diversified and hence not as high. This should have been a rather easy product for the risk unit to analyse. It turned out, however, that the buyers of these products were a subsegment of the large number of CD buyers. To a large extent they have similar investment criteria and philosophy, so their reaction to changes in risk, such as volatility of the product, can be seen as uniform and highly or even fully correlated. Thus the words of the salesmen echoing 'this product has never been put back to issuers' were correct but equally fruitful as the words of E.J. Smith, Captain of the *Titanic*, prior to the eventful journey when he was supposed to have said: *'When anyone asks me how I can best describe my experience in nearly forty years at sea, I merely say, uneventful. Of course there have been winter gales and storms and fog and the like. But in all my experience, I have never been in any accident... of any sort worth speaking about.'*

The risk of this product could not be fully recognized without empirical market experience.

The liquidity management framework is set at a high level by the Board of the bank. It needs to include top-down looking broader statements about the strategy of the bank and reach all the way down to the practical implementation, measuring and reporting level. The top parts of the framework (strategy, governance and such) are the high-level statements that should not change very frequently.

At the next level, which is a strategic one, the framework needs to allow for a regular review and self-assessment of purpose and quality. The next level below is the setting of individual measurements and applicable metrics, which will change as the risk management unit will constantly question whether those metrics are identifying and reporting the potential risk factors, identified at the previous risk level.

5.2   THE HEIGHTENED REGULATORY FOCUS ON LIQUIDITY

Banks cannot rely on regulators to protect them against liquidity shocks. Much has been said about the lack of alertness of the regulatory authorities in spotting the looming liquidity risk in the banking systems coming up in 2007 and in not having implemented a stronger liquidity regime and supervision authority earlier. Passing the blame card around or finding a single scapegoat is not a very fruitful occupation – rest assured that just as many banks were caught by surprise as were various regulatory bodies. Looking at the complexity of the liquidity crises, it is very difficult to determine whether regulators should have foreseen these events.

As the products and the interplay between various markets and players is constantly changing, it is difficult to expect regulators to be one step ahead of the pack. It would be an ideal scenario but in reality it is hardly feasible when taking limited resources into account.

In the publication *Principles of Liquidity Risk Management*, The Institute of International Finance (IIF) put forward a set of liquidity risk recommendations. In their view the elements of liquidity risk policy are:

(a) Governance and organizational structure for managing liquidity
(b) Analytical framework for measuring and
(c) Stress testing and contingency planning.

In 2008 the BCBS quickly turned the lesson learnt from the crises into a fundamental review of their *Sound Practices for Managing Liquidity in Banking Organisations*, published eight years earlier. The outcome was 17 'Sound Principles' published in *Principles for Sound Liquidity Management and Supervision*, issued in September 2008. They are similar to the conclusion the IIF came to and the 17 principles are based around three themes, that is governance of liquidity risk, measurement and management, and finally public disclosure.

The FSA reached a similar conclusion in their updated liquidity regime from 2009, stating that every firm should have overarching systems and controls to manage liquidity, provisions outlining the responsibility of the governing body and lastly provisions on the number of specific areas, such as management of collateral, pricing of liquidity risk and intraday management of liquidity.[2]

Regulatory minimum requirements are not sufficient as a benchmark for proper and functioning risk management. However, banks can benefit from the structural work that has been done by these agencies as they have been required to rethink the concept of liquidity risk. The outcome is the general consensus that liquidity risk is first and foremost firm specific and hence they now require firms to analyse their business as well as going through the reporting exercise. The contribution of the regulatory bodies is a good foundation and can help the risk architect to set the stage and ask the right questions.

A good example where the regulators have contributed to the overall risk framework is the Individual Liquidity Adequacy Assessment (ILAA), which is part of the UK regulatory regime. The assessment, which is a top-down exercise that needs to be performed at least annually, requires the firm to review the fundamentals of their liquidity regime. The assessment includes a review of the stress test assumption, a sense check of the adequacy of monitoring and reporting, and the contingency plans. Effectively, all quantitative and qualitative systems and controls will be reviewed and signed off again. The correct approach to the ILAA is of importance. The exercise should not be conducted in a similar manner to the annual car inspection, which tries to ensure the machine has not materially deteriorated since the last inspection, but should adopt a more dynamic approach. The question to ask is whether the risk profile of the bank has changed over the year, which includes reflecting on external factors as well as internal ones.

If done properly and applied appropriately in accordance with the complexity of the banks, the ILAA is a very good way to provide a firm with a better understanding of its liquidity risk and to assess its business-as-usual operations. This also requires firms to address this risk at a strategic level, but not just something compliance needs to fill out on a regular basis as the finding of the assessment needs to be signed off by the Board.

The 'Sound Principles' gives a good overview of the necessary ingredients of a strong liquidity framework within a bank and as the recommended '6 Step Framework' liquidity framework, which will be built up in the following chapters, makes a reference to the appropriate 'sound principle'. In essence the 'Sound Principles' emphasize:

• The importance of establishing a robust liquidity management framework
• The importance of clearly articulating the liquidity risk tolerance within the firm
• The necessity of allocating liquidity costs, benefits and risks to all significant business activities
• The identification and measurement of the full range of liquidity risks, including contingent liquidity risks
• The design and use of severe stress test scenarios
• The need for a robust and operational contingency funding plan
• The management of intraday liquidity risk and collateral
• The maintenance of an adequate level of liquidity, including a cushion of liquid assets
• The setup and use of a funding strategy that ties into the measurement of Sources of Liquidity Risk
• Public disclosure in promoting market discipline.

5.3   RECOMMENDED LIQUIDITY RISK MANAGEMENT FRAMEWORK – THE '6 STEP FRAMEWORK'

A good recipe is much more than a list of ingredients and simply mixing all the materials together will not get the desired results. The same applies to liquidity management. The list of ingredients for a liquidity management framework is not very hard to find and usually includes:

• Scenario stress testing
• Provisions on cash flow projections
• Contingency planning, early warning indicators and risk metrics
• Policies
• Governance structure
• Funds transfer pricing (FTP)
• Monitoring, reporting and an escalation framework.

It has been pointed out to me that the raw food craze is just about mixing the ingredients together to get the anticipated result and hence disproves the hypothesis. Not entirely. The biggest problem with the raw recipes I have tried is to get the ingredients to stick together. This is also the main issue within liquidity risk management. We have the materials but it is how to make them work together that is the difficult bit.

The most useful guidance to be given when looking at its liquidity is to give sufficient importance to setting the appropriate liquidity management structure or framework, which will make the starting point of a long but, more importantly, a safe journey. This book is to serve that purpose.

Far too often this is not the case and unfortunately there are examples of banks starting at the end point of the journey and trying to work their way backwards. Their liquidity management

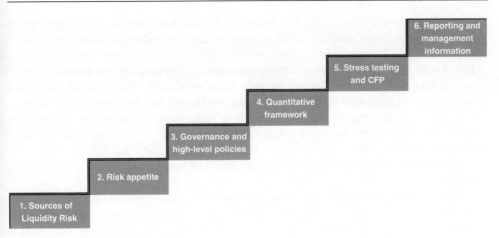

Figure 5.1   The '6 Step Framework'

has been based on reaction and not a proactive approach. What is being tested, why and what assumptions are being used might not be clear, nor what to do if the stress tests start to show danger on the horizon. It is important to start at the beginning, by understanding the bank and its risk profile, and then agree what is the acceptable level of risk the owners and management are confident in managing. The conclusion should be integrated into the necessary policies and translated into the supporting processes and document. By taking the top-down approach the scope for error is smaller and should ensure that the framework is complete and supported by the right pillars.

A bank comes to mind that had a great stress testing methodology, which was detailed enough to project the behaviour of 64 different types of deposits and could apply three levels of severity assumptions to each of them. This was a truly impressive piece of work. It failed, however, to link into the bank's risk framework, escalation was unclear and the actual setting of the stress assumption was thin and did not hold up to scrutiny. The main pitfall was the false sense of security the stress test gave. Surely, a bank that can stress 64 different kinds of deposits in various ways must know what it is doing and be worth its credit, whereas a simple stress with a high-level but thought-through assumption could have provided more protection against liquidity events.

Figure 5.1 shows a suggested structure for an overall liquidity framework for a bank. This is a process in six stages, which we dubbed The '6 Step Framework'.[3] This is not a 'one-size-fits-all' model but rather an approach to liquidity risk management. The guidance and structure, however, holds true for both simple and complex banks, large and small.

The process can be read from Figure 5.1 and starts from the left side with the fact-finding mission on the bank's Sources of Liquidity Risk and then step by step goes through the building up of a framework, ending with the final product – reporting.

To summarize, the first step is for the bank, through a systemic approach, to assess each of its different businesses and the liquidity risk embedded in them, creating the Sources of Liquidity Risk Report. The outcome should be a good overview of the liquidity risk within that specific firm, which is then used (Step 2) by the Board of Directors to set the risk appetite. The liquidity risk appetite statement sets out what amount of liquidity risk the bank is comfortable with running and under what circumstances those limits could be breached.

Step 3 requires the bank to use the finding in the previous steps to set the appropriate liquidity risk governance and agree on the principles used to manage the amount of risk agreed upon.

Step 4 is the most detailed one and sets the quantitative framework, such as detailed controls, system requirements and provisioning, triggers, limits, metrics, etc. An impatient practitioner might be tempted to skip the first three parts and jump straight into the implementation phase, but the danger is then that the bank does not fully understand its risk profile and therefore could be left exposed to unnecessary and unknown risk. One of the lessons we can learn from the bank failures in the recent crises is that the risk assessment was lacking whereas the appropriate tools (metrics and framework) were generally better managed and not usually the limiting factor.

Step 5 takes off from where Step 4 stopped, and is effectively two parallel processes, the setting up of a contingency funding plan and the appropriate scenario stress tests. These are two major features of a robust framework and where the other previous steps all contribute to the assessment.

The final step is reporting, both in the form of management reports to the different layers of corporate governance as well as regulatory reporting, which should give the reader a good overview of the outcome of the liquidity framework and its robustness.

The '6 Step Framework' is a framework but not a to-do list. The objective for approaching the individual features in this particular order is to build up the framework in stages or steps, where each new step on the ladder is based on the previous ones. This is to ensure that the framework holds together and the same assumptions are used throughout. To give an example, the Sources of Liquidity Risk (Step 1) are being used as the platform to build the quantitative projection template in Step 4, which then forms the inputs for the scenario stress testing in Step 5, which again is the key to an adequate contingency funding plan (Step 5). As the book goes through each stage, the references to what has previously been discovered are made as well as highlighting if there are reasons to deviate from the plan. If the six steps, some of which are broken down further into individual actions, are attempted in this set order, the practitioner should clearly become aware if the groundwork or foundation is not sufficiently strong. An example could be if the risk manager finds it difficult to determine the most important liquidity risk factors when setting out scenarios for stress testing or if the assumptions feel more like a guessing game than a thought-out process. The way is then to fix the problem at the right level, which should filter up to the application and output part of the framework.

This is not the only way to attempt liquidity management but there is, however, a shortage of easily applicable alternative approaches. Some start off by setting the stage but then very quickly head into one of the 'cul-de-sacs' and hence do not provide much thought on other areas of liquidity management or how they are all linked.

Each step sets out what the necessary features are within that step to adequately cover that specific risk aspect. The book does not try to provide an exhaustive list of methods and alternative methodologies as the aim is to build a frame that can be added to, if and when needed. This is truly applicable to more sophisticated banking operations, where each step is a field of its own. This does not render the '6 Step Framework' method ineffectual but rather underlines the importance of aligning the various subframeworks to one central idea. The reader is encouraged to expand on each feature as much as is adequate for the size and complexity of the bank's operations, but keep a watchful eye on the balance between assumptions and deduction.

Endnotes

1. The putable CD, also called the extendable CD, is a Certificate of Deposit where the buyer has the option to put the bond back to the issuers with a certain notice. This is usually done in the reverse manner, i.e. the buyer needs to agree to extend the bond at every reset date, otherwise it gets put back to the issuer with the agreed notice period. The product incentivizes the buyer to extend by offering in most cases a coupon kicker (increased coupon) at certain time intervals, making the CD more attractive for the buyer as time passes.
2. See Prudential Regulation Authority (PRA), *Prudential Sourcebook for Banks, Building Societies and Investment Firms (BIPRU)*, Chapter 12. Available at: www.fsa.gov.uk.
3. A 12-step programme has proved to be useful in helping people control some of their addictions and vices. As bankers generally have a low attention span, this programme has only 6 steps. Just as in the other programme, skipping steps will spoil the results.

6

Step I: Sources of Liquidity Risk

The first step in developing an appropriate liquidity framework is to identify all the Sources of Liquidity Risk specific to the firm. Here again, the individual differences between firms are highlighted and the reason behind this approach is the underlying theory that no two organizations have the same liquidity risk profile.

Trying to make a thorough list of all the Sources of Liquidity Risk can be a formidable task. One needs to capture all the different faces the liquidity creature can have but at the same time ensure that the factors or sources are distinctive and idiosyncratic as opposed to being a different symptom of the same cause. This is the tricky bit, but it can be justified by listing what looks like the same factor twice, should it have multiple expressions. Here, it is better to do more than too little and make up a longer list to start with, which can then be consolidated if some factors are indeed one and the same.

There is a method that helps capture all the various sources. Firstly, the overall broad categories should be defined. All Sources of Liquidity Risk fall into the following three types of sources:

- Systemic. This is also called market-wide risk. Under this category fall all risk factors that are external to the bank, such as market disruptions, lack of market or central bank funding or dislocation of the market mechanism of turning assets into cash. This is a market-wide risk so not only the bank in question is at risk. One can agree that the bank cannot influence the systemic risk factors, but has to accept them and align its risk taking according to them.
- Individual or idiosyncratic. These are all the Sources of Liquidity Risk that have their origin within something specific to that bank. The sources that are individual in nature are more likely to be event or crisis driven than the market-wide ones. This could be for various reasons, such as downgrades, announcement of major losses or anything else that makes the bank suffer loss of trust, creating an inability to refinance its obligations and attract new ones.
- Technical or timing. The source of this problem is of a technical nature but not a loss of confidence or a market-wide stress. More specifically, the problem is the timing of cash flows. The situation can be where there is sufficient liquidity within the bank (buffer) and the financial statements do not give any reason to worry but still the bank has an open source of risk. The problem is the timing when the liquidity is available. The bank might have large inflows in distant time periods whereas in the shorter time it has outflows exceeding the liquidity buffer. From a long-term perspective the bank looks to be fine but the short-term cash deficit can be another type of liquidity risk. This is how the mismatch risk in cash flows can create problems, as will be explained later.

To build up a list of Sources of Liquidity Risk for that specific firm, one can use the list provided in Figure 6.1 and complement it with additional factors only applicable to the firm. The question when building up a list like this is always how general the list should be, but each of the items on the list below should be on the to-do list when starting to analyse the possible liquidity risk factors.

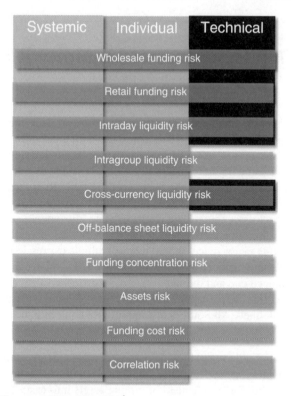

Figure 6.1   The 10 Sources of Liquidity Risk[1]

The 10 Sources of Liquidity Risk have also been mapped to the three overarching categories, systemic, individual and technical. Some belong to one, some to all three.

The list in Figure 6.1 is not the only way to list the liquidity risk factors. Within its regulatory framework, the PRA identified 10 individual Sources of Liquidity Risk for firms to keep in mind when setting up their liquidity management systems.[2] The list in Figure 6.1 is an adaptation of the one from the PRA and the two lists share the first seven items, which are generally agreed to be important and independent sources of risk.[3] The '6 Step Framework' names one category 'Asset risk' whereas the PRA has chosen to separate them into marketable and nonmarketable assets. This is a minor difference, but it is essential to recognize that Sources of Liquidity Risk are not all related to the liability side of the balance sheet and that the asset side also has a liquidity aspect to it. Firms with great reliance on secured funding might find it easier to split the two by the characteristics of the assets, but for most a single category should be sufficient. The '6 Step Framework' identifies correlation risk as a separate risk factor. This is to highlight the fact that the Sources of Liquidity Risk should not only be viewed as independent but correlated in their nature and one risk factor can be the source for another. This reflects what has been said about liquidity risk being a secondary risk.

Instead of franchise-viability risk, which PRA defines as '*the risk that in the stresses required a firm may not have sufficient liquidity resources to maintain its core business franchise and reputation*', this book suggests rather using 'funding cost' risk. One could argue that not being able to maintain the franchise should rather be viewed as consequential risk due to the lack of liquidity, but not as a source of liquidity risk. Conversely, funding cost risk is one where liquidity might be available but only at a price unsustainable to the bank. This ties in with the definition of liquidity risk discussed earlier, liquidity risk being *the inability to meet obligations as they become due and payable or only being able to do so at an unsustainable cost.*

6.1   THE 10 SOURCES OF LIQUIDITY RISK

The assessment needs to be conducted on all major business lines of the bank and those businesses with embedded liquidity risk identified and analysed using the 10 sources list above. When assessing each factor, consideration should be given to the LPHI (low probability high impact) risk of each source, signifying that the analysis should not only give notice to what are the likely shortcomings within the bank's liquidity profile but also reflect on the impact of those risk factors that are unlikely to occur but have dire consequences. If such a factor exists then the Liquidity Policy and Contingency Funding Plan (CFP) is essential to address that problem with mitigation actions or limits. It is a good working method to target each risk factor from both sides, that is the unlikely but severe events versus easily plausible but less severe events. This will help in building up scenarios for the stress test chapter.

It is a best practice to formally review the Sources of Liquidity Risk annually. By going through each source the bank is providing a robust check on the adequacy of its liquidity framework, realizing the framework needs to adapt to changes in conditions. The summary should include detailed analyses of all 10 sources and also any other firm-specific, often event-driven – Sources of Liquidity Risk. A score should be given to each factor or at least they need to be deemed material or immaterial. Those with a high score (the scoring is done by likelihood and severity) are deemed as material and need to be further analysed and addressed in the CFP and be properly reflected in the stress testing. The document Sources of Liquidity Risk can be adequately reviewed as a Level 2 policy (see Chapter 8).

6.1.1   Definition of Retail and Wholesale Liabilities

For most banks, the two most important Sources of Liquidity Risk are retail and wholesale liabilities. Before looking at them separately and focusing on what differentiates the two, the framework needs to decide on their definition. There are different schools of thought around this topic. Basel III has come out with a set of definitions where there is really no differentiation between retail (actual person) and SMEs (small/medium enterprises). According to Article 411 in the CRR 'retail deposit' means '*a liability to a natural person or to an SME, where the natural person or the SME would qualify for the retail exposure class under the Standardised or IRB approaches for credit risk, or a liability to a company which is eligible for the treatment set out in Article 153(4) and where the aggregate deposits by all such enterprises on a group basis do not exceed EUR 1* million'. An SME is generally defined as a company which, according to their last annual report, met at least two of the following three criteria:

- An average number of employees during the financial year of 1 to 249
- A total balance sheet not exceeding €43m
- An annual net turnover not exceeding €50m.

It is up to the risk manager to decide whether this categorization meets their needs and whether it can be firmly assumed their SMEs behave identically to a natural person. This rightly depends on the bank's business model, including where it operates. New research in the United Kingdom found that the average length of time a person has held the same bank account beats the average length of a marriage!! It found that the average bank account relationship lasts just over 16 years compared with 14 years for a marriage. The same survey found that 58% of people keep the same current account for over 10 years, with one in six sticking with their bank for over 30 years.[4] Similar studies show that more than 50% of all UK current account holders have never switched their account. Though not many comparable studies can be found on SME behaviour it can be deduced that SMEs and natural persons behave somewhat differently, if only from the fact that SMEs on average have a shorter life expectancy than humans. In this book we limit retail to a 'natural person' and SMEs are viewed separately. The chapter on Basel III (Chapter 12) argues the need for banks to rethink their categorization approach to match the global standard, but care needs to be taken not to deviate from the bank's own firm-specific characteristics.

Under Section 6.1.3 on retail funding risk, the book introduces a framework to determine the overall stability of deposits and that the methodology is equally applicable to wholesale as well as retail deposits The Sources of Liquidity Risk are given in the following sections.

6.1.2 Wholesale Funding Risk

Before going into details of the characteristics and liquidity risk of wholesale liabilities, it is not out of the way to define the category even further than has been done above as many different kinds of liabilities fall under this large umbrella. In its simplest form, intuitively wholesale liabilities are those that do not come from retail customers. Keeping this wide 'kitchen sink' definition in mind, it comes as no surprise that wholesale funding is a large and wide category and varies dramatically in terms of behaviour characteristics. This is the reason why detailed analyses on wholesale liabilities are needed in the Sources of Liquidity Risk.

New and Recycled Funds

The traditional bank raised deposits to provide funding for lending but the existence and growth of the capital markets have changed and complicated this basic transformation. As the capital markets have grown, the reliance on market funding has increased at the expense of banks receiving their funds from depositors. The increased use of wholesale funding is not only due to the emergence of a wider catchment area via the markets but also as a result of the general growth of the banking system, which has exceeded deposit growth, which could be described as organic growth. This is a key point for the risk manager. There is an argument for viewing some of the liquidity created by wholesale funding as leveraged liquidity; that is the depositor providing the liquidity does not actually own that money but has himself borrowed it from another party. We can therefore have a full circle of these funds, which is the reason why wholesale funding placed by intermediaries is often treated separately and cautiously. Figure 6.2 shows a simple recycle of liquidity throughout the financial system.

It is vital to recognize the risk a part of wholesale funding carries, which has more to do with who the players are rather than the product itself. Liquidity shortages, especially the long-lasting ones, have been the result of this type of leverage funding.

The Increased Emphasis and Benefits on Wholesale Funding

There are a lot of economic advantages for banks not to be solely dependent on deposit funding and wholesale funding helps banks to serve their purpose as intermediaries. Instead of dealing

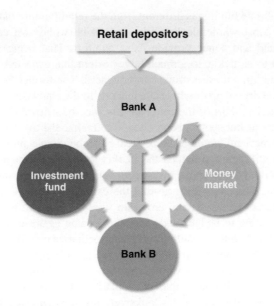

Figure 6.2   Recycle of liquidity

directly and only with their clients in their own markets, banks now have access to investors across the globe if they wish to and the pool of available funding is much larger. Given that the bank has the necessary credentials, usually in the form of a credit rating, which amongst other criteria reflects upon the size of the bank, this can open up alternative funding sources and diversify the funding profile. The creation of capital markets completely changed the liquidity composition of banking and many of the great things banks have accomplished can be attributed to the creation of these markets. The liquidity profiles of larger banks enable them to grow beyond their local franchise and reach. This has also improved their mismatch profile as liabilities from the markets can be for longer tenures than the typical characteristics of the deposit market allow for. The result is a closer alignment of assets and liabilities from a maturity mismatch perspective. Furthermore, banks could then better predict their maturity profile, as bonds have a predetermined maturity (excluding those with put options), and could better estimate their funding needs and further develop their funding plans. The growth of available funds both in traditional Western markets as well as in the newer growing economies meant that market funding became the bread and butter for medium/large banks and for a few years the funding desks turned their focus almost solely on market funding. The excess supply of available funds pushed margins to lower levels than ever seen before, making wholesale funding at times far cheaper than the alternative deposit funding. The markets developed their own issuing standards, set out in the issuing programmes, which increased in number as time passed. These originated in the United States but soon there were available bond issuing programmes to access various corners of the world, from the 'Kangaroo' market in Australia to the 'Maple' programme in Canada.

The other side of the coin is that many of the most serious problems hitting banking systems can be traced back to the same root. It is therefore not possible or even imaginable to classify one type of funding as bad and another one as good. All have their benefits and shortcomings, which if not treated cautiously can backfire. It is therefore more important to keep an eye on why and under what circumstances they tend to go wrong.

The risk from wholesale funding is different from the retail funding risk with its embedded risk of a bank run. Most wholesale liabilities cannot be withdrawn earlier than they are scheduled to be repaid and hence provide extra comfort. That being said, the wholesale markets have proven to be fickle, to a much larger extent that expected. At times they have even completely dried up, with disastrous consequences. The former Governor of the Bank of England likened the drying up of wholesale markets to the equivalent of a bank run, which demonstrates the severity.[5] Part of the cause of this was the general dependence on market liquidity, a trend that was not spotted soon enough to realize the overall risk involved. After the beginning of the new millennium, banks ceased to be simple providers of liquidity to the markets, which until then had helped the market to function. The use of securitization, operations of conduits and other special investment vehicles (SIVs) all added to the imbalance as all relied and were effectively built around the existence of ample market liquidity. At the same time investment banks, having grown in size, all relied on market liquidity, many of them providing funding to hedge funds and thus adding again to market pressure. This new world was based on financial institutions or intermediaries providing liquidity and credit to each other – think again about the liquidity recycling in Figure 6.2. The markets would become characterized by institutions who themselves were reliant on market liquidity and were providing liquidity to that same market. A market like that works well as long as the music plays but the scenario when it stops looks very much like musical chairs – a sentiment attributed to Chuck Prince, former Chairman and Chief Executive of Citigroup, in 2007.[6] A further contagion was discovered as this liquidity was based on the value of the security provided as collateral, creating yet another correlation factor. This fact was also a major contributor to the financial crises as the use of repurchase agreements rose rapidly in the years leading up to the crises.

Box 6.1   The Example of Northern Rock and Countrywide

The story of Northern Rock and Countrywide in 2007 is an example of this type of risk. Northern Rock had changed its business strategy from a traditional mortgage lender, which held on to their mortgages, to a business where they originated, serviced and repackaged the mortgages into securitizations. By doing so it managed to grow fast (annual loan growth of 33% for the previous 5 years), increasing its market share from 6% in 1999 to 19% in 2007. Countrywide was the largest home mortgage provider in the United States, with 17% market share in 2007. Countrywide had asset quality problems in their origination, which, combined with a freeze in the short-term commercial markets, started the downward spiral. Northern Rock got caught in the same storm. In September 2007, their <3 month liquidity gap was more than £25bn as the bank had continued to provide mortgages while not being able to place them into long-term securitizations. Though not faced themselves with asset problems they were not sheltered from the contagion.[7]

The ups and downs of wholesale funding risk can be summarized as:

Pros:

- Good diversification across markets and geographies
- Longer tenure than deposits

- Fixed term (in most cases)
- Bigger pool of funds to tap into
- Can provide a natural hedge against asset–liability mismatch.

Cons:

- If the wholesale funds come from the capital market, they are subject to the market 'herd mentality'. The funding markets, even though far apart, tend to be quite correlated.
- The funding providers can have a limited understanding or relationship with the bank, hence making them less stable.

Box 6.2   The Ups and Downs of the Wholesale Funding Market

When I joined an Icelandic bank late in the year 2005, I joined a bank that was almost solely market funded, apart from the retail deposits it had in its home market. As these were all in Icelandic krona, they could not be used for the growth of the bank, which was mostly away from Iceland. A plethora of investors around the world was willing to buy bonds issued by decently rated banks and the ever-increasing chase for yield had brought down spreads since the turn of the millennium. Until then these bonds were largely bought by 'real money' investors, that is those with their own sources of liquidity, being fund managers or even other banks investing their excess liquidity. As the market started to correct itself, the investor base changed. Hedge funds and more opportunistic players took over from the 'buy to hold' crowd. At that time, it was not widely discussed that these investors were of any less quality in terms of strength, though issuers realized that these were trading accounts, looking to make money by trading the bonds rather than reaping the coupons. Though a prudent treasurer does not like to issue bonds at expensive levels for secondary traders to make a profit out of them, the hedge funds were seen as strong investors and their importance to the market kept on growing. The risk that they themselves would run out of steam was not widely discussed. This contagion of assets and liabilities was also not at the top of everyone's minds.

As the crises in 2008 crystallized, it became clear that this expansion of the banks was not without risk. Growing beyond your own turf and reaching out to investors, some of whom had limited knowledge and ties to the bank or understood the dynamics of its jurisdiction, was a double-edged sword. Funding was no longer client funding but market funding, which could become unpredictable. The structuring teams of investment banks were likewise a new group of bond 'investors', adding bank bonds to their collateralized debt obligations (CDOs), which were then sold on to investors. The reliance on the credit rating agencies meant that many investors bought bonds simply based on their rating without much additional knowledge about the issuer. The fast recycle flow of funds opens up the door for herd mentality and the credit agencies could actually become a liquidity risk factor themselves. An example would be a rating agency that downgrades a bank from investment grade to subinvestment grade. The bank has no problem finding sufficient funding when investment grade rated but could hardly find any if it became subinvestment grade rated. Here the rating agency is becoming the key determining factor and we end up in a 'chicken and egg' discussion.

Analysing Wholesale Funding

When conducting analyses of a bank's wholesale liabilities, the first step is to identify all the different sources of wholesale funding the firm has utilized. Each channel should be analysed by taking into account the relative importance of that channel and how it would behave under normal and stressed conditions, again looking at the risk from a quantity and timing perspective. The difficult part is to analyse and come up with assumptions for rollovers and possible renewals of the obligations. Here the concentration of each market needs to be taken into account, including how many open issuing programmes the bank has and what is the reliance on each of them and the respective market. The past has taught us that some markets act in a binary fashion, that is are either open or closed to a certain issuer, whereas others remain open but readjust the price to entry. In this manner the US bond market has proven more resilient than the European one, most likely due to its longer standing.

The example in Table 6.1 shows how the analyst can get a good overview of the wholesale funding risk, where one of the stress scenarios in the stress testing chapter (Chapter 10) is used to provide the likely outflows under two time horizons.

This basic sheet can be expanded as needed, taking the short-term maximum impact into account versus the longer-term consequence of markets closing. When looking at wholesale funding sources both secured and unsecured need to be analysed. As some of the characteristics that determine stability are similar for wholesale and retail deposits, they are assessed jointly in the subsection on the Stability Framework – How to Categorize Funding Sources, which is set out in Section 6.1.3, Retail Funding Risk, which follows.

6.1.3   Retail Funding Risk

Though retail and wholesale deposits have many things in common it is essential to view them separately when analysing the Sources of Liquidity Risk. The reason for the distinction between retail and wholesale liabilities is obviously the different origins of the two and how we perceive their behavioural characteristics to be different. To start with, retail deposits are a liability to a natural person. Some banks use the further criteria that only deposits can be categorized as retail in order to exclude other products, though being held and owned by individuals will be classified as retail. The reason for defining retail narrowly by taking both the product and client type into account is the general assumption that they are normally less likely to leave under stressed conditions. This dual approach is, however, not recommended as products may change and it is the characteristics of the holder that the Sources of Liquidity Risk report is attempting to define.

Wholesale Funding Bad, Retail Funding Good?

There is a strong bias by analysts, supervisors and rating agencies to view retail deposits as more stable than deposits from wholesale sources. This is reflected in the Basel III prescriptive standards for LCR and many of the metrics the rating agencies apply to banks. As supervisors, just like bankers, learn from the past the boundaries between the two in terms of riskiness are less obvious. Prior to the financial crises deposits were definitely the teacher's pet, but the episode that followed taught the risk practitioners that blunt instruments, such as retail good, wholesale bad, were too simplistic to function properly. The year 2008 saw many examples of how retail deposits can take on the form of a bank run with stories of banks losing more than 50% of their deposits over a six-month period.[8]

Table 6.1 Overview of wholesale funding risk

Wholesale funding source	Outstanding balance	As % of total funding	Short-term maturities, < 6 months	Long-term maturities, > 6 months	Rollover, business as usual (BAU) (%)	Short-term funding gap, stress	Long-term funding gap, stress
SME							
Operational	150	4	100	50	100/45	100	23
Nonoperational	125	3	75	50	90/20	68	10
Euro medium-term notes issuance and Certificates of deposits	500	14		500	90/30		150
Euro medium-term notes issuance and Certificates of deposits	850	23	850		90/10	765	

For some of the rating agencies the LDR (loan to deposit ratio) was the holy grail in the years leading up to the financial crises and banks were strongly encouraged to shift their focus from wholesale funding to retail funding. More focus was given to getting the LDR ratio below par rather than giving consideration to the type of retail deposits that were being gathered. There was very limited empirical evidence on the stability of 'online' deposits and how they could behave differently from the usual deposit accounts. In some countries, especially the Nordic region, there were strong 'traditions' of electronic banking as opposed to visiting the branch. Though the risk was uncertain, it was generally accepted that these deposits as retail deposits were of a better quality than wholesale liabilities such as bond issues. The bank I worked for followed this strategic recommendation to the book and set up deposit-taking units in various European countries. During the crises these deposits proved to be less stable than expected and proved to be the first ones to leave.

However, the generally accepted assumption is to take comfort from banks being retail funded over wholesale funded and a bank should specifically take note should it think that for some reason this assumption does not apply to its retail customer base.

Stability Framework – How to Categorize Funding Sources

To be able to estimate the impact of liquidity stresses to the bank, it is necessary to have an idea of the stability or 'stickiness' of the liabilities. The aim in this chapter is to set out a formalized approach to access the 'stickiness' of funding sources, which is generally defined as their 'tendency to run off quickly under stress'.[9] In order to accomplish this, liabilities need to be aggregated into segments with similar behaviour characteristics under stressed conditions. There are many ways to achieve this, which depend mostly on how granular it is practical to go. This needs to be balanced with the level of assumptions the risk manager is comfortable to make about the behaviour of each category. There are no advantages in breaking down the liabilities into 30 different buckets by various differentiation factors such as size, channel, origin, term, etc., if it turns out to be impossible to come up with more than three or four run-off assumptions. Here a balance needs to be struck.

The question to ask when splitting up liabilities is: Does the identified factor (size, channel, origin, etc.) have an impact on the expected behaviour of the liability under stress and can we quantify or estimate that impact differently from other factors? If we can, then it should be included; otherwise not.

This exercise is vital in the '6 Step Framework' and not only in analysing properly the Sources of Liquidity Risk for the overall risk assessment. The method to rank deposits by their perceived stickiness is also a fundamental component for Step V, the stress testing methodology. It is therefore important to highlight again that in the '6 Step Framework' every step builds on the previous ones.

We will set out two approaches to access the stability of liabilities. One is prescriptive and the other is based on a scorecard.

The UK 2 × 2 Approach

This is a simple but useful approach in categorizing liabilities into four categories, each with their own level of risk. The groups are:

- Retail – Type A
- Retail – Type B

- Wholesale – Type A
- Wholesale – Type B.

The method uses the two factors to rank the deposit base from low risk to high risk. It builds on the assumptions that Type A deposits are less 'sticky' than Type B and retail deposits are more stable than wholesale deposits. By allocating all liabilities into one of the four boxes we have established a ranking system from low risk to high risk. This method is used by the UK regulator and the Type A and Type B terminology is borrowed from them. By having only four categories that already have been ranked low to high, the outcome is at best a two-dimensional framework. However, as wholesale deposits have already been defined as less stable than retail, the framework has effectively only one dimension (see Figure 6.3).

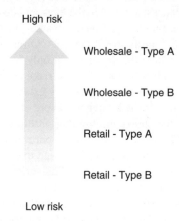

Figure 6.3   The 2 × 2 deposit stability method

In allocating each type of liability to one box we have already started to use stress test assumptions in our mind by agreeing, for example, that all wholesale deposits are less sticky than retail ones. Liabilities are usually ranked by both prescriptive and expected behavioural characteristics. An example would be rate-driven deposits, which are assumed to be of a Type A nature and one would assign all deposits gathered from financial intermediaries to the Type A category based on the funding channel type without taking notice of any behavioural expectations. As long as the assumptions are well founded this simple categorization works well to give an overview of the risk of deposit outflows. This also allows the bank to apply its experience into the risk assumptions, which is the objective of a firm-specific framework.

Even though there are only four overall categories, it can be useful for banks to expand on this model to include further subcategories. If a bank can find good ways to segregate clients then there is no reason for not increasing the number of categories. The categories must, however, be clearly independent and definable.

Deposits are the most common funding for the majority of banks and the point of contact for most of their clients. Therefore, banks usually have a substantial history and data on which to build their findings, which should enable the risk specialist to split, for example, the retail funding sources into two to five overall categories. At one end of the spectrum most banks have a loyal base of clients that have been with the bank for some period of time. Experience shows that this part of a retail customer is stable and reluctant to switch banks. This type of client could form one category. At the other end of the range, the bank could classify retail

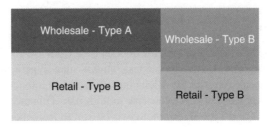

Figure 6.4   The meeko chart

clients that have all the signs of being less sticky. These are clients who come via price-driven products, clients with large balances, are new to the bank and do not have their account linked to any other service of the bank (nontransactional). In addition, the bank can use the delivery channels as one way of segmenting the retail deposits. Offerings through the internet, with little knowledge of the client, where the driver might only be the interest offered cannot be viewed as stable and should be classified in the most risky category. The middle category is populated by those who can neither be viewed as very established stable clients of the bank nor of an especially risky nature. This is a category where most clients would likely end up.

The meeko chart in Figure 6.4 shows the funding profile of a bank with both wholesale and retail liabilities, split into Types A and B. The proportion of A versus B can give a quick indication of the perceived risk of the funding profile and the need for further breakdown.

The 2 × 2 approach has proven useful when making various stakeholders understand that not all deposits are created equal in the eyes of liquidity management and this message can be more easily understood when expressed in such a simplistic format. Banks wishing to rely solely on this type of approach need to expand into subcategories to have a sufficient overview of their risk profile, as it is very difficult to limit the approach to only four types of clients. Expanding the number of categories will improve the assessment within the overall limitation of the method.

The Scorecard Approach

The problem with the 2 × 2 approach is that it is a one-dimensional and binary approach. A deposit is either Type A or Type B, which is highly subjective and belongs to either the wholesale or retail categories that have already been defined as being less stable/stable. There is no given and proven certainty that these rough categorizations appropriately represent the liquidity categories and assumptions of each bank.

By using simple boxes, we are following a binary approach, where the deposit belongs to a certain risk category or not. The risk is to classify the deposit wrongly and incorrectly assign the risk to the categories. A scorecard approach provides a solution to the binary problem and views liquidity risk as a continuous variable ranging from low to high, rather than the simple black and white scenario. By measuring each deposit category against a set of risk factors it is possible to build up a total stickiness score as the sum of various risk factors.

The reason for splitting up the deposits into subcategories is to be able to set and apply a separate stress assumption to each category and view how the funding profile changes along with the assumptions. Figure 6.5 is an example of a liability stickiness scorecard. This includes all the liabilities of an imaginary bank where they have been sorted as comprehensively as possible in terms of capturing different characteristics. The table starts by differentiating between the

Unsecured debt, branch network

	premium (1–5)	covered (+3)	sensitivity (1–5)	to neg. news (1–5)	relationship (1–5)	premium (1–5)	Total score
Unsecured debt, branch network							
1 Retail, branch network – covered by DGS							
1.1 part of an established relationship making withdrawal highly unlikely;	1		1	1	1		3
1.2 held in a transactional account, incl. accounts to which salaries are regularly credited.	1		1	1	1		3
1.3 other, covered	1		1	1			5
2 Retail, branch network – not covered by DGS, but less than €500k	1	3	1	1	2	2	10
3 Retail, branch network – not covered by DGS, >€500k	1	3	2	1	2	4	13
4 SME, branch network – covered by DGS							
4.1 part of an established relationship making withdrawal highly unlikely;	1		1	1	1		3
4.2 held in a transactional account	1		1	1	2		5
4.3 other, covered	1		1	1	2		5
5 SME, branch network – not covered by DGS							
5.1 part of an established relationship making withdrawal highly unlikely;	1	3	1	1			6
5.2 held in a transactional account	1	3	1	1	2		8
5.3 >€500k	1	3	2	1	2	3	12
5.4 Other (i.e. nontransactional <€500k)	1	3	1	1	2	2	10
6 NFC (nonfinancial corporates), branch network							
6.1 part of an established relationship making withdrawal unlikely;	1	3	1	1			6
6.2 held in a transactional account	1	3	1	1	2		8
6.3 >€500k	1	3	2	1	2	4	13
6.4 other (i.e. nontransactional <€500k)	1	3	1	1	2		8
Unsecured debt, internet channel							
7 Retail, internet channel – covered by DGS							
7.1 held in a transactional account, incl. accounts to which salaries are regularly credited.	3		3	2	2		10
7.2 other, covered	3		3	2	2		10
8 Retail, internet channel – not covered by DGS, but less than €500k	3	3	3	2	2	3	16
9 Retail, internet channel – not covered by DGS, >€500k	3	3	3	2	2	4	17
Unsecured debt, treasury							
10 NBFI (nonbank financial institutions),							
10.1 part of an established relationship making withdrawal unlikely;	5	3	3	3		4	18
10.2 held in a transactional/custody account	5	3	3	4	2	4	21
10.3 other	5	3	5	4	2	4	23
11 Governments, central banks and supranationals							
10.1 part of an established relationship making withdrawal unlikely;	5	3	3	3		4	18
10.2 held in a transactional account	5	3	3	4	2	4	21
10.3 other	5	3	5	4	2	4	23

Figure 6.5 Liquidity stability score for Bank A

three major funding channels the bank has: its branch network, the internet deposit platform and deposits gathered by the treasury operations. The bank assumes that the local deposit guarantee scheme is an influence factor and segregates covered deposits from uncovered deposits. It uses the Basel III template to further split up covered deposits into established relationships (prime deposits) and those that are for transactional purposes. The template also takes the size of a deposit into account as a behavioural factor and again uses the Basel III proposal from the European Banking Authority (EBA) to create a separate high-risk deposit group for deposits between €100k and €500 and the very-high-risk group for those above €500k.

The bank has decided not to follow the Basel III categorization completely and does not group retail and SME deposits together as it believes, in the case of this bank, that the two categories do not fully behave alike. This underpins the fact that no two banks are alike and the stress testing models need to be tailor-made. The treasury deposits are split into two major categories, which are nonbank financial institutions and governments, central banks and supranational organizations.

The second phase in creating the stickiness framework is to list all the determination factors and assign a score range for each of them. This is where the process becomes subjective, which is unavoidable, unless the bank can rely on data on a historical stress event. The first risk factor is the channel premium where deposits gathered from the branch network received the lowest score, the internet deposits gain a higher score and finally the assumption is that deposits gathered through the treasury desk are from sophisticated professional clients and hence are less sticky. Each risk factor adds a charge to each liability category (0 if not applicable) and by adding all the scores together a total risk score for each category can been established. As a result, a multidimensional framework has been created, which is more dynamic in nature than the 2 × 2 method. In the case of this hypothetical bank, one can see how the results can differ from the other 2 × 2 model. Under the scorecard method there is, for example, a situation where the most stable wholesale deposits are viewed to be stickier than some of the retail ones, which are price driven, large and not covered by the deposit guarantee scheme. The 2 × 2 assessment could never provide these results.

As mentioned earlier, the scorecard method is not without flaws as both the absolute and relative scores are subjective. The outcome could have looked different if the scale used was not from 1 to 5 or if, for example, the 'penalty' for not having a deposit guarantee was higher or lower than the number 3 that is being used in the example.

At last it is possible to aggregate together the categories that have the same stickiness score. The bank has created seven categories where each can be applied its own relative stress test assumption. In essence this aggregation is not necessary as the bank can use the individual scores to set the relative stress outflow propensity.

The risk managers will need to see if the model loses its 'prediction power' when balances are aggregated. However, the aggregation makes the stress testing easier, which is the main purpose of going through the ranking framework. The categorization used in Table 6.2 mirrors the groups used in the cash flow analysis in Section 10.1.11 on liquidity scenario stress testing. Apart from that, this bank ranks all deposits 'as if they are the same' but the cash flow stress test projections have separate headings for corporate deposits versus retail ones.

There is no single method of identifying all the various risk drivers for wholesale and retail deposits but the following features should at least be included:

- How 'professional' is the counterparty? There is a large difference between the behaviour of a small-sized company placing their surplus cash with a bank than with a large pension fund.

Table 6.2   Categories used in the cash flow analysis

	Total score	Amount $	%
Stability I	<5	4,500	29
Stability II	5–10	3,000	19
Stability III	>10	1,500	10
Stability IV	<10	4,000	26
Stability V	>10	1,500	10
Stability VI	<20	300	2
Stability VII	>20	700	5
Weighted average score	6.5	15,500	100

- Are these his own funds or funds held on behalf of a third party?
- How good or long-standing is the relationship? Is it based on price or other factors? How was the product sold to him? Directly or through a third party?
- Does the counterparty have many other products with the bank?
- How large is the deposit/liability with the bank?

It is also important not to confuse the maturity of liabilities with their propensity to leave under stress. Due to their nature, on-demand deposits can more easily leave the bank than term deposits, but that does not make them more likely to do so. It depends on the relationship the client has with the bank and the purpose of the deposit account. An example would be individual current accounts, which are on demand but quite sticky, as most people show remarkable reluctance to switch their bank, as discussed earlier.

The risk for a bank that has a large part of its liabilities in short-term deposits is that the liquidity situation of the bank could change quickly. This is being dealt with in the stress test chapter (Chapter 10) and the correlation risk, discussed later in Section 6.1.11.

By assigning or ranking wholesale and retail deposits the analyst gets a better understanding of the funding profile and the different behaviour categories become visible. It is worth noting that the term wholesale funding is used for various types of clients – from a long-standing small business client to a bond issue sold to a large investment fund that does not have a relationship with the bank.

6.1.4   Intraday Liquidity Risk

The latest type of liquidity risk hitting the spotlight is intraday risk. The intraday liquidity risk is the inability to meet intraday payments and settlement obligations on a timely basis under both normal and stressed conditions. Here it is not only the amount that is important but rather the timing of the payment, that is when during the day the payments happen.

Banks with access to payment systems like BACS in the United Kingdom have multiple payments coming in and going out throughout the day. The intraday risk is not about the net total amount going through each day but is rather concerned about the gross liquidity outflows, which could create a temporary net funding shortfall at different points during the day. These might not be large amounts compared to the overall size of a bank's liabilities but a failure of one bank honouring its settlements can have a knock-on effect on other banks and stop the payment and settlement systems from functioning smoothly. Therefore, intraday risk is of great concern to the regulators.

The regulatory developments in Europe with the introduction of the LCR and NSFR are specifically set to measure the risk of funding outflows and how well the bank is prepared (by maintaining a liquidity buffer) to sustain those outflows. The topic of intraday liquidity risk is not part of that effort or, as BCBS themselves state, in their consulting document monitoring indicators for intraday liquidity management: *'Although the LCR is designed to promote the short term resilience of a bank's liquidity profile, it does not currently include intraday liquidity within its calibration.'* Therefore the BCBS has set out a number of reporting and monitoring requirements to address those instead of trying to introduce a specific liquidity requirement for intraday liquidity risk. There are various ways to analyse the intraday liquidity risk but the method recommended here is largely based on the consultative document from the BCBS on intraday liquidity risk, which encompasses all of the critical components.[10]

When assessing its intraday liquidity risk the bank should first identify its intraday liquidity needs, which can be defined as *'funds which can be accessed during the business day, usually to enable financial institutions to make payments in real* time'.[11] A business day in this concept is when the settlement systems are open for making and receiving payments. What the amount is depends first and foremost on whether a bank is a member of the general payment system in its area and as such is making payments on a client's behalf. The risk stems from the cash flow streams or, more precisely, when payments need to be made to other participants in the payment system, or to other systems, and finally to payments arising from providing contingent intraday liquidity liabilities to clients. To meet those payments the bank has its own sources of liquidity, such as:

– Cash balances or collateral pledged with the central bank.
– Its own unencumbered liquid assets on the bank's balance sheet, which can be repaid to the central bank if needed.
– Cash or credit lines with other banks (these need to be available intraday).
– Finally, for banks that do not have direct access themselves to the settlement systems but instead rely on other banks to provide the service, they rely on collateral placed with that settlement bank (or credit line) if needed.

Before using the above-mentioned sources to cover outgoing payments the bank will rely on intraday payments received from other system participants. Therefore, when an intraday liquidity requirement is analysed it should take into account the fact that outflows can be netted against inflows, but there will be timing differences between those making the bank a net receiver and net payer vis-à-vis the system. Therefore it is not sufficient to analyse the intraday flows on a net cash basis.

When assessing the bank's intraday liquidity requirement the bank should look at the likely liquidity usage both under normal circumstances and stressed conditions. Consequently, no single measurement or indicator can measure the intraday liquidity risk embedded in the business and such an approach is not adequate. The BCBS has suggested a few indicators, which if applied give a good overview of the risk at large. They are:

(a) *Daily maximum liquidity requirement.* This is completed by calculating the daily net cumulative position over a period of time. Confusing as it may sound, this is the difference between the value of payment received and paid out during the day. The largest negative cumulative position is called the 'daily maximum liquidity requirement' for that day. To establish its maximum exposure the bank will conduct this experiment over a period of time. As the traffic going through the settlement systems is cyclical and depends on economic

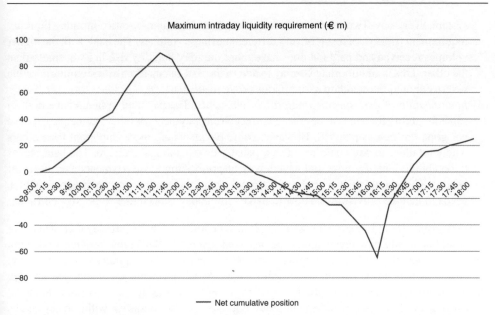

Figure 6.6   Intraday cash flows

activity (salaries, VAT payments, etc.), the period analysed needs to be sufficiently long. It should cover periods of likely high outflows, such as month ends, quarter ends, tax payment days (e.g. VAT deadline) and any other expected spikes the bank can reasonably expect. Figure 6.6 shows how the daily outflow maximum number is calculated. As it is the liquidity requirement that is being analysed, it is the largest negative number we are concerned about. In the example it is –€63 m.

When these analyses are done over time, the bank should be able to determine the largest single negative cumulative intraday requirement in its regular business. This is the minimum number the bank needs to be able to have available (assuming the bank has a negative number) on any given business day. As seen from the graph, this reflects the net change from the opening balance of that day with either the central bank (for direct participants to the payment system) or the settlement bank (for indirect participants). These analyses reflect the amount of risk under normal conditions and should be performed regularly as the business volume of the bank will change over time. It is important to stress that this scenario reflects only normal circumstances and takes into account payments coming in through the systems. In times of stress the payments from certain banks might not happen, hence increasing the net cumulative intraday liquidity stress for our bank. The quick domino effect is the reason why regulators are now putting increased emphasis on intraday liquidity risk.

(b) *Available intraday liquidity*. This measurement summarizes the amount of liquidity the bank has ready to cover its intraday exposure as calculated under point (a). The sources of the liquidity were listed earlier and as the requirement is calculated under normal conditions the buffer available needs to be somewhat higher to account for any market liquidity risks happening simultaneously.

(c) *Total payments*. This is for the bank to establish the intraday liquidity risk, which is not only subject to the largest cumulative negative balance but the amount that goes through the system, every day. Two banks could have the same maximum negative intraday liquidity requirement (peak) as a result of very different business volumes. The bank with the higher volumes received and paid out does have more intraday liquidity risk in its business than the other. This is an important overlay to add to the risk calculations as it signifies possible severity should the standard assumptions prove inadequate.

(d) *Identification of time-specific and critical payments.* The payment systems have built in some flexibility for banks to be able to correct wrong payments or other payments that have not gone through as planned. However, some payments are more important than others where a failure to pay could result in a penalty or reputational damage. The bank needs to be able to identify those and have a way of prioritizing those payments over others if needed. This should tie in with the operational part of the contingency funding plan, which needs to include provisions on how to make critical payments under stressed conditions.

These points should give a bank good guidance on how to view its intraday risk, where the risk could arise and how much should be provided against it. Banks that provide settlement services on behalf of other institutions carry heightened intraday liquidity risk as they can be viewed as part of the overall settlement system. As all payments are channelled through them and their business is to provide settlement and payment services to other financial intermediaries, they need to address intraday liquidity as a business risk with greater details and measurements than described here.

The above-mentioned framework is for managing and monitoring intraday liquidity risk under normal circumstances. As the payment patterns might be quite different during stressed conditions, it needs to be stressed how the intraday risk could be established under adverse conditions. That is being shown in the stress test chapter (see Chapter 10, Stress Testing and the Contingency Funding Plan).

6.1.5   Intragroup Liquidity Risk

Understandably, this source of liquidity risk is only applicable for banks operating within a group structure or with subsidiaries. However, as the business of banking is becoming more sophisticated with companies being set up in various jurisdictions for tax purposes, the concept of intragroup liquidity risk and trapped liquidity is becoming more significant.

Intragroup liquidity risk arises in two ways. Firstly, intragroup liquidity risk is present if a bank relies on other group entities for liquidity support, either as a part of its own liquidity buffer or as a contingency requirement. In some jurisdictions the requirement is not for each entity to be self-sufficient in terms of liquidity but rather it allows them to rely on each other for funds. As an example, in the United Kingdom the general rule is for self-sufficiency unless a bank has applied for a modification to that rule, which then allows the bank under certain restrictions to rely on its parent for support. This is, however, a limited support and a certain amount of reserves need to be available in the jurisdiction.

Secondly, the reverse setup also needs to be acknowledged; that is a bank may be subject to other parts of the group calling on its liquidity sources, through informal or formal agreements. This is the more difficult part as circumstances within other entities might not be as clear as the bank's own conditions and the bank is also reliant on the quality of the risk management framework within the other entities to alert in a timely manner if conditions have changed. As a part of the bank's risk assessment, it needs to ensure that the other frameworks are adequate and a communication channel to the contingency fund provider is clearly set out.

This risk is best analysed by mapping out the reliance on others for liquidity and from others to the bank. It is then measured by assuming that the group will not repay money owed to the bank but the bank will meet the obligation to other parts of the group – a kind of worst case scenario. The outcome can give a good indication of the risk at hand. It should be noted that the risk is not only that the group will not be in a financial position to honour its obligation but that it is not allowed to do so. There can be legal restrictions enforced in other jurisdictions that under times of stress do not allow funds to be channelled to other group entities. These restrictions need to be looked at closely and taken into account. The bank should discuss the intragroup framework with the regulator with the aim of getting a better understanding of how the regulator will react under market-wide liquidity stresses. Regulators work closely together but their duty is first and foremost to their own jurisdiction, which might not always align with the objectives of other regulators. The examples from the financial crises of funds being trapped or up-streamed to parent companies, even in other continents, still hang on the wall in the regulator's office and they will do their utmost to ensure that they are not repeated. Therefore, the channels and conduct might be very different under stressed conditions compared to the business-as-usual environment, where the sequence of actions and its framework are clear.

The results from the intragroup analyses form a part of the base for the general liquidity stress tests and the liquidity buffer requirement.

As a part of the intragroup liquidity risk the bank can also assess the possible contagion from other parts of the group. It is an understandable tendency to look at the relationship through the lens of a lawyer, but under times of stress the bank might have no other options than to support subsidiaries far beyond the contractual obligations to avoid the risk contracting the parent as well. This is discussed further later on, but from the liquidity management perspective the risk under severe conditions is likely to be linked to the name but not the legal structure.

6.1.6 Off-balance Sheet Liquidity Risk

Off-balance sheet risk is easy to understand but more difficult to account for. Here it is possible to draw some lessons from what happened in 2007. The ESCB (European System of Central Banks) data show that the total off-balance sheet credit commitments of EU banks amounted to close to 17% of on-balance sheet assets in the year 2006, up from 2% in 2001.[12] In March the next year, the Senior Supervisors Group concluded in their report that '*several firms did not properly recognize or control for the contingent liquidity risk in their conduit businesses or recognize the reputation risk associated with the SIV business*'.[13]

In assessing the off-balance sheet contingency liquidity risk, the risk specialist needs first of all to identify all the off-balance sheet items that could have cash flow impacts on the bank. These following categories outline the main possible sources of off-balance sheet liquidity risk:

– Undrawn overdraft and other credit standby limits
– Undrawn credit card limits
– Contingent liquidity support to investment vehicles and securitization programmes
– Lending pipeline and 'unavoidable' underwriting of new business or extension of existing loans
– Liquidity commitments provided
– Collateral requirements of derivatives positions.

The list shows the off-balance sheet items either being of a credit or liquidity nature, which is a good starting point to differentiate as the likelihood for sudden drawdown is quite different for a liquidity line than a credit line.

As these factors are different in nature the same assumptions cannot be applied to all. The probability of all the credit cards being fully drawn to the maximum limits is far less than a single investment vehicle needing liquidity support. As the aggregate number from the off-balance sheet items can be quite high, the assumptions on the possible utilization play a key role when analysing the risk at hand.

To start with, the bank needs to know the amount of all its off-balance sheet commitments should they all be fully drawn. To increase knowledge of the likelihood of drawdown and the off-balance sheet implied, the bank would have to perform a historical analysis of the different sources and their stability through stressed conditions, if possible. To further understand the risk, it is necessary to assess how these factors would perform under stress. The method of how the analyses are best done is to break up the off-balance sheet commitments into each of their subcategories and then later on down to a sufficiently detailed basis. This should reveal the various different types of off-balance sheet items and customer categories the bank has, which will enable the risk specialist to get a firmer grasp on the risk and likely behaviour. The question to ask is under what circumstances is the category likely to draw down and are those circumstances likely to be firm, specific or correlated to other firms having the same problem? Then the bank needs to assess whether it is only bound by legal requirements or if its support to the receiver is critical and hence the bank will not be able to reject the support without severe consequences. The more comprehensive breakdown that can be provided the better, as this contributes to a better understanding of this type of risk. Special attention should be given to the type of commitments that are likely to be correlated with the bank's own financial health and might fall on to the bank at the same time the bank is needing liquidity to serve its own business.

Box 6.3   Contract for Differences – an Example of an Off-balance Sheet Risk

'An easy risk to understand but more difficult to account for' is how we choose to describe the off-balance sheet liquidity risk. An example of this paradigm is of a bank that offered CFDs (Contract for Differences) to their clients, which is effectively a derivative on a certain stock. The long and short of it was that the bank got into trouble when off-balance sheet commitments related to those derivatives surfaced. What happened was the unexpected correlation between two types of liquidity risk. At the same time the underlying shares took a dive (the worst daily drop in the FTSE for over 20 years), the few counterparties the bank was reliant on to provide lines for this business increased their 'haircuts' for doing business. The combined market-wide and firm-specific risk required the bank suddenly to post a much greater amount of collateral than expected.

Under this category it is also useful to include the uncertainty on the volume of new requests for loans or loan renewals. Banks can in principle refuse to extend loans or grant new loans but in reality lending does not really stop, even in dire times. This is an obvious problem if the lack of liquidity is a company-specific problem but not a general credit crunch. For one bank to stop lending to its customers while others continue to do so is a situation bankers do not want to face and could send out a signal to the market. The risk specialist should allow for other interests to come into play when managing liquidity and expect to need to make certain compromises from what they expect to be the ideal course of action.

Additionally, it can be expected that contagion risk is at play and one face of the liquidity problem would be a borrower who cannot pay back the loan or get it refinanced elsewhere, which effectively could make the client's problem inherently the problem of the bank.

6.1.7   Cross-currency Liquidity Risk

For most countries with established foreign exchange markets the cross-currency risk might not be the most pronounced one. However, in 2007 and again in 2011 banks faced unexpected challenges obtaining US dollar funding and it was only after the European Central Bank (ECB) involvement that the foreign exchange spot market became liquid. This cross-currency risk with regard to the major currencies has somewhat dwindled after the central banks from the G7 nations agreed that the emergency currency swap lines established in the crises were to be made permanent to provide a backstop to the market. For banks operating in small monetary systems this is, however, truly a large risk factor. This was, amongst other things, the reason for the fall of the Icelandic banks; they had liquidity but it did not help very much as it was denominated in an obscure currency called Icelandic krona (ISK) while their liabilities that needed to be refinanced were in the major currencies USD, EUR and GBP. As the foreign exchange market evaporated, the liquidity denominated in ISK could not be exchanged into any usable currency. Iceland is not the only country that this has happened to. Examples from the emerging economies, both in Eastern Europe and Latin America, show the same type of risk. So when it comes to currency liquidity risk the prudent treasurer cannot rely on viewing all currencies as one but has to review the overall currency mismatch and the largest gaps for each material currency. The currency risk is not only limited to the liabilities but also the assets that the bank holds as a liquidity buffer or even within its contingency funding plans. Long-dated assets in certain currencies can be difficult to use to cover short-term liabilities in that same currency and even more so if the plan is to account for them to match liabilities in other currencies. Extra attention should be given if the bank has no funding channels in a currency it is lending in and is hence fully reliant on the currency markets.

A good principle for banks exposed to cross-currency risk is to run the stress tests separately for every material currency. It is not uncommon for regulators to ask for separate returns for all currencies accountable for over 20% of the bank's balance sheet and that can be used as a starting point. Most banks will have 'shortfalls' in some currencies and surpluses in others and need to look at the historic currency volatility (and worst case scenario) to gauge whether sufficient funds can be moved from one currency to the other.

6.1.8   Funding Cost Risk

Funding cost risk could be classified as a secondary liquidity risk. It comes into play when liquidity is available but only at a price that is unsustainable for the bank and will jeopardize the bank as an overall going concern. It might in the short run not be as serious and knee jerking as the other types of liquidity risk described earlier, as the bank can get funds if needed. However, this type of liquidity risk is a very good sign of rising market liquidity risk, which plays a large part in the overall liquidity risk assessment. If the short-term or deposit markets rise suddenly it is a clear sign that the market forces are at play and the excess demand over supply of funding is pushing up the rates. This is more often than not a sign of credit risk (or perceived credit risk) transforming itself into liquidity risk.

If a bank continues to reprice liabilities at a higher rate, it can eventually lead to going concern issues. Therefore, in liquidity management, even though the funds are available it does not mean they are usable in the long run and this needs to be kept under observation.

There are some difficulties in measuring if the funding cost is putting the franchise into difficulty and the questions to ask are whether the situation or conditions will persist or whether they are only temporary. There are always those who will argue the latter and soon the bank will find cheaper funding or manage to reprice the loan portfolio. Notice should be given as to how long this abnormality exists and if market conditions allow for the lending to be adjusted to the increasing borrowing cost. This can be a wider problem and could inflict damage on many banks or even the whole market when market adjustments are taking place. In the UK market in 2012, banks experienced increased competition in the deposit market and deposit rates for on-demand deposits even exceeded long-term mortgage rates. Even though the liability side of the banks in general became more and more expensive, the lending did not reflect those increased costs. Perhaps there was a general reluctance to make loans that impacted on the lending market but it was obvious that the marginal deposit rate paid by the high street was far too high to support current lending practices.

As the funding cost risk is secondary and usually is not acute, the tendency is to put it a notch lower than the others. This should not be the case. Out of all the various Sources of Liquidity Risk this one has the most predicting power. It is widely argued that liquidity crises do not come out of the blue and signs and strains can most often be picked up from the market place. Therefore, having a good grip on rising funding spreads is an important indicator of liquidity risk and banks should assess how sensitive they are to price changes. This is something that is discussed in detail in Chapter 10, where the early warning triggers are analysed.

6.1.9   Asset Risk

Here it is useful to look at what the UK regulator has done. It differentiates between the risk embedded in 'marketable assets' and 'nonmarketable assets'. The reason the PRA chooses to view marketable assets separately is that some of them can be counted towards meeting the overall liquidity requirement and a drop in pricing of those assets (or increased haircuts) may lead to the bank failing to meet its requirements. The PRA defines 'marketable assets' as those that can be sold outright or repoed.

The value of those types of asset is dependent on various things such as the depth of their market place, the amount being held, etc. In essence it can be said about almost all assets that they can become illiquid on a bad day and therefore the approach in the '6 Step Framework' is not to split the assets into two buckets. The best way to estimate the risk embedded in the asset portfolio is to look at the position the company holds in relation to the amount sold each day in the market place, both under stressed and normal conditions. If these assets are being held for repo, then the depth of that market needs to be known, by checking the volumes and how reliant the bank is on certain counterparties to provide repos. This is especially important if the assets do not have an outright price themselves and can only be realized via repos.

The liquidity risk originating from the asset side has been widely viewed as systemic risk. When a certain type of behaviour is taken across an industry as a whole the risk becomes pro-cyclical. Market participants tend to mirror each other's reactions as many of them are bound by the same constraints. Therefore, when few participants start to sell and unwind positions, it can trigger others to start selling as well, creating a self-made inflicted market drop.

The case of Bear Sterns in 2008 is a case of liquidity risk derived from assets and asset valuations. At the time of need counterparties were unwilling to provide funding even against high-quality assets. Prior to 2008, the general consensus was that secured funding markets were strong as long as there were underlying assets. The experience in 2008 proved the assumption wrong; the availability of secured funding is always a mix of the asset quality (and the perceived asset quality) and the counterparty involved. The aftermath of 2008 revealed why counterparty risk is still significant as getting the asset (collateral) delivered to cover the exposure was far from a straightforward process. It could even be argued that the practical experience of 2008 exhibited the condition that, even though the documentation and the setup of the secured financing is done to preserve the right of the lender, when it comes to unwinding of positions and making the loans whole, the process is more complex than anyone expected. This extra layer of uncertainty and surely delay for the borrower is another reason why some types of secured funding will carry a premium. This can be interpreted in such a way that as long as banks still have a bad taste in their mouth after 2008 the secured funding markets will remain fickle, something that liquidity planning needs to take account of. Needless to say, there are different kinds of secured funding and one should not draw parallels between the repo market for unlisted assets and, for example, the AAA/Aaa rated RMBS (residential mortgage backed security) market. The method of providing a lien over an asset also plays a significant part and there is a difference between having pledged an asset and actually having delivered it to the lender.

6.1.10   Funding Concentration Risk

Funding concentration or rather funding diversification is everyone's favourite and simply puts more diversification into funding between counterparties, markets, currencies and products – the more the better. The listing of all funding sources described earlier in this chapter makes it easier to recognize if this is a material risk factor for the bank or not. There is no simple way of measuring funding concentration, let alone to compare it between banks, but some have experimented with a variation of the Herfindahl concentration ratio.[14] The Herfindahl index is usually calculated as the sum of squares of the proportion (share) of each of the funding categories in relation to total funding. The higher the concentration of funding the higher the index becomes. Empirical research supports this risk assessment.

Most banks look at this risk by listing the exposure they have to their largest funding providers (like a top 10 depositor list). This gives a good indication of how reliant the bank is on others and if funding concentration is relevant. Subsidiaries or groups of banking entities, operating under a centralized funding model where one entity provides funding for the others, is an example of where this risk needs special attention. Funding concentration risk should not only be looked at from a static analytical point of view but should also play a large role when setting the bank's funding strategy. The diversification aspect of liquidity risk should not be underestimated; the lesson learnt from the credit crunch was that no single type of funding can be viewed as riskless and an assumption on what is risky and what is not can easily change quickly. The concept and assessment of diversification is further dealt with in Section 8.5,

Funding Strategy, under the title 'The myth of diversification', which warns against taking too much comfort from a single measurement of diversification.

6.1.11   Correlation and Contagion Risk

There is a good reason for not starting off by trying to define this source of liquidity risk as it deals with the risk when one source of liquidity risk materializes in another type of liquidity risk. This can be explained with an example. On Thursday 13 September 2007 people started queuing outside Northern Rock branches in the United Kingdom to withdraw their deposits. The first bank run in the United Kingdom since 1866 had begun.[15] The origin? Material losses 3 months earlier, of two highly levered hedge funds sponsored by Bear Stearns in the United States, were revealed. One cannot immediately spot the link between those two events, one being a retail bank run in the middle of England, the other a wholesale liquidity risk event happening thousands of miles away. What was the link? Firstly, with the correlation and contagion risk, there is hardly ever a straightforward relationship between factors. The 'if A, then B' train of thought does not apply and one should not expect to see the public starting to queue next time a hedge fund sinks. The contagion factor is changeable and very dynamic. What happened in June 2007 was that a highly leveraged hedge fund, sponsored by Bear Stearns, suffered material losses on their $20bn ABS portfolio as it contained direct and indirect exposure to subprime RMBSs. Margin calls resulted in a sale of ca. $4bn of assets in a week, driving down prices and drying up the secondary market, even for AAA rated tranches. The spiral continued as haircuts were increased. The market turbulence soon caught the interbank money markets and the ball started rolling and growing in size. Northern Rock, not having been able to securitize its mortgages for some time, funded its assets in the short-dated market waiting for things to improve. It is worth noting that Northern Rock was a mortgage lender in the United Kingdom, and not in any way associated with US subprime mortgages. The short-term funding became increasingly difficult and Northern Rock ended seeking emergency funding from the Bank of England. The stigma attached to this fuelled the retail markets and a bank run took place. The relationship between these two events is not obvious and is covered by many 'what if' questions. What if the funding profile of the hedge funds had been different, could the immediate sell have been avoided? What if the general public had understood the deposit guarantee in place and what if the word 'bail-out' had been avoided in the media, etc.? Just as in the comparison to the *Titanic* disaster in Section 5.1, many things could have prevented what happened but did not.

This is what the liquidity source risk of correlation and contagion is about. There is no simple formula to follow to gauge this risk, but some guidance can be given and the risk specialist should focus his efforts and analysis on the material funding sources. Once they have been laid out (as demonstrated earlier in this chapter) a SWOT (strengths, weaknesses, opportunities and threats) analysis needs to be conducted for each of them. Looking at the strengths, weaknesses, opportunities and threats of each funding channel, the analyst can understand better what external factors could come into play for the weaknesses and threats. But why include the strengths and opportunities part as well? Firstly, they give a good input into the Funding Strategy the bank needs to set out (see Section 8.5) and, secondly, by highlighting the opportunity of one funding channel its shortcomings should become clearer. To provide an example, the opportunity of issuing bonds in a new market is mirrored by the threat that these investors are not close to the bank or share a relationship, and hence these bonds are less stable. This assessment will provide increased understanding of the bank's funding fragility but will not be a quantifiable measurement, but rather a qualitative assessment.

Endnotes

1. Adapted from Matz, L. and Neu, P. (editors) (2007), *Liquidity Risk Measures and Management, A Practitioner's Guide to Global Best Practices*, John Wiley & Sons Ltd, and Prudential Regulation Authority (PRA), *Prudential Sourcebook for Banks, Building Societies and Investment Firms (BIPRU)*, Chapter 12.5.14. Available at: www.fsa.gov.uk.
2. See Prudential Regulation Authority (PRA), *Prudential Sourcebook for Banks, Building Societies and Investment Firms (BIPRU)*, Chapter 12.5.14. Available at: www.fsa.gov.uk.
3. The PRA's list of ten Sources of Liquidity Risk is: wholesale secured and unsecured funding risk, retail funding risk, intraday liquidity risk, intragroup liquidity risk, cross-currency liquidity risk, off-balance sheet liquidity risk, franchise-viability risk, marketable assets risk, nonmarketable assets risk and funding concentration risk.
4. Survey commissioned by Santander, April 2013. See http://www.which.co.uk/news/2013/04/customers-stick-with-bank-account-for-16-years-317991/ for details.
5. See Llewellyn, D. (2009) The Northern Rock Crises: A Multidimensional Problem, from *The Failure of Northern Rock: A Multi-dimensional Case Study*, SUERF – The European Money and Finance Forum, Vienna, 2009, p. 18.
6. See *The Financial Times* on 10 July 2007, '*When the music stops, in terms of liquidity, things will be complicated. But as long as the music is playing, you've got to get up and dance. We're still dancing,*' said Chuck Prince, former Chairman and Chief Executive of Citigroup.
7. See Eisenbeis, R. and Kaufman, G. (2009) Lessons from the Demise of the UK's Northern Rock and the US's Countrywide and Indymac, from *The Failure of Northern Rock: A Multi-dimensional Case Study*, SUERF – The European Money and Finance Forum, Vienna, 2009, pp. 73–94.
8. See Senior Supervisors Group (2009), *Risk Management Lessons from the Global Banking Crisis of 2008*, 21 October 2009, p. 8.
9. See Basel Committee for Banking Supervision (2008), *Principles for Sound Liquidity Risk Management and Supervision*, September 2008, p. 11.
10. Basel Committee on Banking Supervision (2012), Consultative Document, *Monitoring Indicators for Intraday Liquidity Management*, July 2012.
11. Basel Committee on Banking Supervision (2012), Consultative Document, *Monitoring Indicators for Intraday Liquidity Management*, July 2012.
12. See European Central Bank, *EU Banking Sector Stability*, February 2003 and November 2007.
13. See Senior Supervisors Group (2009) *Risk Management Lessons from the Global Banking Crisis of 2008*, 21 October 2009, p. 5.
14. See, for example, Praet, P. and Herzberg, V. (2008) Market Liquidity and Banking Liquidity: Linkages, Vulnerabilities and the Role of Disclosure, from *Banque de France, Financial Stability Review*, Special Issue on Liquidity, No. 11, February 2008, p. 95.
15. Lastra, R. (2009) Northern Rock and Banking Law Reform in the UK, from *The Failure of Northern Rock: A Multi-dimensional Case Study*, SUERF – The European Money and Finance Forum, Vienna, 2009, p. 133.

7

Step II: Risk Appetite

Now that the risk assessment has been concluded the risk specialist should have an overview of what kind of liquidity risk is material, what the funding profile of the bank is, etc. The next step is to formulate a high-level liquidity risk appetite statement. One might argue that setting the risk appetite should happen first, before the bank starts its operations and accepts liquidity risk. That would be the case if we were starting up a bank, but the reality is that the banks came first and risk management was introduced much later.

7.1 THE RISK APPETITE STATEMENT

A risk appetite statement is the overall 'mission statement' for liquidity and funding. The aspect we are concerned about here is the 'micro' angle focusing on an individual bank. If one subscribes to the view that the appetite for risk goes in cycles, then the liquidity risk appetite can also play a 'macro' role in creating liquidity cycles that can pose threats to the financial stability. Benoît Cœuré, Member of the Executive Board of the ECB, pointed out how the increased appetite for liquidity risk eats up liquidity and creates at the end a liquidity shortage, which in turn decreases risk appetite. Benoît calls them 'global liquidity cycles', where liquidity fluctuation exacerbates the underlying weaknesses in the economies.[1] This is a valid observation but for this book we limit ourselves to a single bank.

7.1.1 Eggs, Omelettes and a Free Lunch in the Board Room

The risk appetite can be described as the nature and extent of risk the financial organization is willing to take in pursuit of its business objectives. One has to break an egg to make an omelette and running a bank cannot be done without taking risk. As simple as this may sound, this is still widely misunderstood and the root of some fundamental misconceptions of the role of banks. Unlike some other businesses one is able to get a rough idea of a bank's risk profile by looking at its funding cost.[2] For example, Bank A is funding itself in the deposit market at 1.5% in 1 year. Another bank, Bank B, much smaller and with a lower credit rating, is offering better rates of 2%. The difference in return to the investor is the higher risk for placing his/her money for 1 year with Bank B but not the generosity of Bank B. A bank with higher returns on its assets should generally be expected to be riskier, though other things like efficiency, size, etc., do play a part. This simplistic and rather obvious risk–return example should act as a reminder to those who set the risk appetite – without any risk the bank does not make any returns. Subsequently, higher expected returns demand higher risk, which experience has taught is closer to the reality, rather than accept as true that the bank is just smarter and better than the rest.

This also means that the risk appetite does not only describe the risk the bank is willing to take but also to accept and tolerate. If banks take on risk according to their risk appetite, then the difference between the spread between the two above-mentioned banks should lie in their stated willingness to take risk and their risk versus return approach.

Agreeing on the appropriate risk appetite is no easy matter. The Board needs to balance and weigh the different perspective of the various stakeholders and, as P.G. Wodehouse put it, '*it all depends from where you are looking*'.[3] The equity holders require returns and might have a different appetite for risk than the rating agencies, which are predominately concerned about the safety of the creditors, etc. There is no easy task for the Board to find the golden middle ground that satisfies everyone.

Then there is the problem of articulating the risk, which can be an interesting exercise. Most Board members have little problem when asked to define what is an acceptable minimum return for the bank as there are many comparables against which to set the benchmark. Fewer hands are raised when the question is asked about how much risk the bank is willing to take and accept in exchange for those returns. There is no free lunch, not even in the Board room. Many are uncomfortable underwriting acceptance or acknowledgement of risk, especially liquidity risk, and view risk as some unlikely and unexpected random event, which should sit next to the word failure in the dictionary of banking. In reality, as mentioned earlier, risk is the heart of a bank and without it we have no banking. Credit risk is the most basic of all risk types within the risk appetite statement and the one the Board usually can accept without difficulty. It is easily understood as the bank suffers when someone does not meet their payments, etc. Boards spend their time looking at credit quality of large exposures and are well aware what can go wrong and how it will impact on the bank. This has already been filtered into the regulatory requirements through the setting of capital ratios that are set as a proportion of risk-weighted assets.

When it comes to less tangible risk factors, such as liquidity risk, it can be more difficult to obtain a general consensus on what is the tolerance limit. Many feel that the bank should under no circumstances be able to fail due to liquidity risk. This becomes more apparent when doing reverse stress testing, which is an exercise to draw up a risk scenario and define a risk level at which the bank admits it will fail (see also Section 10.2).

7.2 DRAWING UP A RISK APPETITE STATEMENT

The risk appetite statement needs to be clearly articulated and understood. This might look like an obvious statement but nevertheless it needs to be put forward. A risk appetite statement built around complex metrics or models is not something the stakeholders and risk owners will relate to. It should be formalized at the highest level of the bank as this defines the purpose of the organization just as much as how much credit risk the bank is willing to take in its business activities. Setting the risk appetite at the Board level ensures that the undertaking of liquidity risk is adequate to the overall business strategy and interlinked to other risk taking within the bank. By providing a Board approved risk appetite statement, the Board also takes on the responsibility to see that these limitations are met and consequently liquidity is put on the Board's agenda to enable the Board members to execute their oversight duties. The second BCBS Sound Principle echoes this top-down approach: '*A Bank should clearly articulate a liquidity risk tolerance that is appropriate for its business strategy and its role in the financial system.*'[4]

The liquidity risk appetite can be defined in various ways but they should be articulated through both quantifiable and qualitative measures. The importance of qualitative measurements should not be neglected as it defines the approach to risk taking. A risk appetite based solely on some quantitative rules that cannot be broken does not send the right message to senior management and employees on how the bank wants to conduct its risk taking. The credo that everything is fine as long as you do not break the limit can lead to excessive risk taking and an approach to circumvent the metrics. The Board needs to set the risk–reward relationship at a high level to make sure that additional returns are gained from good execution but not additional risk.

Example 7.1   The Risk Appetite of Barclays Bank[5]

Barclays Bank is an example of a bank that has 'done things in the right order' and its annual report tells us much more than the bare numbers and readings from risk metric calculations. We can, for example, see that the Board Risk Committee spent 61% of their time in 2012 discussing the bank's risk profile and risk appetite and only 6% of the time on risk policies and internal control. In different words, the Board spend their time on setting the future course rather than ticking off risk reports. Barclays seems to keep a strong discipline in their camp and even report how well each member attends meetings, something which is becoming a more popular disclosure.

Barclays defines its liquidity risk appetite (LRA) as: the level of risk that Barclays is prepared to sustain whilst pursuing its business strategy, recognizing a range of possible outcomes as business plans are implemented.

A part of Barclays LRA are three primary defined stress scenarios, the outcome of which defines the size of the liquidity buffer. The stress scenarios are:

- a three month market-wide stress event;
- a one month Barclays-specific stress event; and
- a combined one month market-wide and Barclays-specific stress event.

Source: Barclays plc Annual Report 2012.

A few words will follow on what to aim for when making the liquidity risk appetite statement. The overarching goal is to prevent the earnings of the bank or even its going concern from the impact of liquidity events. It needs to be recognized that the bank is not in control of all the factors that influence liquidity risk and there could be random market events or changes in external factors, the impact of which the bank cannot avoid. The bank has, however, two ways of limiting its risk exposure, which need to be differentiated.

It can control its *exposure* to these uncertainties and, secondly, its *sensitivity* to the possible changes. The risk appetite statement controls the afore-mentioned amount of exposure but the sensitivity can be measured and managed with active liquidity management and liquidity policies. When the risk appetite statement is written it is useful to keep these two limits in mind, exposure and sensitivity. They are both under the power of the bank and the risk appetite statement needs to express how the bank will set the parameters under its control. There is no use including other parameters in the risk appetite statement, especially those the bank has no control over. A statement like 'the bank shall not lose more than $600m of deposits a month' might at first glance have captured the risk, but when looked at more closely it is impossible for the bank to arrange its affairs in such a way that the scenario will never happen – that is simply not in its power.

7.2.1   Risk Appetite Set at the Appropriate Level

The risk appetite needs to be applied at the appropriate level within the bank. Notice needs to be given to the legal structure, the setup of subsidiaries and all other factors that can hamper the free flow of funds. Any restrictions of fund flow require the bank to split itself up into liquidity entities, which effectively all need to be viewed on a stand-alone basis. This is something banks can fail to do adequately by not linking the separate entities together into one in terms of risk taking. The aggregation of liquidity risk is not always as straightforward as one would expect, as not all restrictions are legal or geographic. As an example material exposure in various currencies requires the bank to consider if a single goal is sufficient or if further breakdown is necessary. The test that the risk appetite statement needs to pass is whether it encompasses the whole bank and the risk within it.

Again, the setting needs to be done according to a top-down approach. A risk appetite statement done using the bottom-up approach can often easily be spotted and shows a clear sign of the tail wagging the dog. There are a few methods that can be applied that usually start by assessing the risk capacity of the organization. Below is guidance for some qualitative and quantitative measures that can be used to build the risk appetite.

The qualitative measurements should:

- Recognize that not all risk factors can be measured or quantified.
- Set the approach to risk taking and acceptance, where the focus is on substance over form.
- Tie the risk taking to the business plan, strategy and objectives.
- Set out what type of risk the institution has zero tolerance for.

The quantitative measurements need to:

- Be fixed and finite measurements, easily quantifiable. They should not change in order to change market conditions or other external factors.
- Be set in relation and applied to major and relevant sources of risk to the bank and its business plans.

The quantitative measurements are supported by sets of metrics and indicators, which confirm the risk appetite compliance and also act as early warning indicators (see also Chapter 9, The Quantitative Framework). The above guidance could be applied to most types of risk within a bank, which should help the liquidity risk taking to be set in the same way as other risk elements and should also aid comparison. This will enable the bank to have an integrated approach to risk taking as opposed to a sum of various factors.

The quantitative part of the liquidity risk statements can be set out in the following way:

(a) *Liquidity risk tolerance limit approach.* It is important to quantify the tolerance by some means, if for no other reason than focusing on what are the most likely liquidity pitfalls the bank would find itself in. This can be built on simple metrics such as a loan-to-deposit ratio and be expanded depending on the complexity of the bank's operations and risk. A straightforward single limit can capture the risk of a one-dimensional saving and lending institution but will become less reliable as the business becomes more complicated. However, a balance needs to be struck, where the liquidity tolerance statement should try to be as overarching as possible and should not confuse the various metrics the bank can use to measure and manage its liquidity. One can think about this as a mission statement versus a business plan. That said, appropriate risk limits applied on measurable and relevant risk factors are the single most effective risk control tool but belong in the liquidity policy rather than the statement. The appetite statement should therefore include larger, broad tolerance limits which will cascade down the organization and divide into smaller metrics, limits or observation points.

(b) *Minimum survival period or scenario-based limits.* Setting the risk appetite as a minimum time period the bank needs to be able to function without external funding is a popular and useful method as it brings in the time aspect of liquidity risk. Furthermore, this measurement captures all types of liquidity risk (or rather their impact) and hence should be a strong guard against unforeseen and unexpected events. The downside is that most banks have substantial amounts of on-demand or other short-dated liabilities, which require the policy maker to set assumptions on their expected outflows under stress. Consequently, the risk appetite becomes a function of the assumption, which can be seen as a drawback but is difficult to avoid.

The minimum survival period could be expressed as a single statement that at all times the bank should maintain enough liquidity to withstand a severe but plausible shock. An alternative statement is to have enough liquidity to meet all outflows for a certain amount of time. The former is again based on the setting of assumptions but the latter usually does not work for banks with considerable exposure to on-demand liabilities and is better suited for wholesale funded banks.

(c) *Minimum liquidity reserve amount.* To set the risk appetite as a minimum liquidity requirement (a fixed amount to be reviewed regularly) or as a certain proportion of liabilities is a simple but effective way to ensure some sort of limit to the risk taking. The approach of using a single amount or a fixed percentage does, however, have its limitations in practice and can be seen as too general or blunt for all except smaller banks. There are ways that can be used to be more specific by taking the following into account:

- Banks with higher liquidity risk would generally agree on a higher number than less risky banks. The setting of the appropriate level is therefore always subjective but can be quantified as well.
- Type of reserve. The amount also needs to be decided, taking the type of collateral into account, under the view that less liquid collateral would justify a higher buffer than if the reserve is being held in cash only.
- Cash flow projection. Again, liquidity is a function of time and banks with low net inflows in the near term will aim at a higher reserve amount.

The risk appetite statement does not need to be overly complicated or sophisticated. Again, a well-understood short and simple statement is better than a complex description of risk models. Remember that this is set at a high level and therefore needs to be useful for strategy purposes. The liquidity risk management framework will fill out the further details and limits to individual businesses or products. Those limits are to expand on the risk statement and encourage appropriate risk taking and direction so that risk undertaken is consistent with the overall risk appetite. It is not recommended to rely only on method (b) or (c) as they only deal with the amount of liquidity as a reactive management to mitigate liquidity risk, rather than a proactive measurement. Any bank worth its weight will include some metrics and limits to be included in the business strategy rather than trying to solve the situation by maintaining a liquidity buffer.

7.2.2 Liquidity Risk Statement – Tolerance Limit Approach

When defining the risk limits one should try to think of broad limits that would capture the different ways the demon of liquidity risk can raise its ugly head. They can be balance sheet driven or limit driven. A few suggested tolerance limits are:

- Ceiling on borrowing or a maximum loan-to-deposit ratio. For a bank with a rather simple business model, the overall cap on borrowing or a limit on the loan-to-deposit ratio sets a clear stage for the risk taking. The implicit assumptions are that the deposits are valuable in their own right and more stable than other types of funding. Furthermore, by linking the deposit side to the asset side, the bank has created a good foundation to work from. A bank with limited access to the wholesale markets might choose this approach. This would be the case for small banks that have a good natural deposit franchise but lack the size and rating to seek regular funding through the markets. If this bank has more assets than deposits the bank must seek other funds than deposits to close the funding gap. It has three primary sources to do so: firstly, available cash or cash-like instruments that can be easily and quickly turned into cash; secondly, short-term borrowing limits with other financial institutions; and, finally, the wholesale funding markets. For this bank, which has defined deposit funding as its core, the fall-back solution is to fund itself from the external wholesale markets and the LDR limit is to prevent the bank from taking on this type of risk. A larger bank of strong credit quality with good market access might not find the LDR useful and prefer wholesale funding over deposit funding. The credit crunch, however, demonstrated that no matter how big a bank is the markets can shut down for everyone. There are other ratios that are similar to the LDR, such as core deposit/loans, which can be equally useful. Another way to capture the risk is to set a limit on unsecured borrowing. This assumes that secured borrowing carries less risk as the amount is equal to the assets (when haircuts have been applied) and hence the bank has created a liquidity risk hedge by this matched funding. Unsecured borrowing, on the other hand, would then be defined as the missing piece to fulfil the funding needs and by applying a limit the bank is setting its appetite for unhedged liquidity risk. This method only works if the balance sheet of the institution is of the quality and nature that it can be used for funding purposes.
- Concentration limits. Caps on exposure to a single market or a source of funding are an example of limits set to prevent concentration risk. Diversification is always a positive thing but by putting a cap on certain funding sources, the bank must access and conclude that limiting one type of funding will actually decrease funding risk and not push the bank to use less stable sources of funding to a greater extent. If this is only one of many good and healthy metrics to have, then the liquidity policy is a more appropriate home for this measurement rather than the risk appetite statement.
- Cap on funding the maturity gap (maximum gap risk or minimum cash flow coverage ratios). This is a popular way of describing the liquidity risk. There are various ways of measuring the gap, both static and dynamic. The static approach is a snapshot of the imbalances created by the different maturities of assets and liabilities with the nondated assets usually excluded from the measure. The static gap is then the asset–liability mismatch within each time bucket, where the bank can set a limit (or coverage ratio) for each bucket. This method was recommended by BCBS in their first attempt to set out general principles of sound liquidity management in the year 2000, but for some reason this recommendation is not to be found in the updated version in 2008.[6] The limit or the coverage ratio should be at 1:1 and generally higher for the near-time periods than for later periods. The method can be taken a step further by arguing that the cumulative gap is more important than the status of each maturity bucket and hence a cumulative limit should be set. This highlights the importance of the time value as a positive gap further out on the curve is of little use if the bank cannot

overcome the shorter negative mismatches. This allows the bank to 'carry forward' the excess surplus and is therefore a better indicator of the overall situation. The gap limit can be set over a particular time, such as always >0 for the first 6 months. This method can be expanded even more into a more dynamic approach. Where the static method is only a snapshot, the dynamic method tries to project the funding gap under various scenarios, both normal and stressed. This method is set out in detail in Chapter 9, Step IV: The Quantitative Framework.

The drawbacks of the cumulative method need to be recognized as it assumes the marketability of assets and that they will be paid back at maturity. Moreover, the maturity profile of the asset side of the balance sheet is made up according to contractual maturity, which hardly ever reflects the actual behaviour of the loan portfolio. On the one hand there can be assets like long-dated mortgages that are subject to refinancing, even sudden ones should rates move. On the other side, corporate lending is frequently done under the assumption that the loan will be rolled over and not repaid at maturity. Even though the bank had the right to demand payment, the business plans of the borrowers usually do not take this into account and the borrower may be unable to pay. It is therefore important to do some sensitivity analysis on the behaviour maturities, looking in detail into the loan categories and estimating the refinancing needs for each of them. Each asset class has its own attributes and it is possible for the bank to assign a haircut to each one of them. The haircuts should also take into account the market sensitivity the assets could have if they are at all marketable.

Just like any other measurements the balance sheet limits described above need to be applied while keeping their limitations in mind. Firstly, they should not be used unaccompanied to measure liquidity risk as they:

- Are retrospective in nature and use historical accounting data and therefore do not capture fully the expected funding needs.
- Do not measure the available funding sources or the ability to turn assets into liquidity.
- Unless being modified, most of them do not allocate off-balance sheet commitments, which can be large users of liquidity.
- View cash and deposits kept with other banks as liquidity at hand and available to meet outflows.
- Most importantly, they fail to capture the time dimension of liquidity risk.

We therefore need to take them for what they are: a limit based on a point in time snapshot, which needs to be augmented with more dynamic forward looking measurements. This is explained further in Chapter 9.

7.2.3   Liquidity Risk Statement – Survival Time Period or Scenario-Based Approach

Another approach to risk limit within the liquidity risk statement is to define a minimum survival period in accordance with a predefined risk scenario. A bank following this approach would, for example, state its risk appetite as a minimum liquidity buffer to be able to make the bank survive for a certain period of time without any access to new funding. The benefit of this approach is its practicality; it takes time into account thereby realizing the importance of liquidity problems being a function of time. The second benefit in this approach is that it is the impact of liquidity risk that is subject to a limit not the sources, which gives this measurement a wider 'protection'. This means a survival time horizon can be used to protect against various types of liquidity risk rather than a one-dimensional problem, which the balance sheet ratios are set to prevent. The pros of this method can also be seen as its drawback. The impact of a liquidity event is to some extent subject to the set and agreed assumptions. To give an example, a bank could have defined the survival horizon to have sufficient liquidity to cover all outflows for the next 60 days. This would work well for all term liabilities but it would be very difficult for a bank to hold liquidity against all on-demand deposits. An alternative and a very common approach, which is also based on assumptions, is to determine the survival time period from the bank's own internal stress tests or even the regulatory requirement. The survival horizon would then be defined as the requirement to withstand a predefined shock for a predefined time.

Of the above-mentioned methods, the one using a defined survival time period is the main method banks use in the risk appetite, some with the help of further balance sheet limits. A risk appetite stated as a survival period is easier to understand and put into perspective rather than the balance sheet limits. As it ties in with the results of the stress test scenarios it forms a part of the overall '6 Step Framework' approach, which should ensure that it is dynamic in nature and changes along with the outcome of the stress tests.

7.3   THE LIQUIDITY RESERVE

The other side of the setting of risk limits in the risk appetite statement is how the need for liquidity should be adequately covered, which brings the size and composition of the liquidity buffer into play, usually referred to as HQLA (high-quality liquid assets).

The size and composition of the liquidity buffer can be a science in itself. This book will only touch base on the main principles by establishing a clear understanding of the trade-off between risk and returns by recognizing that banks play a balancing act between principles of risk prudence and the income principle, which requires them to make a return on assets.

There are two major aspects of the liquidity buffer or reserves: its size and its composition. To determine the appropriate size we should review the reasons for the liquidity buffer (in addition to the one being there to satisfy the risk limit statement). The liquidity reserve is *liquidity available to cover additional funding needs for a defined period of time under stressed conditions*. So the liquidity needs first and foremost to be available when needed, which is dealt with under the composition of the liquidity buffer. Unavailable liquidity is understandably of no use, but one of the principal guidances for buffer composition is to keep in mind the fact that an asset that is available under normal conditions might not be so under stress market conditions. We note that the definition for the buffer is to cover additional funding needs, that is not the regular ones arising from business-as-usual transactions, and it furthermore is clear that those additional needs arise from stressed liquidity conditions as opposed to business activities such as growth.

Now knowing what the buffer is for, it is easier to set out what its appropriate size should be. The main principle involved is that the size of the buffer needs to correspond to the liquidity risk of the bank. 'Obviously!', one might say. The top-down approach will tell us to look at the maturity transformation within the bank. The larger the maturity transformation the higher is the liquidity risk and hence we should cover that with an appropriate liquidity reserve. However, there is not a single measurement for maturity transformation and even if we had such a standardized scale, it would be difficult to translate that into a 'hard' buffer amount. An experienced treasurer would also challenge such a formula by stating that not all maturity gaps are created equal and maturity transformation is fine as long as the funding is stable. Almost by ruling out options that are either 'impossible' or inadequate it becomes clear that the only way to set the liquidity reserve amount or the liquidity requirement is with a multidimensional model, where one dimension is time and the others would be characteristics of the liabilities and assets. This is drawn from the liquidity stress testing, which is discussed in Section 10.1, Stress Testing. One of the reasons for stress testing is to determine exactly an appropriate amount of liquidity reserves.

Now we will look at the composition of the buffer. When constructing the liquidity buffer it should be kept in mind that the buffer is only there to be used under stressed conditions, where other sources are not easily available. This should be remembered when the quality of collateral is being assessed and how quickly it can generate liquidity. Needless to say, the standard assumptions about the liquidity and the depth of the markets might not hold true at times of widespread turbulence.

The liquidity buffer or reserve must first and foremost be built using cash and assets that are liquidity generating within a short period of time at a predictable value.[7] The risk appetite statement should spell out the bank's view on what is eligible collateral and what is not. The BCBS has provided good guidance on what they consider to be of sufficient quality to be used as liquidity when complying with the liquidity coverage ratio.[8] The assets within the liquidity reserve need to have the following characteristics:

- They have to be able to be converted into cash at little loss of value in private markets. The BCBS calls these assets HQLA, or high-quality liquid assets, and state that ideally they should be central bank eligible.
- They need to be unencumbered to the entity relying on them.
- They need to pass the low-risk, transparent in nature test.
- They need to be easily valued, which brings into play the size and activity of their market, its volatility and general level of recognition.
- Preferably they should not have high correlation to the financial institution holding them as HQLA.

It can be useful to follow the BCBS guidance and allocate the reserve assets into different levels according to the Basel III LCR criteria. Level 1 assets are the ones of the highest quality, such as cash, central bank reserves and securities issued by sovereigns and governments of good credit standing. Level 2 assets are typically of slightly lesser quality and include some government securities as well as corporate debt securities, residential mortgage-backed securities and equities that meet further conditions. The BCBS has set out the maximum proportion of the reserve that can be from the Level 2 category. The publication is also a good starting point when analysing how liquid the HQLA are in order to determine their worst case valuation should the bank need to access them under times of stress. Applying the appropriate haircut to the assets is of importance as the bank will only rely on them in times of difficulty when a market-wide liquidity stress could have spilled over to the value of assets.

If liquidity dries up in one place, it usually has a wider impact. Many banks have built models to express an opinion on the value of the HQLA. The models provide a more sophisticated approach than applying a straightforward, one-dimensional haircut percentage. A useful model will give consideration to at least two factors, which in a way mirror the two types of liquidity risk, that is idiosyncratic and market wide. The model will assign a haircut based on the credit worthiness of the bond (rating, etc.), which will include a haircut ladder, increasing the haircut as the credit rating is lower. It is usual to include a higher haircut (jump) if the credit rating drops below the minimum threshold acceptable to be included as an HQLA. The duration of the instrument should also be included in this individual (idiosyncratic) matrix assessment, reflecting the PV01 sensitivity of the bonds. Then the market risk factor needs to be added to the haircut assumptions. High-quality government bonds have a higher market liquidity than corporate bonds and the size of each market place is an additional factor. As we are drawing parallels from the liquidity risk definitions it is not out of the way to add a component for correlation risk. Each bond should be assessed on a stand-alone basis but also with correlation to the risk of the bank. As an example, a large Danish bank holding a substantial part of its HQLA in Danish government bonds should expect some correlation between itself and the sovereign.

7.3.1   A Liquidity Reserve or a Liquidity Buffer?

The golden standard is that a bank should not use the liquidity reserve unless faced with stress and usually the regulators take it seriously if a bank dips into the liquidity reserve. How conservative the rule is depends on the country.

In 2012 the UK regulator moved the goalposts, splitting up the reserve buffer into two portions, a lower tier and an upper tier. The lower tier proportion is equal to 40% of a full liquidity requirement (most banks in the United Kingdom are only required to maintain a liquidity buffer to cover a proportion of the full requirement, all depending on their risk profile) and the upper tier is the amount which is beyond the 40% requirement. Banks are allowed to use the upper tier portion more freely and without any regulatory consequences, but the lower tier buffer (i.e. 40% of the full requirement) is not to be used unless the bank is facing severe stresses and the regulator has been advised. The decision to allow banks to use their buffers is obviously more of a monetary easing measurement than a risk-driven decision.

The argument to use the liquidity buffer under defined circumstances is, however, a valid one. Requiring banks to maintain an asset that cannot be used under any circumstances (like insurance) can be costly and even unnecessary from a systemic point of view. The other view is that the liquidity reserves should be used when a bank suffers stress, which is after all their main purpose. Here the reserve takes on the function of a countercyclical buffer. The requirement would then be to maintain the set regulatory minimum only under normal conditions but to use the reserve when needed.

Both schools of thoughts have a point. To have at all times an untouchable reserve is a good insurance against liquidity risk. The counter-argument is that the reserve is there to be used against outflows; thus requiring banks to maintain full compliance during stress periods has a doubling effect. One can also argue that the use of the buffer can lead to the bank not meeting the minimum requirements for long periods of time and the banking system as a whole will become riskier. If the term 'under stress' is not defined, the risk is that banks will use the buffer more freely and even for purposes that are not liquidity stresses, leaving the bank worse off if a real threat emerges. The UK regulator has chosen the middle ground, which might be an agreeable solution, but does not take away the risk. A better solution, both for individual banks and supervisors, is to have firmer guidance on when the buffer can be used. For the '6 Step Framework' we recommend that banks define how they view the usability of the buffer and whether it can be used under stressed conditions, and then define within the risk tolerance what these conditions are. It is not good practice to change the rules when the funds are needed.

7.3.2   How to Review the Risk Appetite?

Again it is useful to look at what the BCBS sets out with regard to risk appetite. The second principle is '*A bank should clearly articulate a liquidity risk tolerance that is appropriate for the business strategy of the organisation and its role in the financial system*.[9] This implies that the risk appetite should not be viewed as a static measure as both strategy and general risk tolerance change over time. This could be due to external reasons such as a change in market conditions, market liquidity or even regulatory requirements, etc., or as a result of a change in the business strategy and balance sheet composition. Rest assured that the bank needs periodically, and at the right level, to review whether the risk appetite is still appropriate. An annual review is adequate and the changes or the decision to keep it unchanged should be backed up by reason and documented properly.

By setting the risk appetite as a survival period, which in turn is determined by the outcome of certain stress scenarios, the bank is taking a good step towards having its risk appetite flexible to changing conditions. This is one of the reasons why the survival horizon method is best practice and good arguments are needed not to utilize its benefits.

Endnotes

1. Speech by Benoît Cœuré, Member of the Executive Board of the ECB, called *Global Liquidity and Risk Appetite: A Re-interpretation of the Recent Crises*, at the BIS–ECB Workshop on Global Liquidity and Its International Repercussions, Frankfurt am Main, 6 February 2012.
2. Other things come into play in determining the funding spread, but at least for comparative analysis this argument is useful. This gives importance to the theorem that the markets are 'always' right. Though not infallible, they have often been more right than wrong and their smoke often indicates there is fire somewhere. It seems to hold true that wherever market participants have great stakes in the results, the truth somehow manages to air itself. There are a number of examples of firms trading as outliers in the credit default swap market unlike their peers, without any obvious reason.
3. I am sure this is the first time P.G. Wodehouse is quoted in a risk management book, but as his fans understand, Wodehouse is useful to all aspects of life. The quote is from *Heavy Weather* (1933).
4. Basel Committee on Banking Supervision, *Principles for Sound Liquidity Risk Management and Supervision*, September 2008, p. 3.
5. Barclays PLC Annual Report 2012. Available at: www.group.barclays.com.
6. See Basel Committee for Banking Supervision, Principle 3, in *Sound Practices for Managing Liquidity in Banking Organisations*, February 2000.
7. See Committee of European Banking Supervisors (CEBS), *Guidelines on Liquidity Buffers and Survival Periods*, December 2009.
8. See Basel Committee on Banking Supervision, *Basel III: The Liquidity Coverage Ratio and Liquidity Risk Monitoring Tools*, January 2013.
9. See Basel Committee for Banking Supervision, *Principles for Sound Liquidity Risk Management and Supervision*, September 2008, p. 7.

8

Step III: Governance and High-Level Policy

The bank's appetite and tolerance for liquidity risk have now been defined. Ahead of the details of liquidity management it is necessary to agree on some high-level principles and policies on how to manage liquidity risk within the bank. This section can be viewed as the interpretation or further expansion of the risk appetite, taking something that is crafted out in a short form to be expanded into a wider detailed framework. Both the Institute of International Finance (IIF) and the BCBS have come up with good lists of major principles applied. They emphasize how critical a firm-wide risk governance is. This becomes evident when the largest risk management failures are being reviewed. Since 1994 we can find at least 10 separate risk management incidents, each causing losses in excess of $500m, where risk management failed. This is excluding the systemic meltdown in 2008. In all of these cases, 'management failure' is cited as one of major reasons for the losses and failures and in their summary of findings the Group of Senior Supervisors point out that '*the failure of some boards of directors and senior managers to establish, measure, and adhere to a level of risk acceptable to the firm*' was one of the major weaknesses resulting in the 2008 liquidity crisis.[1] The regulators have done their bit in increasing the importance of governance. Under the UK regulatory regime the Board is made responsible for conducting an annual individual liquidity adequacy assessment (ILAA) and discuss its outcome with the regulator. This ensures that liquidity risk stays on the agenda at the highest level within the firm and quantitative as well as qualitative measures are being put in place and maintained. This also requires the Board to sign off their approval to the liquidity framework and assumptions used.

Proper governance might not be rocket science but rather a prudent approach and a cornerstone when building up a risk culture. It will always be impossible for risk management and regulators to move at the same pace as the sophistication of the various trading instruments and strategies. As long as banks and other market participants are remunerated for taking risks, they will strive to make it more advanced and complex. Risk management will play catch-up but the greatest comfort can be taken from a proper governance of risk taking and the top-down approach it sets.

Figure 8.1 shows an example of liquidity management governance structure, where each governance layer has an input and an output. The Board is at the top setting the overall risk appetite and maintain its regular oversight. In order to do so it is provided with set of reports which are review regularly. The next level below is the entity carrying a delegated authority from the Board. In this example it is the asset liability committee but most banks have a layer in between the Board and ALCO, which would be the executive committee (Exco). At the bottom is ALM and treasury which handle the operational aspect of liquidity management according to the strategy set by ALCO (within the risk limits set by the Board) and filter up their information and risk reports.

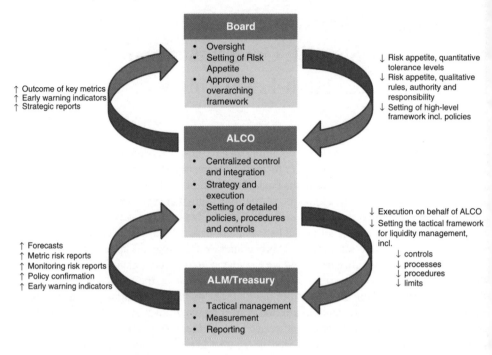

Figure 8.1   Liquidity management governance structure[2]

8.1   THE ROLE OF THE BOARD OF DIRECTORS

The first step of the governance is to define the roles and responsibilities. The Board of Directors have effectively two major roles, the role of oversight and, secondly, the role to establish the structure to support the risk appetite statement. In their role of oversight, the Board of Directors have the ultimate responsibility that the bank's risk is within the set limits and they do so by regularly reviewing the outcome of the various monitoring reports. This is an on-going task, which needs to be performed at each Board meeting.

Then the Board has an even more complex responsibility, which is to establish and approve the risk management structure, which includes strategy, policies and practices. It is usually the senior management that writes and proposes the organizational framework and the set of procedures, but the ultimate responsibility to assess its appropriateness lies with the Board. Lessons learnt from 2008 show that a key weakness in governance was a disparity between the actual risk that the some banks took and the risk that their Board of Directors thought they were taking. The following items should be checked by the Board and senior management when determining whether the framework and their function within it are appropriate:

Output:

- Is the framework in line with and supports the risk goals and appetite set by the Board?
- Does the framework define responsibility and authority at all levels?
- Are the escalation processes and control functions clearly set out?
- Is the limit process rational? Do the smaller limits support the larger ones agreed by the Board?

- Does the framework allow for multiple lines of defence? Is there a clear differentiation between those managing, monitoring and controlling?
- Are the operational processes detailed enough to ensure risk is adequately reported?
- Does the framework monitoring change and expand with the overall risk status?
- Does the framework comply with all the regulatory requirements and the best practices as laid out by the BCBS?
- Does the framework use models as appropriate and allow the bank to learn from experience?
- Does the framework set out a periodical review and adaptation to changes in strategy?
- Does the liquidity framework fit into the overall risk structure (including internal control or audit) and are all stakeholders aware of its content? Is there a process to communicate any changes?

Inputs:

- Are the reports and information provided appropriate, so the Board can be certain that the bank's risk is within the risk appetite?
- Does the information provided give the Board an overarching view of the liquidity risk and positions within the organization?
- Do the quantitative metrics provide a forward looking view on the liquidity risk or only static ones? Are the metrics reported frequently enough and do they measure all relevant major risk factors? Can they be described as overviews or snapshots?

8.2   THE ROLE OF SENIOR MANAGEMENT

The senior management has the role to establish and maintain the strategies and policies described above. Again, the task here is to create an overarching framework that translates into the goals set by the Board and to make sure that the execution and monitoring is fully aligned to the risk objectives. One of the important aspects within the framework is for the Board to divide the responsibility and authority between the senior manager and divisions. There is no one-size-fits-all approach but many banks have been moving towards increasing the authority of the CRO at the expense of finance or treasury. By 'senior management' we could be referring to the Exco or the ALCO. In the structure set out in Figure 8.1 the ALCO is shown as the next layer beneath the Board within the liquidity framework. In many cases the composition of the Exco and (group) ALCO is not very different so this segregation is not of importance. Other banks, usually the larger ones, place more authority in the Exco and give the ALCO more of a tactical liquidity management role. It is good governance practice to try to segregate the function of policy setting and strategy from the business-as-usual liquidity management (tactical). In addition to the checklist above, shared with the Board of Directors, the ALCO (or Exco) needs to give further details for the execution and tactical part of the liquidity framework. The ALCO must themselves develop the detailed controls, processes, procedures and detailed limits to ensure that the framework is supporting limits and objectives set at a higher level. Things to consider include:

- Is the framework sufficiently broken down into subpolicies, each with its own objective but all part of an integrated model?
- Is the authority for execution defined and adequately broken down into a hierarchy?
- Is the detailed responsibility defined and is there an effective segregation of duties?

- Have areas of overlapping duties (treasury/ALM/regulatory team) been identified by the teams and concluded?
- Is there an appropriate importance on forward looking measurements, which the bank can react to, as opposed to monitoring only static ex post information?
- Are the early warning indicators relevant to the liquidity strategy and profile?
- Are all the processes documented in detail to ensure that the bank has sufficient contingencies to sustain staff turnover?

8.2.1   First Down Then Up Again

When the governance structure is set the starting point is always at the top to make sure the limbs move according to the commands of the head. This top-down approach is useful and captures the 'military' approach needed. However, a second chain of command or rather information is needed, which is sometimes the part that is being left out. Each entity should not only concern itself with pushing downwards and making sure its orders are being executed. It also needs to consider if its output, in most cases information sent upwards in the management structure, is appropriate. This is where experience has shown processes to fall short of expectations. Each level within the governance chart needs to make sure that the information it passes to the next level above is sufficient for that body to shoulder its responsibility and perform its duties.

8.3   HIGH-LEVEL LIQUIDITY POLICIES AND STRATEGIES

The liquidity management framework is built on a set of strategies and policies. Staying faithful to the top-down approach, the aim is to delegate the risk defined in the risk appetite into an effective scheme of policies and strategies. From the schematic viewpoint we can break down the various functions of a liquidity framework into the levels shown in Figure 8.2.

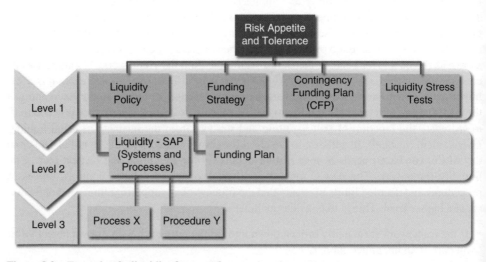

Figure 8.2   Example of a liquidity framework

The policies and strategies are ranked by their importance. The most important policies (Level 1) need to be approved at the highest level (Board of Directors) and consist of principles the bank does not change frequently or lightly. The second level are the plans that complement the Level 1 policies, such as an annual funding plan, which is derived from the overall funding strategy, which should not be altered every year even though it gets reviewed. At Level 3 are the detailed functional and tactical procedures. They could be on delegation of duties, level of authority, etc., but still need to cohere to the proper governance and should be approved by the ALCO.

The diagram shows what would be considered the minimum set of comprehensive policies and procedures, but more complex institutions will require a further breakdown. This structure can be broken down to country or subsidiary levels as appropriate, realizing the changes in authority. There is an argument for having the liquidity stress tests as Level 1 policy if the liquidity appetite statement is measured by the outcome liquidity stress test and is hence subject to stress test assumptions.

When laying down the framework for the first time, there will unavoidably be items that at first sight might not be easy to fit into the structure. For some practitioners, and keeping in mind that risk professionals tend to be risk averse, there is a tendency to kick all decisions up the ladder, leading to unbalanced duties of the Board. The opposite is also just as bad a habit and counterproductive. The test to apply is to ask: is the measurement/principle or process of major importance? Is it one that will not frequently change and changing would mean a shift in the liquidity profile of the bank? This should help the appropriate balance to be found. One also needs to consider what level of understanding can be expected at each level. A Board member might not have a view on whether it is appropriate to stress test stable retail deposits by 10% or 20%. This is a question for the risk specialists, not because they are by any means smarter but because their duty is to propose adequate assumptions and the duties and responsibilities of a Board member are different.

8.4 LIQUIDITY POLICY

The Liquidity Policy is the main document within a liquidity management framework and the one to which most consideration needs to be given. It is best approached in stages whereby the overall objective of a liquidity management and the risk under consideration are defined first. The objectives could be:

- To ensure adequate liquidity at all times. One can elaborate further and state that the policy is to ensure that sufficient funds are available at an attractive price to meet claims and promote asset growth, etc., but the main principle is to have sufficient funds for the bank.
- To comply with risk appetite and tolerance as defined and set by the Board of Directors.
- To comply with regulations at each given time.

If the bank is a part of a wider group or has subsidiaries or branches in multiple markets, it is worth the effort to define the scope of the Liquidity Policy in more detail and how other liquidity policies, if any, fit into the structure.

(a) *Scope of the Liquidity Policy.* For the policy to be effective it needs to set out what are the main forms of liquidity risk the bank is exposed to. This should be derived from the critical assessment on the Sources of Liquidity Risk, from Step 1 of the '6 Step Framework'. A part of that assessment could be to distinguish between the funding risk and market risk and what is the liquidity risk profile in terms of tactical, structural and contingency. As the Liquidity Policy is in most cases the cornerstone of the framework, it is appropriate to include the governance structure of the framework here, that is which are the documents used and what is their approval process, frequency and audience. The policy should also emphasize that compliance with the risk appetite by itself is not sufficient and liquidity management needs to comply with regulatory requirements, both quantitative and qualitative.

(b) *Articulation of risk tolerance and quantitative requirements*. The policy needs to set out how the liquidity risk is being measured and how the overall risk appetite is effectively supported by further limits. This is where the risk limits are spelled out as well as providing a clear escalation process in case of noncompliance or likely noncompliance. The next chapter will expand further on the liquidity monitoring and measurement framework but the Liquidity Policy should include all the quantitative requirements that the bank needs to adhere to. This could include the overall guidance on how liquidity is measured. At first glance, it might seem an unnecessary and laborious process but it is vital to ensure that the measuring technic and definitions cannot be changed on a tactical level, especially if the bank is having problems meeting the requirements. This could include the gap limits, setting out the timeframe for liquidity measurements, etc. The composition of the HQLA needs to be defined and to find what the overall liquidity requirement is and what is viewed as being a sufficient level of reserve. It should also articulate whether the minimum threshold is a hard limit and if not under what circumstances the bank would be allowed to use up its reserves and how quickly the gap needs to be replenished. Best practice would also set out the escalation process under these circumstances and provide a list of those who need to be notified or otherwise consulted.

(c) *Qualitative requirements*. A part of the Liquidity Policy is used to define qualitative measures. Here the monitoring and reporting function is set out and this part should make sure that even though the quantitative measurements would not necessarily capture a risk event, the qualitative approach would do so.

(d) *Responsibilities*. Now that the limits and requirements are set out, the next step is to pin down the responsibility for the various parts of the liquidity management framework. It could start by defining what aspects of the liquidity framework the Board of Directors is responsible for, as well as what level of information they should receive and how frequently. Then the next level, the role of the ALCO or Exco, should be defined both in terms of what their responsibility towards the Board is as well as what responsibility they can delegate further down the hierarchy. Finally, the mandate of the ALM and treasury needs to be set out along with their responsibilities.

A clear definition needs to be agreed upon with regards to the power of each committee if there are multiple jurisdictions, each with its own liquidity management or decision powers. This is usually addressed early on in the document when the bank has agreed upon a centralized or a decentralized liquidity management structure. The degree of centralization of liquidity management should be aligned with the bank's overall risk framework, taking issues like regulatory guidance and compliance into account. Even the most decentralized model keeps the main risk setting centrally. As mentioned previously, the risk appetite should always be done centrally and apply to the whole group, with communications to satellite offices.

A local ALCO is usually the way to link together the local management and authority to the group functions or group ALCO. This is a good platform for the group functions to exercise their centralized oversight. Care needs to be taken in a decentralized structure, so all key metrics are reported not only to the group but also up the ladder to the Board of Directors, which needs to be aware of any material developments in subsidiaries. This should be done even though the numbers are not consolidated. Furthermore, the approach taken at the group level in terms of processes, governance and procedures needs to be properly incorporated at the subsidiary level. Rather than having its own policy, which could invite a misalignment between the subsidiary and the parent company, it is worth using the group policy as a reference and marking the parts not applicable or where the local management proposes a different structure. This will make it easier for the group to ensure that local policies are kept in line with group ones and are updated. I have recently come across a policy for a subsidiary of a large bank that still includes processes around F/X risk between French francs and the German deutschmark. Hopefully this is just a documenting issue for surely the policy has been updated more frequently than once a decade.

When setting the responsibility it is useful not only to outline the power to make decisions but also who has the responsibility to get it done (execution) and who needs to be informed and who to be consulted. Some decision tree approaches give these roles different names, the decision maker being called 'accountable' but the person actually executing being named 'responsible' for reporting into the 'accountable' body or person. The day-to-day strategy needs to be described in the Liquidity Policy but the detailed processes can be referred to in Level 3 documents. This might be viewed again as a tedious process but there are probably as many instances where things went wrong due to lack of organization as there are instances of failures to carry out duties accordingly.

The exercise of writing and agreeing on a Liquidity Policy does not only have the benefit of creating a guide for all liquidity participants but it also forces and disciplines the organization to clear up areas where responsibility has not been agreed upon between divisions. Overlap of duties needs attention and should be sorted out. There is always a tendency to delay having different points of view coming head to head, but the policy makers cannot shy away from tough decisions. A document that requires the reader to have inside knowledge about the organization and to be able to figure out how things are done is a document that fails it purpose. I have come across some interesting policies that seemed to have been built around individuals rather than a contribution to a proper governance framework. Rather than segregating the authority, the same person was responsible for the supervision, decision, execution and finally control, which looked strange to everyone but those who had lived within the organization.

The clear management structure is one that is made to avoid mistakes, and one only needs to read about some of the most costly fiascos in the past to see that many of them would have been avoided if the responsibility had been properly structured and segregated. While things are fine, everyone accepts 'dotted lines' between various functions, but when trying to comb through the chain of command after something has gone wrong, the lines of communication or authority can become blurred, which is essentially why they were only drawn dotted in the first place.

When setting the appropriate responsibility, it is also necessary to segregate the committee's responsibility from the individual responsibility of the senior managers, such as the CFO or CRO. As members of senior management they are ultimately responsible for the decisions and duties of their divisions, but some of the decisions lie with the committees, like the ALCO. Again, nobody is done any favours by keeping the areas of responsibility unclear and reporting lines vague. Another alternative is to make the chair of the ALCO fully responsible for its decisions. However, if the ALCO chair is not the CEO, but the CFO or CRO, then this could create more problems than it solves.

8.5 FUNDING STRATEGY

One key element of a strong liquidity framework is the establishment of a funding strategy. Even though a funding strategy is a stand-alone document it needs to be built up as a part of the bigger picture. It should specifically complement the liquidity policy and risk appetite of the bank and these two cornerstones should be used as the platform to build from. Unlike most of the other parts of the liquidity framework, the topic is future planning and the strategy is probably the most forward-looking policy that the ALCO is responsible for. It is therefore a critical piece of work. A bank with a strong thought-through funding strategy, one that is successfully implemented and executed, should have a far lower liquidity risk than a bank that deals with the problems as they come along. The funding strategy is in another way an opportunity for the bank to set its tolerance and approach proactively for liquidity risk. Therefore, if a bank understands well the risk embedded in its funding profile, it should be more aware of what are the weak points and areas for attention. By the same token, the funding strategy should tell the bank where the more detailed observation and early warning indicators are needed and what kind of events the contingency funding plan should prepare the bank for. All in all, the funding strategy should not only be seen as a long-term funding strategic plan but also a plan and weapon to curtail risk.

The importance of having a laid-out funding strategy is becoming increasingly recognized. As an example, Australian financial legislation requires banks to develop and document an annual funding plan and a three year funding strategy, which need to be submitted to the regulator. Moreover, the requirement is for the best case estimate used in the strategy to be accompanied by sensitivity analyses.

The Institute of International Finance (IIF) strikes a similar note, recommending firms to have established and robust methodologies to manage the different parts of their funding strategies, which include a wide range of transactions and ensuring proper diversification to maintain a relationship with investors. They also make a good suggestion for banks to measure or estimate their secured and unsecured funding capacity both at the aggregate level and for each subset.[3]

The funding strategy can be built on using the following steps:

1. Examination of the business strategy/plan requirements.
2. Assessment of funding sources and their attractiveness.
3. Medium and longer-term funding plans.

Before embarking on the components of the funding strategy it is worth repeating the value it has to the business. If a bank proactively and strategically manages its funding it can decrease its overall liquidity risk with all the associated cost benefits. Banks finding themselves with a high and costly liquidity risk, more often than not, could blame insufficient strategic planning in the past.

8.5.1 Examination of the Business Strategy/Plan Requirements

There is a difference between a funding strategy and a funding plan and they should not be mixed. The focus should be on the strategy first and then implementation through the plan.

Doing things the other way around or jumping straight into the planning is a quick fix in an attempt to come up with something that can be put into action speedily. This is, however, the wrong approach and can have a detrimental impact on the bank's long-term viability. By rushing into the planning the bank forgoes having a thought-through strategy and the funding approach becomes reactive rather than proactive. A clear sign of such an arrangement is when the starting argument is of the nature: 'Gather around!! We are to fund $6m in the next 18 months. Let's figure out how to do it. Any thoughts?' By following this path the business strategy (asset strategy) or plan becomes the sole driver and the funding strategy only means to fill up the funding gap. This faulty approach of an asset-dominated strategy has been the road to a self-inflicted extinction for banks and even banking systems.

By having a stand-alone funding strategy built up on an assessment of what is available, at what price and risk, the bank will have a stronger overall approach rather than that of building the asset and liability plans separately and realizing later on that they do not match or that one has damaged the other. A strategy is determining which direction to take and a road down which the firm will travel. Therefore, and perhaps unlike other decisions with the framework, the repercussions of getting it wrong are neither easily nor quickly mendable. Banks have found themselves being cornered in their funding due to overly ambitious asset plans that were not met and being challenged by a funding strategy.

These words of warning do not, however, change the fact that the starting point for a funding strategy is the bank's overall strategic business strategy and plan, especially in terms of growth. A bank with limited growth plans will require a different strategy from a fast growing bank. Even though the tools of the trade are the same, the funding strategy set for growth is quite different from a strategy set to maintain and prune the funding franchise. The growth plans of the bank are always a key factor in the funding strategy and will determine its focus.

The key objectives of the funding strategy can be married to the business plans to create a balanced scheme. The key objectives of a funding strategy are listed below. For those who think and memorize life in acronyms, we can call the list **MARS**:

- **Maturity**. To raise funds in various maturities to manage the bank's funding gap, creating a prudent funding mix.
- **Appetite**. To raise funds from sources that are within the bank's overall risk and cost appetite.
- **Risk**. To ensure the bank has sufficient funds to meet its liabilities as they fall due, both in ordinary and stressed business conditions (the definition of liquidity risk).
- **Stability**. To raise funding through various stable and diversified funding channels, thereby making the bank better able to withstand various liquidity shocks.

We should also require the funding strategy to contribute to a profitable business and meet all regulatory requirements.

The Myth of Diversification

Diversification is a magical word. This, along with the concept of cost, is usually the first things that come to mind with regards to funding. All banks want to diversify their funding and fund cheaply. Diversity of funding has become a sweet term that all should hail, but it is not always the cure-all remedy it is held out to be.

In the blueprint of a funding strategy the diversity of funding is addressed and is important enough to be one of the 10 Sources of Liquidity Risk. No one disagrees with the importance of diversity but the limitations come from how the diversity is being dealt with and reached, which can create an impression of unwarranted safety. A usual metric, which can be found in Step 4 of the '6 Step Framework' in Chapter 9, The Quantitative Framework, is the concentration of funding calculated as the amount of funds received from the top 10 or 20 largest funding providers. The greater the distribution, the better the funding stability should be. The same diversification is sought in each funding channel, being deposits, money market funds, credit lines, etc. The underlying key assumption is that each provider is to a great extent idiosyncratic in its decision making. This can, however, be a questionable assumption and we have mentioned markets where all participants act as being one, which gives no diversification. A recommended tactic by Sungard is to diversify by type and not by the name of the counterparty and to apply a wider approach by looking at the diversification between counterparties, groups of similar counterparties and markets.[4]

It is therefore vital to understand the risk of false safety that diversification can producee if not properly thought though. Nevertheless, banks should diversify their funding as much as possible, trying to reach the diversification from various angles. They could include:[5]

- Diversified retail and commercial deposit franchises.
- Wide range of funding maturities.
- Diverse funding programmes between different markets.
- Variety of wholesale funding products, ranging from CP, CD short-term issuance to longer-dated programmes, such as EMTN, 144A, etc., and covered bonds and securitizations.
- Diverse wholesale investor base from a customer type and geographic perspective.

We can conclude on a health warning, which goes something like: adding more of the same does not help increasing the diversification of the funding.

8.5.2 Assessment of Funding Sources and Their Attractiveness

Here is where the work in Step 1 of the '6 Step Framework' again comes in handy. The Sources of Liquidity Risk will give the risk managers a good idea of the bank's funding weaknesses and relative strength of each channel. This should be used to build the funding strategy from keeping in mind how the funding strategy could impact on the overall liquidity risk profile.

Nowadays, all banks have control over their funding strategy and even the smallest local players can influence and manage what type of funding providers they seek and the products they have on offer. The funding strategy can be seen as a tug of war between what funding is readily available and how attractive the funding is. As with so many things, the easy wins are the most costly and funding that is difficult to source is also funding that is unlikely to leave. There is a simple method that can be used to approach this problem in a formalized way, which is to construct a funding scorecard.

Funding Scorecard – Availability and Attractiveness

After going through the hoops of the Sources of Liquidity Risk, the riskiness of the funding franchise should be clearer, which gives a good input into setting the details of the strategy. It is worth giving further consideration to what kind of funding is available to the bank and what the attractiveness of each of those channels is. This will give at the outset a good overview of the current funding options available and put a risk factor next to each of them. This effectively gives the necessary connection between what the bank would like to do versus what is possible.

We start by setting out each funding channel and assess it by its attractiveness and availability. These two separate factors are not two single measures but an aggregate outcome of the assessment where further factors are taken into consideration. Under attractiveness we include subfactors like:

- Possible diversification within the channel
- Relative pricing levels and price elasticity
- Other on-going costs of issuance and market maintenance
- Stability of customers
- Available tenors
- HQLA requirement and impact on LCR and NSFR.

By taking each of the subfactors into account it is possible to give each funding channel a crude attractiveness score. In the same way we can assess the availability of each funding channel, taking into the overall score factors like:

- Size and depth of the funding channel
- Competitive landscape
- How easy it is to access the market
- Stability of fund flows from the channel.

We can express these two factors in a spider web, where we have simplified the results into a scorecard (see Figure 8.3), giving each channel a score between 1 and 5, separately, for attractiveness and availability.

The hypothetical example above shows five funding channels identified for Bank A. Each channel is given a score from 1 to 5, 1 being the lowest and 5 the highest. The more attractive the channel, the less risky it is. On this scale, the retail deposit channel is the most attractive option with a score of 5, but the assessment shows the bank has limited access to that market, or a score of 2. The European bond market (EMTN) has been viewed as an available option for the bank, but scores low on the attractiveness scale (which could be due to adverse pricing). The aim of measuring and accessing each channel is to see whether the available area can be better aligned to the 'attractive zone'. The gap between what we like to get and what we can get needs to be deemed to be fixed (e.g. the bank could be a securities house) or something the bank can move towards (i.e. the bank could set up retail deposit channels). This will give the strategy maker a good overview of what can be done now and what the bank could move its strategy towards instead of doing more of the same, which is the pitfall when working on a funding plan rather than a strategy. The score system is always subjective, but should still be helpful in providing a better understanding of the funding platform.

8.5.3   Medium- and Longer-term Funding Plans

After all the assessments and setting of strategic goals the funding strategy is translated into medium-term and long-term funding plans.

The medium-term funding plan should include issuance schedules for all major bond issuance as well as the redemptions of existing ones, which should under business-as-usual conditions be able to provide a monthly net inflow of new money for the next 12 to 18 months. The plan for new funding is prepared so the bank maintains a certain amount of cash or free funds or alternatively enough funds to cover a set period of time (i.e. the outflows during

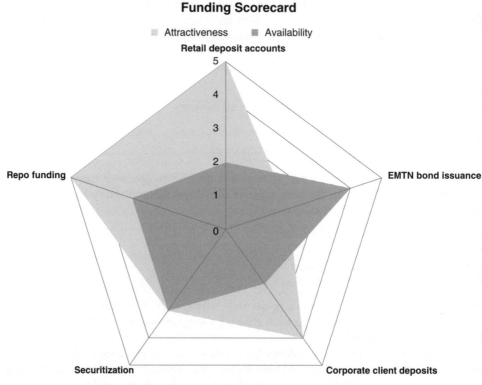

Figure 8.3   Example of a funding attractiveness/availability scorecard

that period). As pointed out in the following chapter, the lessons learnt from the financial crises show that the coverage plan cannot only be built on normal external conditions but has to be augmented using stress assumptions. These should encompass both liability and asset (repayment) behaviour.

The funding plan sets out the details and tactics for each funding channel. Figure 8.4 is an overall summary of funding sources for banks and is broken down into the main four categories

	Time horizon	
	Short-term funding	Long-term funding
Unsecured funding	– Central bank discount facilities – Repo – Securities lending	– Covered bonds – Securitization – Bilateral loans (committed lines) – Syndicated loans
Secured funding	– Sight deposits – Short-term deposits – CD/CP paper	– Longer-term deposits – Term bond issuance

Figure 8.4   Funding sources

by time horizon (short and long) and product type (unsecured and secured). This summarizes the instrument that is available.

There is very limited value in going beyond the 12–18 month time horizon as asset assumptions and overall plans will have shifted. For security houses and others with their funding franchise limited to short-term funding, the funding plan horizon needs to be much shorter as longer-term funding is not available. Not every detail or execution can be written into the funding plan, which should adopt a descriptive method to set the guidance. Therefore, instead of relying on hollow numbers like 'issue $30m in the money markets each week', a more appropriate guideline is to set the amount outstanding as a proportion of the funding needs in that time period. Notice should be given to not having too much long-term debt maturing at the same time, causing an unnecessary 'cliff risk'. Furthermore, one should differentiate between actual maturity of longer-term debt (public debt) versus medium-term money market instruments coming in for rollovers.

As the illustration above displays, funding can be obtained from both sides of the balance sheet. On the liability side, firms can obtain funding with a variety of methods, both secured and unsecured, from a range of lenders and for a variety of maturities. On the asset side, liquid securities, and to some extent other securities, can be converted to cash through the use of repurchase agreements (repos and securities lending) or posted as collateral to support trading that demands funding. As discussed in detail under the Sources of Liquidity Risk (Chapter 6) and the availability and attractiveness assessment, each funding source, whether from the asset or liability side of the balance sheet, has its own individuality in terms of availability, cost, maturity and stability.

Chapter 12 lays out the new liquidity requirements banks need to take into account under the Basel III regime. As the requirements are quite descriptive and could be challenging for some banks, it is important to have them included in the funding strategy and plans. So far Basel III has only set out the definite parameters for the LCR but banks need to think about their alignment to the NSFR as well as more structural changes that might be needed to comply with the NSFR rather than the LCR. The LCR has an impact on both the type of funding the bank should prioritize as well as its maturity. As it is a 30 day liquidity coverage ratio, the short funding plan needs to pay strong attention to the impact it might have.

From Funding Strategy to the Funding Plan and Back Again

The longer-term funding plan is effectively the strategic goal of the bank and will constantly be replaced by more tactical short/medium-term plans. It does, however, play an important part in resetting the course if the plans fail to stay on track. To reach the longer-term goals, the short-term goals need to be reached and this gives the practitioner the opportunity to see how the bank did in keeping to the plan and which parts are usually the outliers. This becomes more natural once it has been done a few times and should provide the management with the assurance that the funding is progressing as planned. By overlaying the 'actual numbers' on the longer-term goals, it is possible to test the viability of the funding strategy; it will clearly demonstrate whether there is a difference between what is practised and what is preached. If the analysis shows a consistent gap, then the funding strategy needs to be rationalized as there is no use maintaining a document of rosy dreams. This is a relevant point to raise as in some cases, and even against the backdrop of the financial crises, the funding strategy has resembled a Christmas wish list or at best a decorative document to give the reader what he/she likes to read.

The Shift of Funding Sources

It can be said that before the inroads of the capital markets, the funding strategy of the bank was to some extent included in its DNA. A bank funded itself on its home market, having limited power to set its own plan and differentiate from its peers. We have already discussed how the capital markets opened up a variety of opportunities for unsecured and secured funding from market places, where some are measured in trillions of dollars. This holds true for larger operators but one might think that the situation for a local bank is not very different from what it was two decades ago. This is only partly true. The local and 'simple' deposit markets have also developed with technology and increased product offerings. Savers and other depositors are becoming more aware of the value of their deposits and can now compare offers from banks close and further afield. As we can expect this trend to continue as traditional clients become more educated and more demanding, this will mean that 'traditional' banks, which might have got their funding easily and even without a strategic approach, will need to rethink their game. Therefore, even the smallest bank can differentiate its funding from what others are doing and pick its strategic preferences with price, growth and risk in mind. A bank that does not take a proactive approach will be left with a lack of funds (hampering growth and viability) or competing on price only to survive. This will unnecessarily increase liquidity risk.

Lessons Learnt

It is not possible to finish a chapter on banking funding strategy without mentioning some of the lessons learnt from the financial crises. It can be said that the problems were largely down to inadequate liquidity risk management, which is true as long as one includes the funding strategy within that space. The stress tests, early warning indicators and other features of the liquidity management structure certainly did not manage to capture and remedy the problem, but they would not have happened in the first place had the funding strategies served their purpose. Asserting that the funding strategies failed in 2007 and 2008 might be a symptom of perfect hindsight, but at least it is possible to conclude that the assumptions completely broke down. There are numerous stories of the secondary effect of deposits flowing out, but it was the breakdown of a certain funding channel that created a snowball that turned quickly into an avalanche of previously unknown magnitude. As is now well known, the avalanche even knocked over banks that had no exposure to the underlying problem but were caught at the wrong place at the wrong time.

The reason for touching upon the faults of the past as a lesson learnt is to exhibit the importance of an adequate funding strategy and the pitfalls to avoid. The lesson learnt for risk managers is not to focus idiosyncratically on the channel that broke down but the wider lessons this might have for the liquidity management forum. It is a natural inclination to pay the most attention to the factors that broke down last time, sometimes at the expense of other risk categories. It is impossible to predict what the next liquidity shocks will look like, but it is unlikely they will emerge from the same source as last time. The lesson should therefore be a general one. From a funding strategy standpoint the failures during the financial crises were mainly:

- Secured funding (repo). Some banks were overly dependent on easy and uninterrupted access to the secured funding markets to fund their asset portfolios. The problem crystallized in a spiral when the main collateral became more difficult to price, leading to tighter definitions of eligible collateral and higher haircuts and finally a decreased risk appetite from the funding providers for secured funding.

- Interbank market. As funding providers to the interbank market became aware of looming idiosyncratic risk, this funding channel came quickly to a halt. Contrary to popular belief, the interbank market (especially in Europe) was quite concentrated in a number of net fund providers.
- Increased risk aversion of money market mutual funds to ABCP. Another similar problem to the one of the interbank market was the increasing uneasiness amongst fund managers to accept ABCP paper from SIVs due to the uncertainty of their subprime exposure. The decreased lending and shorting of tenor when rolled over led to these vehicles experiencing increased funding problems, impacting on many of their liquidity providers in the banking systems.

These are features of where the funding plans or assumptions failed. Assumptions on the relative merits of secured lending over unsecured did not prove adequate. Secondly, the established interbank market, which had until then shown resilience, dried up and was perhaps not as deep as it was thought to be. Lastly, the huge ABCP market, which had taken a lot of comfort from high issuer ratings, demonstrated much less diversified investor behaviour than expected.

The lesson learnt is that even the best thought-out assumptions on each funding market can prove to be wrong. This brings up the need for proper diversification between markets, instruments and client types. This will decrease the dependence on assumptions being adequate under various external conditions.

The funding plans also had their deficiencies. Firms relied on business-as-usual plans for outflows and inflows, underestimating their real funding needs in the short and medium terms. The calculated number of weeks/months of outflow being covered was in some instances based on contractual maturities and normal business conditions. Under stress the behavioural assumptions broke down and diverged from the contractual maturities.[6]

Act Two of the crises was when funding problems resulted in unexpected demands on the firm liquidity and liquidity management, which were in many instances not ready or adequate to meet the increased liquidity demands. These problems are the ones the '6 Step Framework' methodology is set to prevent.

8.6 FUNDS TRANSFER PRICING

When taking stock of the various tasks the ALM performs within banks, Funds Transfer Pricing (FTP) is probably the area where the ALM and Treasury provide the most direct value to the businesses, management and profitability of the bank. Unlike some of the tasks within liquidity risk management, which might look like a passive second line of defence, the FTP is the opposite. By having the appropriate, effectively implemented FTP method, the ALM unit provides a proactive tool to manage the largest contribution of income for most banks, the Net Interest Margin. Unlike many other roles the ALM plays, this one is outward facing, where ALM partners with the businesses. This is most likely one of the major reasons why FTP implementations have been described as an organized minefield and an area where most banks can share stories of unsuccessful attempts, grievances and misunderstandings between divisions and management.

Part of the bad reputation FTP has can be blamed on its preachers. Picking up a paper or textbook on Funds Transfer Pricing you will quickly learn this is where financial risk gurus have had a field day, leaving the rest of us behind.

A synopsis of the FTP method and its application and usefulness follows. It serves the purpose of briefing the reader on the topic, and shows how to set the principles correctly and what steps to take to implement it.

8.6.1 Funds Transfer Pricing in a Nutshell

In one sentence, FTP (Funds Transfer Pricing) is a mechanism that assigns the cost, benefits and risks of liquidity to the respective business units within the bank. This is of importance as most units in a financial institution share one common resource: liquidity. One can easily imagine the large-scale problems that could occur if banks did not apply a process to charge for liquidity. As it turns out, many banks did not. A survey conducted in 2009 by a group of prudential regulators covering 38 large banks from nine countries revealed various shortcomings within the industry. Most banks lacked FTP policy and some even treated liquidity as a free commodity, applying no liquidity charges to businesses. It was pointed out in the findings of the survey that this failure to realize and attribute the cost of liquidity led to banks accumulating long-term assets to be funded only with short-term liabilities, creating a massive market-wide maturity mismatch that was not accounted for.[7] This weak and risky setup was unable to weather the liquidity drought, with seismic consequences. In the survey banks acknowledged that if sound funds transfer pricing models had been in place they would not have carried on the significant levels of illiquid assets that ultimately resulted in large losses and, moreover, would not have built up the substantial contingency risks.

Regulators are also becoming aware of the importance of FTP as a risk mitigating tool and have started to require banks to operate models where cost and rewards are distributed. The regulatory framework in the United Kingdom sets out what should be a minimum internal requirement for any bank of almost any size. The requirement is twofold. Firstly, in relation to all significant business activities the cost, risk and benefits of liquidity should be incorporated into product pricing, performance measurement and the new product approval process. This should also apply to off-balance sheet activities. Secondly, banks are required to ensure that these charges are applied in a transparent fashion and are understood by the businesses.[8] This guidance is not very specific but is sufficient for banks to know what should be the main features in their internal funding framework.

The experience in 2008 might be an extreme example of things going wrong on a large scale, which will not be repeated, but FTP also serves as the business-as-usual process to allocate cost and measure profitability. The largest part of income for most banks is the interest income from their lending. Allocating the correct liquidity cost to the lending is paramount to measure the correct net interest income and consequently the profitability of the bank. This is where FTP adds tremendous value. As will be explained later, FTP uses the economic cost to measure liquidity cost, rather than historical or accrued cost. This difference in approach from standard accounting methods, which use historical cost, is what makes FTP powerful to measure real profitability and even viability. This is of importance in a volatile environment where market conditions have quickly shifted the cost of funding, which puts a question mark beside the prices charged for loans. Banks need to be able to quickly realize the impact of a change in future funding costs and make costs visible in the lending decisions. Failure to do so will distort profit assessment, making the management believe costs are being met and profits are being made.

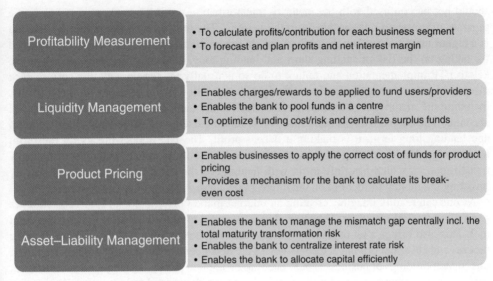

Profitability Measurement	• To calculate profits/contribution for each business segment • To forecast and plan profits and net interest margin
Liquidity Management	• Enables charges/rewards to be applied to fund users/providers • Enables the bank to pool funds in a centre • To optimize funding cost/risk and centralize surplus funds
Product Pricing	• Enables businesses to apply the correct cost of funds for product pricing • Provides a mechanism for the bank to calculate its break-even cost
Asset–Liability Management	• Enables the bank to manage the mismatch gap centrally incl. the total maturity transformation risk • Enables the bank to centralize interest rate risk • Enables the bank to allocate capital efficiently

Figure 8.5   The usage of FTP models[9]

8.6.2   The FTP Principles and Objectives

The term FTP is being used in various ways: as an accounting tool, management device and risk measurement method. The four main uses for FTP can be categorized as shown in Figure 8.5.

As FTP can mean various things to various people it is critical to establish an agreement and consensus on what FTP does and what it does not do. This might sound like a normal health warning and not something unique to FTP. However, a practitioner's guide must point out the pitfalls for the manager to avoid and this is truly one of them. There are many stories of failed implementation attempts, so it cannot be too often repeated: to be able to construct a fit-for-purpose FTP method followed by a successful implementation, the FTP principles need first to be agreed and understood, not only with the ALM but much more by those who will be measured by it.

The following are generally accepted as the main objectives of an FTP:

1. To improve profitability by identifying liquidity costs and provide a mechanism to minimize (optimize) the cost across the firm.
2. To be able to measure business unit profitability (independent of interest rate risk) and set their targets.
3. To provide a consistent product pricing guidance to businesses.

To be able to accomplish the above objectives, the business units need to be matched in funding (back-to-back funded) with the treasury centre. As an example, should the businesses provide a 5 year loan, they will get a 5 year internal financing from the treasury. This results in all the interest rate risks being centralized, which enables the bank to quantify how much maturity transformation it is taking on and what the business margin is without the impact of maturity mismatches. As will be explained later, this feature is the centre of funds transfer pricing and the reason why it is sometimes misunderstood. The profit the businesses make by lending should not be confused with the maturity transformation profit the bank makes, which is a separate risk–reward relationship from the lending. The businesses make money by lending at a higher margin than they themselves are charged, whereas the treasury centre is rewarded for taking on the risk of funding short and lending long. Understanding this concept is the key to FTP implementation and failure to do so is usually the reason why this performance measurement can struggle. Businesses might be used to looking at their own profitability, including the maturity transformation risk, which is the view one would find in the financial accounts. The business might think that as it is funding itself with cheap short-dated deposits and lending long term, it is making a decent profit. The FTP model breaks up the profit into its ingredients, which can show that the lending profit is largely made up of maturity transformation, which has little to do with lending, as the bank could get those returns by investing the money further out on the interest rate curve.

As one can readily imagine, creating an internal market place is not an easy task and does require substantial resources. However, this is essential to make FTP an active management tool. This also brings a lot of leverage to the ALM on the businesses as the decision-making process and customer pricing at the businesses are dependent on the transfer pricing. However, this 'match funding' of businesses only needs to be applied through management accounts for performance measurement and no actual deals or fund flows need to be applied. This makes the implementation easier.

8.6.3   Construction of an FTP Model

Once the goals and uses for the FTP are in place, the calculation method needs to be laid out. It should be based on the following principles:

- The method should reward providers of liquidity and charge the users.
- The method should include all relevant liquidity and funding costs, benefits and risks. This includes the cost of maintaining the liquidity buffer.
- The method should be based on a price curve as opposed to a single price.
- The reward/cost rate should include the relevant incentives to encourage management behaviour that supports the funding strategy.
- The FTP method should use the marginal cost/reward as opposed to historical or average cost/reward. The FTP should not be viewed as the only measurement applied to manage businesses. It has a single objective: to measure the actual cost (cost of funds) in order for the bank to be able to minimize its cost base. By using the FTP tool, a bank is heading towards minimum cost but not necessarily maximum profit or lowest risk. Profits are derived out of revenue generating strategies, which identify where risk and reward are acceptable, with cost minimization being only one of them.

The FTB method has limitations as it does not provide incentives towards reaching other types of business objectives such as lending growth. However, once the objective has been set the FTP can minimize the cost associated with reaching the target. It is important to realize these constraints of the FTP, which do not make it any less useful. Businesses always have more than one goal and cost minimization is only applicable with certain constraints, being growth or the level of acceptable risk.

Another example is the one-dimensional approach of the FTP, which will guide businesses towards the cheapest sources of funds but not taking their riskiness and stability into account. There are two ways of dealing with these constraints. If they are few and relatively simple then they can be incorporated into the FTP model by adding corresponding transfer pricing curves or adjustments. The reward rate for unstable deposits can be set lower than for stable ones, wholesale deposits lower than retail ones, etc., and by doing so other strategic objectives can be incorporated. To incentivize lending over deposit growth, lending can be assigned a separate curve from the liability curve, where a lower threshold rate is applied to boost lending. Care needs to be taken that the amended rate is based on realistic assumptions; assigning a zero transfer price to lending just to increase the asset base of the bank is not a sensible strategy and works against the objectives of an FTP. Should these other constraints or objectives be too complex to be mirrored into a proxy within the FTP, then they need to be set outside the method. Thus, should the goal for the bank be to increase deposits by a certain amount (which could be for regulatory reasons), then the FTP could be used to minimize the cost in reaching that objective, even though it goes against the optimum. The FTP is also a powerful tool to quantify the cost associated with reaching the nonoptimal objective.

Most banks apply other restrictions or strategies on top of the FTP mechanism to alleviate the shortcomings of the FTP. As business units can make profit through the performance measurements, both by raising deposits and by providing lending, they might switch their focus towards one of the targets over the other. If unmanaged this can lead to excessive imbalance between assets and liabilities and thus not support the bank's strategic goals. To prevent this from happening the business units are given certain targets for assets and liabilities (assuming they do both), which will guide the bank towards a balance.

8.6.4   The FTP Method in Two Steps

The FTP has two steps (see Figure 8.6). The first step is to create a funds transfer price by adding together the various funding cost components. In the second stage, the funds transfer price is assigned to the business or product in the form of a reward or a cost charge. By doing so the businesses can review and compare funding options and minimize cost, which is one of FTP's main objectives.

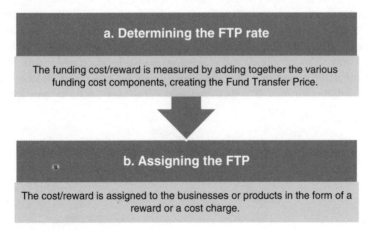

Figure 8.6   The two steps of the FTP

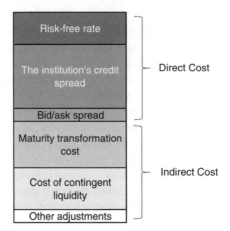

Figure 8.7   Direct and indirect costs

Determining the **FTP** *Rate*

The funding cost is measured by adding together the various funding cost components, creating the funds transfer price. The FTP has two major components, direct and indirect costs (see Figure 8.7):

1. Direct cost (or market cost) of raising funds, which can be further split into:
   (a) Interest rate component (the risk-free rate).
   (b) Add-on, representing the institution's credit spread.
   (c) Bid/ask spreads associated with the management of liquidity.
2. Indirect liquidity cost or liquidity adjustments, which are:
   (a) Maturity transformation cost (based on the maturity tenor).
   (b) Cost of contingent liquidity.
   (c) Other adjustments, such as optionality and fees.

By adding all the ingredients together a curve is created, shown in Figure 8.8. For practical reasons banks can in most cases assume that the maturity transformation cost is included in their own market credit curve, which makes it easier to create an FTP curve. The FTP uses economic (marginal) cost as opposed to historic or average cost; that is how much it would cost the bank to raise new funds. True to the economic cost methodology, the FTP methods recognize the time value of money and charge/reward for longer-dated tenors. As explained earlier, the time value premium is charged even though the bank itself chooses only to fund itself in short-dated maturities. It is this time value of money (maturity transformation) that

Figure 8.8   The FTP curve

causes the FTP curve to be upward sloping. Even though the funds transfer price looks at the cost of raising new funds, it is imperative not to think of it as a cost-charging method in the traditional understanding where the method is supposed to allocate costs that have already incurred by the users.

The above-mentioned components highlight the difference between the FTP approach and standard accounting as the FTP calculates economic cost as opposed to historical or average cost.

When the FTP is used to price a new product or determine profitability, the direct cost component applies the actual funding cost of the bank, that is the cost should the bank need to go out and raise the funds needed. It does not give consideration to the historic cost, even though cheaper funds may have been raised in the past. This difference between the FTP and historic cost methods is also apparent when calculating the indirect liquidity cost. The maturity transformation cost is charged against the business for that particular tenor regardless of whether the bank actually raises funds in that maturity.

The contingency liquidity cost includes the cost of maintaining a liquidity buffer. There are various ways to construct an appropriate FTP curve. The key assumption to make is that the direct cost must reflect the bank's marginal cost of funds available to the bank. The marginal cost, as previously explained, is defined as the cost of making new funding transactions in the market. While long-term money costs more than short-term money the cost needs to be calculated for various maturities (the FTP curve). This can be hypothetical or estimated cost if the bank does not raise funds in various maturities. In the matched funding model a single rate is not appropriate, unless the bank does all its lending and funding in the same single maturity (fully matched), which is not realistic.

In the absence of having price data points in various maturities, a hypothetical or synthetic curve needs to be built. There are various ways of constructing such a curve, most of which try to make a distinction between the risk-free rate and the credit spread for that institution. Methods vary in sophistication and complexity. There are methods for building a curve to include factors like the market liquidity of the funding instrument, optionality, type of interest (floating rate note (FRN)/fixed), basis risk, etc. Some banks even construct multiple curves for secured, unsecured and pledgable funding. A balance needs to be struck between usability and sophistication. A simple but well-implemented FTP framework has advantages over a more complex system that has failed to be accepted and used.

A centralized funding model is the prerequisite for adopting an FTP mechanism. It is possible to identify the funding cost without a centralized funding centre, but to reap the benefits from the method an internal market place for funds needs to be created. A centralized model also allows for the indirect cost to be added and distributed, such as interest rate risk, the cost of maintaining a liquidity buffer and the cost of complying with regulatory requirements. The benefit is also that cost items such as interest rate risk can be centralized and each business unit can be measured independently of interest rate risk.

Assigning the FTP

When the funds transfer pricing curve has been established, it then needs to be applied to the businesses. The FTP method has three profit/cost centres: the treasury and the businesses where funding and lending functions have been separated, as seen in Figure 8.9.

The treasury sets the funds transfer price in the form of an upward sloping pricing curve, taking into account the direct and indirect components. The transactions between the businesses

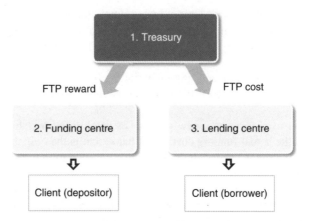

Figure 8.9   The three legs of the funds transfer pricing stool

and treasury are priced off this curve. In a simple variation of the FTP method, the same curve is used for cost and rewards (the financing and investments of the businesses).

The businesses are matched in funding and do not underwrite any interest rate risk or maturity transformation risk; that is they borrow from the treasury at the same maturity they lend to their clients. They make a profit by lending out at higher rates than their funding rate (FTP) or taking on deposits cheaper than the FTP rate. It is the treasury that assumes the reward of maturity transformation (funding mismatch) and manages the associated risk.

This can be explained by the example in Figure 8.10. The business (lending centre) grants a 4 year loan at 5% and funding is raised through the funding centre by a 2 year deposit at 2.5%. The FTP curve set by the treasury is 2 years at 3% and 4 years at 4%. The three T-accounts for each centre show the profit.

The single transaction of granting a 4 year loan funded by a 2 year deposit creates profit in each of the three segments.

- The lending centre has a contribution margin of 1% (5% from the loan against the 4% funding they received from the treasury).
- The funding centre has a contribution margin of 0.5% (3% - 2.5%), as it raised the deposit at a cheaper price than the FTP price.

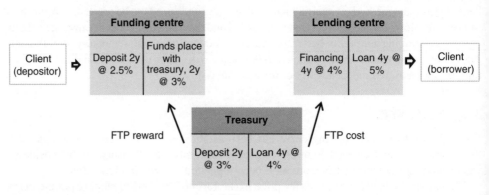

Figure 8.10   Example of funds transfer pricing[10]

- The treasury contribution is 1%, which is the maturity transformation profit by lending in 4 years versus funding in 2 years.
- The overall net interest margin is 2.5%. The businesses are 'squared off' with matched funding.

8.6.5   The Pooled (Average) Cost Method

The most basic form of FTP mechanism is the average cost method or pooled method. Under the pooled approach the cost of funding across all funding sources is aggregated and used as an FTP and charged to lending. This method has limited functionality, but is better than applying no funding cost to lending. It also creates a market place for funds and drives a kind of cost minimization, which is of benefit. Due to its limitations it is not suitable for most banks, but is good as an introduction to more advanced methods. The first and obvious flaw can be seen from Figure 8.11, where a single rate is used for assets and liabilities, regardless of their maturity. The use of historical cost figures is also a major disadvantage, as change in market conditions can take a long time to impact on the average cost and the business underwritten in the meantime could be wrongly priced or even loss making.

The pooled method can be enhanced and made more useful by applying separate curves for deposits and lending. Instead of a single rate in the previous example, the fund providers are rewarded with a different rate from the one the lenders are charged. By having the charge rate higher than the reward rate, the business is focused on deposit raising rather than lending. This can be useful to set out management action and an agenda for growth.

The enhanced method still has a major flaw in ignoring the benefits of attracting longer-term funding and the increased liquidity risk of long-term lending. This defect promotes excess maturity transformation and increases the structural liquidity risk by encouraging long-term lending and discouraging the attraction of long-term funding. Consequently, the net interest income measurement becomes inaccurate and the use of average rates distorts a profit assessment.

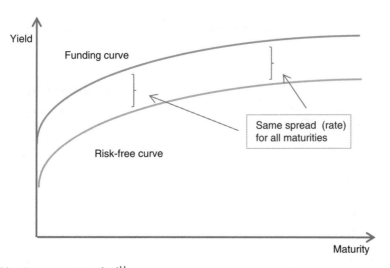

Figure 8.11   Average cost method[11]

8.6.6 The Matched Funding Method

The FTP is normally explained with the matched funding approach, which is the only method that fully captures all the functionality we expect from the FTP. Other methods are a trade-off between simplicity and efficiency. The matched funding method accomplishes the task of assigning a transfer rate to each financial instrument, which mirrors as closely as possible the instrument's cash flow. It is also the most demanding method in terms of resources systems. Few things set the matched funding method apart from other processes, which is explained later. Under matched funding:

- Every financial instrument needs to be valued separately, allowing the bank to break down its income into contributing parts, as explained in the worked-out example earlier.
- The cost of the funds curve is the marginal (market) cost of a funds curve that recognizes the term liquidity premium. The marginal cost increases with time, recognizing the maturity transformation cost.

The pooled method reflects the three legs of the funding transfer price mechanism explained in the example earlier, where the maturity transformation profit can be isolated from the profit generated by lending or raising deposits. The difference between the pooled method and matched funding method is shown in Figure 8.12. The matched method properly recognizes the maturity transformation cost by being steeper than the risk-free curve, realizing the time value of money. The pooled method, on the other hand, applies a single rate across all maturities and is parallel to the risk-free curve.

It is possible to compare the outcome for these two methods. Figure 8.12 shows that the two curves cross at time T_1, where they would show the same results. For maturities shorter than T_1 the pooled method is higher and overcharges, but for instruments with maturity greater than T_1 the pooled method is charging too little for the longer maturities compared to the marginal price indicated in the matched method curve.

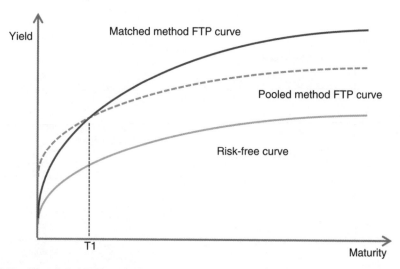

Figure 8.12   The pooled FTP method

8.6.7 Funds Transfer Pricing in Application

I am sure you will find a sentence like this one in most ALCO meeting note folders: 'ALM to improve internal funds transfer pricing'. Banks are currently paying a great deal of attention to the need for FTPs and the benefits they provide. This is, however, the part of the overall liquidity framework that is least understood and accepted by people outside the ALM clan. One could compare the situation to how the first car salesman in the world felt on his first day at the job. The product might have been there but the understanding of its merits might not have been.

The ALM will set the pricing curve(s) which will immediately raise eyebrows. *'Why am I being charged a 4 year rate when we don't issue any bonds greater than 2 years? Is this a contribution to the ALM retirement fund?'* The answer is the matched funding mantra. There is usually a pressure to keep the FTP rate as low as possible to help the lending businesses in their efforts. This is perhaps more relevant now than it was prior to 2008, as currently the lending margins have not caught up with deposit prices and most banks are operating on very thin margins. It is therefore very tempting for banks to ignore the signs of the FTP and let other objectives overtake them.

Box 8.1   The Lesson Learnt from UBS in 2007

In 2007 UBS reported large subprime-related losses in connection with the closure of Dillon Read Capital Management in May 2007. The bank ultimately reported net losses of ca. \$19bn in relation to US residential mortgage exposure that year. In a shareholder report published in May 2008 and another transparency report to shareholders from October 2010 the past was confronted, which gave other practitioners the opportunity to learn from their mistakes. In a nutshell, the short-term funding obtained in the markets by UBS was distributed internally without any additional risk premium, which enabled the business units to make risky investments with funds that were not adequately priced. Though the bank operated via a centralized treasury and liquidity management process the model *'resulted in significant funding being available to the businesses with prices within the ordinary external market spread (i.e. internal bid prices were always higher than the relevant London Inter-Bank Bid Rate (LIBID) and internal offer prices were always lower than relevant London Inter-Bank Offered Rate (LIBOR))'*. Effectively the businesses were funding themselves at more favourable rates than the bank itself. Needless to say, the lack of funds transfer pricing fuelled the problems that later happened.[12]

A simple funds transfer pricing chart is introduced in Figure 8.13, which should demonstrate how the transfer pricing mechanism can appear for businesses and how it should influence their behaviour. The numbers in the example are for illustration purposes only.

Unit A is the retail unit of Bank B, which is a typical savings–lending bank without any trading activities. The funds transfer pricing is done separately for resources and advances with the objective of calculating the unit's net interest income independently from group treasury or the maturity mismatch profit. To make the FTP 'profit' more understandable it is compared to the actual interest income of the divisions. This will show us how business units can 'make money' from both the lending and deposit business.

Full year 20xx $ 'm

	A	B	C	D = (C/B)	E	F	G (=C+F)
Liabilities	FTP assumptions	Balances	Margin $	Margin %	Fund transfer reward %	Fund transfer reward $	Net Interest Income
On demand deposit							
– Retail/SME	behavioural	2,800.0	4.2	0.2%	0.9%	9.8	14.0
– NFC (nonfinancial corporates)	behavioural	1,400.0	–6.3	–0.5%	0.2%	7.0	0.7
– NBFI (nonbank financial insti.)	behavioural	300.0	–0.2	–0.1%	0.0%	0.1	–0.1
Term Deposits							
– Retail/SME	actual	3,700.0	–11.1	–0.3%	1.0%	18.0	6.9
– NFC (nonfinancial corporates)	actual	4,000.0	–36.0	–0.9%	0.3%	23.0	–13.0
– NBFI (nonbank financial insti.)	actual	150.0	–0.2	–0.2%	0.1%	0.1	–0.1
Other deposits							
– Retail/SME	behavioural	50.0	–0.2	–0.5%	0.4%	0.2	–0.0
– NFC (nonfinancial corporates)							
– NBFI (nonbank financial insti.)							
I. Total Liabilities		**12,400.0**	**–49.8**	**–0.40%**	**0.5%**	**58.2**	**8.4**

	A	B	C	D = (C/B)	E	F	G (=C+F)
Performing loans	FTP assumptions	Balances	Margin $	Margin %	Fund transfer charge %	Fund transfer charge $	Net Interest Income
Personal and corp. loans	actual	6,100.0	192.4	3.15%	–1.7%	–103.7	88.7
Overdrafts	behavioural	1,400.0	60.2	4.30%	–0.7%	–9.8	50.4
Mortgages	behavioural	3,400.0	71.4	2.10%	–1.3%	–44.2	27.2
II. Total loans		**10,900.0**	**324.0**	**2.97%**	**–1.4%**	**–157.7**	**166.3**

Net Interest Income (NII) (I+II)							**174.7**

Figure 8.13 Example of a funds transfer

Unit A is measured on its ability to raise cheap deposits and lend at margins above the FTP price. We start on the liability side. It is broken down into three categories depending on their origin and stability. Each group has different liquidity requirements and run-off assumptions, whereas Bank B could either use their internal models to assign the corresponding factors or use Basel III categories. Bank B is using the three major Basel III categories, retail/SME, NFCs (nonfinancial corporates) and NBFIs (nonbank financial institutions), each with a separate FTP rate that takes into account the liquidity requirement. Retail/SME deposits have a low outflow propensity and need the least amount of liquidity buffer to be set aside. The wholesale deposits have a higher run-off assumption and the deposits from other financial institutions receive the lowest reward rates due to their lack of stability. To figure out the appropriate requirement the bank can use the LCR run-off factors or its own assumptions. In this example there are only three categories, whereas in reality they would be multiple, both on the liability and asset sides. The appropriate breakdown into categories is important as it demonstrates the differences there are in values of deposits to a bank and they will see from the rewards they are given which are the ones they should target.

The balance sheet does not only have to be ranked according to stability but also to maturity, as we are applying an upward sloping FTP curve. On-demand deposits are separate from term deposits. Each category of liabilities is either assigned a hypothetical funds transfer pricing rate based on behavioural assumptions (expected maturity) or the rate derived from the funds transfer pricing curve is adjusted for a liquidity requirement corresponding to their actual maturity. For on-demand retail/SME deposits Unit A has applied the assumption that the deposits have a 3 year average life, whereas the on-demand deposits for the NFCs and NBFIs are assumed to be much shorter and hence attract a lower reward rate. Bank B is equipped with good systems and is able to assign a corresponding FTP rate to each term deposit. Should that not be possible some average life assumptions need to be done.

We see from the table that Unit A has paid out $49.8m (column C) in actual margins for deposits in the year 20XX, which equates to an average margin of 0.4% (column D). Some of the retail/SME on-demand deposit bears no or a very low interest rate and hence the bank is actually receiving a margin on them but is not paying out.

Column E is the FTP rate taken from the Bank B FTP curve. We can see that the reward rate is higher for retail/SME deposits than corporates and term deposits are of more value than on-demand deposits (i.e. more stable). The average FTP reward rate attributed to Unit A is 0.5%. As the total funds transfer pricing reward is higher than the margin paid, Unit A is actually making a net interest income on their liabilities. This means they are paying less in the margin to their deposits than the FTP benchmark indicates. Their net interest income from liabilities is $8.4m.

Unit A has only three categories of assets: personal and corporate loans, overdrafts and mortgages. The model is a match funding model, assigning a corresponding FTP rate to the maturity of each asset (each loan being priced off the corresponding FTP rate from the curve). The overdrafts are 'nonmaturity' and mortgages usually get refinanced before their maturity. Consequently, Bank B is applying behavioural assumptions to both categories. The average FTP rate charge to Unit A is 1.4%, which indicates that the asset side has a longer duration than the liabilities, which were rewarded with a 0.5% rate on average. The lending operation of Unit A made $324m in margins in the year 20XX and is being charged $157.7m from the centralized treasury unit for the match funding. The net interest income from lending is therefore $166.3m.

In total, Unit A is making $174.7m in the net interest margin, with the bulk of it coming from the lending business. If we just look at the funds transfer pricing transactions, then the unit has received $58.2m in reward for its deposits and is being charged $157.7m for the usage of funds. This FTP 'loss' of $99.5m will have a corresponding 'profit' in the treasury unit, as this is the maturity transformation profit the bank makes, which should not be assigned to Unit A.

The application of this simple model will influence the decision making and strategies at Unit A. The lending business, which at first glance might look profitable, might not necessarily be so when the appropriate cost of funding is applied. On the other side, Unit A is providing a service to the overall bank by raising deposits at a cheaper rate than the corresponding FTP rate, and as it has a funding surplus this increases the overall profitability of the bank (assuming there is another business unit with a deficit).

The steering the FTP methodology makes needs to be aligned with other business goals. It holds true from the above example that Unit A is making money by raising deposits. It could therefore set its focus on that part of the business and neglect the lending business. This becomes more actual if the FTP curve is generally higher. This activity of Unit A to raise deposits rather than lend money can only benefit Bank B as a whole if there are uses for the funds, either within other divisions with a funding deficit or if the treasury has the risk appetite to take on more maturity transformation risk by placing these funds further out in the curve for a profit. Therefore, in reality business units are set overriding goals on deposit and lending volumes to keep the bank in balance.

The above example is only one of many ways to apply an FTP, but it is important to keep in mind that no single method is without any downsides and the models need to be adjusted to the funding profile of each firm. It is, for example, questionable for a bank that is largely customer deposit funded to price 'reoccurring' or existing business according to the prevailing marginal rate alone, especially if the deposits are in the form of 'free' current accounts. Under those circumstances (where the average cost of funding is always going to be lower than the marginal cost), it could lead to the wrong behaviour, if the lending businesses were required to apply the marginal rate without any adjustments. If the funding curve is steep this can lead to some irrational lending pricing decisions.[13] It is therefore important to adjust the models to the environment and funding profile, but still keep track of the maturity transformation cost.

Endnotes

1. See Senior Supervisors Group, *Risk Management Lessons from the Global Banking Crisis of 2008*, 21 October 2009, p. 1.
2. Adapted and expanded from Choudhry, M. (2007), *Bank Asset and Liability Management: Strategy, Trading, Analysis*, John Wiley & Sons, Ltd, p. 331, and Matz, L. and Neu, P. (editors) (2007), *Liquidity Risk Measures and Management, A Practitioner's Guide to Global Best Practices*, John Wiley & Sons 2007, Ltd, p. 97.
3. See Institute of International Finance, *Principles of Liquidity Risk Management*, March 2007.
4. See Sungard, *Liquidity Risk – New Lessons and Old Lessons*, 2008. Available at: www.sungard.com.
5. Adapted and expanded from Institute of International Finance, *Principles of Liquidity Risk Management*, March 2007, p. 28.
6. See Senior Supervisors Group, *Risk Management Lessons from the Global Banking Crisis of 2008*, 21 October 2009.
7. See Senior Supervisors Group, *Risk Management Lessons from the Global Banking Crisis of 2008*, 21 October 2009, p. 21.

8. See Prudential Regulation Authority (PRA): *Prudential Sourcebook for Banks, Building Societies and Investment Firm (BIPRU)*, Chapter 12.3.15, Pricing Liquidity Risk. Available at: www.fsa.gov.uk.
9. Adapted from Ernst & Young, *Fund Transfer Pricing, Roadmap to Managing Pricing and Profitability for NBFCs*, undated.
10. Adapted from Moody's Analytics, *Implementing High Value Funds Transfer Pricing Systems*, September 2011.
11. Adapted from Grant, J. (2011), Financial Stability Institute, Occasional Paper No. 10, *Liquidity Transfer Pricing: A Guide to Better Practice*, Bank for International Settlement, December 2011.
12. See Transparency Report to the Shareholders of UBS AG, UBS, October 2010, p. 22, and Shareholder Report on UBS's Write-Downs, April 2008, p. 25.
13. See, for example, Sinclair, Mark, *ALM Risk Management Observations*, Presentation at the ALMA 2013 Summer Conference. Available at: http://www.ukalma.org.uk/.

9

Step IV: The Quantitative Framework

The fourth step of the '6 Step Framework' is the quantitative liquidity risk framework. Liquidity risk, like any other field within risk management, relies on various quantitative measures. This is sometimes stamped as 'liquidity risk management', which should not be confused with the general task of managing liquidity, which is a tactical function undertaken by the treasury division. The chapter covers first and foremost the systems and processes for identifying, measuring and monitoring liquidity risk.

This part of the '6 Step Framework' is an integrated part of the framework. By defining the Sources of Liquidity Risk (the first step), it has established what specifically is to be measured while keeping in mind measurements and metrics that need to be tailored to the bank's risk profile. Included in this quantitative framework is the cash flow analysis platform, which is used in the scenario stress testing in the next step, Step V. Furthermore, many of the metrics defined and used are also included in the Contingency Funding Plan, also in Step V, in the form of early warning indicators (EWIs). Both the balance sheet metrics and cash flow forecasts (through stress testing) provide the limits used when setting the risk tolerance in Step II, so it can be concluded that the quantitative framework is a key factor in the '6 Step Framework' and is well integrated.

9.1 DIFFERENT WAYS TO MEASURE LIQUIDITY

There are a few different methods used to measure liquidity from a risk management angle. This area, along with the increased focus on funds transfer pricing, is where liquidity risk management has developed the most over recent years. The features that newer approaches in measuring liquidity and FTP have in common are that they are forward looking and not based on financial statements, which is not a coincidence as liquidity management is increasingly adopting economic value tools.

Liquidity risk management started by analysing balance sheet figures from the financial accounts and mainly through applying various ratios tried, in order to measure liquidity riskiness. Although good for what they are, the balance sheet ratios are static in their nature and thus do not include the time factor of liquidity. As explained before, liquidity risk is about quantum and time and practitioners soon realized that they could not measure the impact of time by using this method. Liquidity management therefore borrowed many of the principles from management accounting and started to develop more dynamic measurements. This also led to the development of funds transfer pricing as a management tool.

We will introduce three different approaches to quantify liquidity and discuss how each one of them can be appropriately used and adequately adopted. The three methods are:

(a) Balance sheet analysis
(b) Cash flow analysis
(c) Cash capital calculations.

There is yet another hybrid approach called cash capital calculations, which in this book is covered under the balance sheet analysis.

Basel III also includes a set of metrics that will become a global standard in 2015 and this chapter will look into how they can be of use to the risk specialist. They should not be devalued into a simple regulatory reporting exercise as they can be very useful if applied effectively. We will then look at some of the lessons learnt from the crises, where in some instances the metrics applied fell short of expectations. To aid the user, examples are given of widely used metrics as well as an overview of how banks have approached quantitative measurement.

Firstly, yet another health warning. No single method or quantitative measures can provide full adequate protection. Again the bank needs to build up parameters suited to their business model and sources of funds and what is appropriate to one bank might be rather useless to another. This is echoed in the regulatory requirements of various supervisors and in best practice guides. The fifth BCBS principle sets out a good foundation to work from where it states that *'a bank should have a sound process for identifying, measuring, monitoring and controlling liquidity risk. This process should include a robust framework for comprehensively projecting cash flows arising from assets, liabilities and off-balance sheet items over an appropriate set of time horizons'*.[1] The Australian regulator, the Australian Prudential Regulation Authority (APRA), has set out a more precise guide than many other regulators, which defines more closely what good measurement tools should accomplish. In addition to the requirement for 'sound processes for measuring liquidity risk' the regulator expects banks to 'employ a range of customized measurement tools for this purpose' and ends up by stressing that cash flow projections are the critical tool for adequately managing liquidity risk.[2]

Before heading into the details of each method we should establish and summarize the main components a good measuring system should have, which support the overall objective of identifying potential future mismatches and current imbalances.

- The measurement palette should be tailored and firm specific. The 'one size does *not* fit all' mantra has been used before but for measuring it is of great importance to align the measurements to the business. The adequacy of the measurements is not only determined by the risk profile and sources but also by the system constraints the bank has and its capacity to produce reliable information.
- Needs to prioritize the dynamic nature of liquidity risk rather than static attributes.
- Should be forward looking and not retrospective.
- Should mirror and match the stress testing methods. If the quantitative measurements start to show indications of threat, the stress testing methods need to be able to model that threat and provide the possible impact under different scales of severity.

9.1.1   Balance Sheet Analysis

As the name indicates, the balance sheet ratios draw out the difference and relationship between certain types of assets and liabilities. There are a number of these ratios but most are there to cast a light on stability or instability. As an example, by knowing the quantum of illiquid/liquid assets and stable and instable liabilities we can get a useful estimate of the balance sheet liquidity risk. The various ratios derived from the balance sheet number are there to quantify the risk and enable monitoring over time. The balance sheet analysis focusing on the assets and liabilities has obvious limitations as items not found on the balance sheet statement are not included. These items can, however, be of great importance, such as

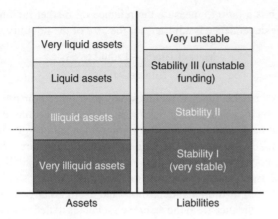

Figure 9.1   The liquidity balance sheet

off-balance sheet commitments that have been met by adding some off-balance sheet figures to the measurements if available. To enhance the benefit of the balance sheet ratios, it is useful to construct a liquidity balance sheet listing items according to their liquidity, as shown in Figure 9.1.

At the bottom we align the most stable funding next to the most illiquid assets. The stability of funding is discussed in Chapter 10 on liquidity stress testing and the ranking of assets is quite similar. The very illiquid asset class consists of long-term loans and loans ineligible for securitization or other types of asset sales. At the top are the very liquid assets such as the HQLAs, which we can view next to unstable funding. This is a very simple way of viewing the balance sheet and the categorization is obviously subjective. This point in time ratio will, however, reveal any major structural imbalances within the balance sheet and should give more guidance than the usual two segment split (short dated and long dated).

The Basel III NSFR ratio is an example of an advanced balance sheet ratio measuring stable funding against illiquid (longer-term) assets and if the illustration above is compared to the NSFR illustration in the Basel III chapter (Chapter 12), one can see where its origins lie and how, if adapted and implemented thoughtfully, the balance sheet ratios can provide substantial value in risk management.

Logically most of the balance sheet ratios are retrospective in nature and reflect past liquidity positions. They therefore do not provide the best insight into what the future might look like and should not be solely relied on. At a first glance it is easier to spot their shortcomings than their benefits. They cannot provide any information on expected future cash flow mismatches or future funding needs or funding sources. By the same token they do not provide information on the liquidity of the balance sheet, that is how easily assets can be converted into cash. However, they should not be excluded from the framework as point in time measurements can reveal structural weaknesses and imbalances, as touched upon earlier. The imbalances between the composition of assets and liabilities that the balance sheet ratios reveal will also create a need for forward-looking projections.

The rating agencies apply balance sheet ratios to measure liquidity risk within banks. Thought not to be very advanced measurements and with the limitations described earlier, they allow the agencies to obtain a quick view of the bank and moreover to use the outcome to benchmark the bank against its peers, which is part of the rating agency approach. Included in Moody's approach is a ratio to measure the reliance on market funding when funding the asset base, where the dependence is adjusted for the size of the liquidity buffer:

$$\frac{\text{Market funds} - \text{Liquid assets}}{\text{Total assets}}$$

Moody's definition of market funding includes, amongst other noncore deposits, long-term debt, short-term borrowings and trading liabilities. Liquid assets consist mainly of cash and balances with central banks, amounts due from other financial institutions and available-for-sale securities. In Moody's scorecard the range of outcome is from −10% for the strongest banks (where liquid assets exceed market funding) to 20%. Other similar measurements are the liquid assets/total assets and core deposits/total funding. Moody's defines core deposits as deposits not sourced from institutional depositors and excludes large-ticket deposits, making the banks use the local guidance from the insurance schemes to define what large deposits are, for example, in the United States, those deposits exceeding US$100,000.

The focus of the rating agencies is on the reliance on short-term money and how risky these funding sources are. This is a useful approach to use when assessing whether a bank is in the vulnerable position of having an insufficient liquidity buffer to cover short-term obligations. Fitch applies a measurement on short-term liquidity coverage, defined as

$$\text{Liquidity coverage} = \text{Liquidity pool} - \text{Cash outflows}$$

The definition of a liquidity pool is similar to the HQLA and includes cash, unencumbered assets, government securities, liquid financial assets at fair value and committed credit lines. Most types of outflow are included in the cash outflow definition, such as short-term unsecured debt, retail and brokered deposits, trading liabilities, etc. As this is an all-encompassing definition Fitch applies run-off rates on each category from 10% to 100%.[3]

Standard and Poor's have a similar approach to Moody's and calculate and publish various balance sheet ratios. The ratios try to cast a similar light on the problem as those already mentioned, such as how short the wholesale funding is, what coverage HQLA provides if short-term unsecured wholesale markets erode, as well as how strong the long-term funding structure of the bank is. The ratios are:[4]

- Core deposits/funding base
- Customer loans (net)/customer deposits
- Long-term funding ratio
- Broad liquid assets/short-term wholesale funding
- Net broad liquid assets/short-term customer deposits
- Narrow liquid assets/3 month wholesale funding
- Net short-term interbank funding/total wholesale funding
- Short-term wholesale funding/total wholesale funding.

Moody's Cash Capital Position

Another useful tool from Moody's is their calculation of the cash capital position. Whereas there are various methods that predominantly look at the shorter end of the funding structure, this tool looks at the amount of long-term funding to fund illiquid assets. This is however a 'stock'-based approach and as such has much in common with the balance sheet ratio methods.

Generally, under a liquid assets (stock) approach, the firm maintains liquid instruments on its balance sheet that can be drawn upon when needed, including a pool of unencumbered assets (usually government securities) that can be used to obtain secured funding through repurchase agreements and other secured facilities.

The scenario for the cash capital position is one where the bank has lost its short-term unsecured funding and needs to rely on its long-term funding and unwinding of its HQLA to fund its illiquid assets. The cash capital position can be defined as:

Cash capital position = Stable funding sources − Contingent outflows − Illiquid assets

In this measurement stable funding sources are defined as long-term funding, core deposits and equity. Illiquid assets would include both loans and securities.

A positive cash capital position means the bank can continue to operate without the short-term funding whereas a negative outcome signifies that the bank needs to sell down its liquid assets to create funding. It is possible to realign the equation and also calculate the cash capital position by measuring how much of the unencumbered liquid assets are left after they have been used to pay back short-term funding and noncore deposits, taking into account the appropriate haircuts. What remains is then available to contribute to fund illiquid assets. The equation will then look like this:

Cash capital position = Liquid assets − Short-term funding − Noncore deposits

The resemblance to the NSFR is obvious and though this measurement has been succeeded by other policies at Moody's it is still a useful tool and benchmark, especially for securities firms, which have a built-in reliance on short-term funding. It is valuable to be able to estimate how the bank copes without access to short-term funding and needs to fund itself on its assets. This simple equation falls short by not taking off-balance sheet commitments into account and is subject to definitions of what is long-term debt. It also does not provide any guidance on when the liquid positions can be liquidated and turned into cash. Some of the shortcomings can be overcome and a more advanced ratio created from this base case approach.[5]

9.1.2   Cash Flow Analysis

Forward-looking cash flow analyses are key ingredients to many aspects of liquidity risk management, reaching from stress testing to planning. While measures of liquidity focusing on balance sheet ratios are necessary, the best practices require more advanced measures to assess future funding needs within certain time periods. The importance of cash flow analysis can best be understood if the liquidity risk definitions are revisited. Liquidity risk is defined as the ability to obtain cash for operations when needed. The liquidity needs result from the cash flow projections, covering expected cash inflows and outflows. For this reason the cash flow analysis or simply the maturity mismatch approach is the bread and butter of the daily function of a liquidity management unit and provides the template for scenario stress testing and maturity mismatch gaps. It therefore has many uses for risk management. To summarize, the main advantages of using a multiperiod cash flow analysis are as follows:

- The single largest advantage this method has over the other techniques is introduction of time. Whereas the balance sheet ratios at best use blunt categories such as short-term debt and long-term debt, the cash flow projections are fully dynamic.

- By introducing the time dimension it allows the projection of funding needs and identification of funding sources (both quantum and time). This becomes important in liquidity stress testing.
- It allows the bank to identify when it is most exposed to liquidity risk and a possible negative event.
- It enables the bank to determine the need for an appropriate liquidity buffer.
- It provides the link between liquidity risk management and planning and funding strategy.
- It can be enhanced as needed to include behavioural assumptions, consideration of off-balance sheet risk and the liquidity impacts of trading and derivatives, to give an example. As such it helps the risk specialist to see which part of the balance sheet is contractual and what amount of cash flows are subject to assumptions and uncertainty.

Most banks combine the two schools of measurement, that is the liquid asset approach (liquidity as stock) and the pure cash flow method. This gives a more realistic overview of the risk at hand and the possible mitigating factors. The table will then match cash outflows in each time bucket against a combination of contractual cash inflows plus inflows that can be generated through the sale of assets, repurchase agreement or other secured borrowing. Assets that are most liquid are typically counted in the earliest time buckets, while less liquid assets are counted in later time buckets.

Section 4.2 dealt with the liquidity gap concept, which derives from the cash flow projection idea. The most basic cash flow approach creates the static liquidity gap. It is a mismatch report incorporating only balance sheet items that have a maturity or expiry date and consequently does not include equity or other items without a specific time value. The dynamic liquidity gap, which is the best practice standard, on the other hand, includes the elements included in the static gap analysis and in addition all items without a set maturity date applying appropriate behavioural assumptions. It therefore offers a dynamic projection into what the liquidity risk profile could look like under normal and stressed conditions.

Understandably it is more difficult to forecast the dynamic cash flows. The predictions start with the base case, which reflects the business-as-usual cash flow projections including the contractual cash inflows and outflows due in each time bucket. It should also include the best estimates of the noncontractual cash flows, keeping in mind that the behavioural assumptions are only valid for a short period of time and need to be updated frequently.

Section 10.1.11 on scenario stress testing takes a closer look at the appropriate granularity and breakdown of balance sheet items and the proposed roll-off assumptions. Therefore this chapter will provide more understanding on the cash flow conception rather than the implementation details. There are, however, few details that need to be discussed at this stage. The scope of the projection needs to be adequate and reflect the free and undisturbed flow of funds. The natural restrictions to those are legal entities, different jurisdictions and currencies. The bank accordingly needs to conduct cash flow projections at the top level and in each subsidiary (if there are actual or hypothetical restrictions) as well as cash flow forecasts in each material currency.

The most common gap mismatch report separates a customer-driven transaction from a treasury transaction, and contractual cash flows are separated from cash flows that are subject to behavioural assumptions. Banks with a simple balance sheet largely funded by customer deposits might break down the forecast into monthly periods, but banks with larger exposures

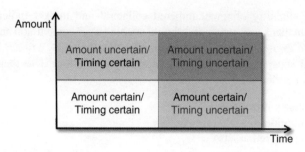

Figure 9.2   The uncertainty of cash flows

to the money markets, such as security houses, usually have daily buckets for the first week or 14 days and weekly buckets up to 1 month and monthly thereafter.

The Four Types of Cash Flows

When constructing the cash flow analysis we generally think of four types of cash flow elements, as illustrated in Figure 9.2. The most predictable cash flows are where both the timing and quantum of the payment are certain, of which a fixed rate bond could be used as an example. At the other end of the spectrum are cash flow transactions where both timing and amount are uncertain. On-demand deposits are an example of a liability with this difficult feature.

In between these two extremes we have flows of cash where the timing is certain but the amount is not. The floating rate loan would be an example of this or the typical subordinated bond with a call option. Then the opposite can also be true, that is timing unknown but amount determined. Each one of these four categories requires a different level of assumptions. The first category is the clearest one but the one with both factors uncertain needs the most attention and thought on assumptions. This is the reason for the research focus on the behaviour of on-demand deposits. Off-balance sheet items are also a factor that needs great attention as the size of off-balance sheet commitments is material for many banks, even exceeding the size of the liquidity buffer. In those instances special care needs to be applied when determining the most appropriate draw down assumptions. To complete the picture we also need to include the cash flow impact of the banking operations in the future, which include future expected cash inflows (new issuance) and new loans and loan renewals.

Basel III Metrics

It has been mentioned how the NSFR ratio bears many similarities to the cash capital position. The other Basel III measurement, the liquidity coverage ratio, is also an advance version of the balance sheet ratios described earlier where the objective is to measure the liquidity coverage for the next 30 days. It adds behavioural assumptions to the asset and liability categories, which makes it a more useful tool than the simple balance sheet ratio. The NSFR and LCR are discussed further in Chapter 12.

In addition to the LCR, the new Basel III rule book sets out what it terms 'consistent monitoring tools', which are expected to capture information related to cash flows, balance sheet structure, availability of unencumbered collateral and market indicators. These are measurements many banks are using and should enable easier comparison and benchmarking between banks and even countries. The hope is also that the ratios will act as early warning indicators to local supervisors when they can aggregate them next to their assessment on systemic risk. The metrics are:

1. Contractual maturity mismatch
2. Funding concentration
3. Available unencumbered assets
4. Market-related monitoring tools.

1. *Contractual maturity mismatch.* This measurement is the static maturity gap table discussed earlier. By listing all the contractual inflows and outflows of liquidity in predefined time bands, it is possible to analyse the mismatch in each time period and how much liquidity the bank would potentially need to raise in each bucket. By only including the contractual cash flows, the table will isolate the maturity transformation of the bank, which by itself is a risk indicator. For most banks there will be a negative cap in the short end (liabilities > assets) followed by a positive gap in the mid and longer date time periods, where the bank has more assets maturing than liabilities. As already discussed, this does not only exclude the behavioural angle of liabilities, being either stable on-demand deposit or time deposits that are expected to be renewed, but also the expected rollover of renewal of loans. For most banks, the asset side of the balance sheet is much longer dated than the contractual maturities indicate and it is far from likely that the bank could expect the loans to be repaid at their due date. This problem is even more pronounced from the regulator's point of view if this applies to the whole banking sector. Regulators are left to define the templates to be used but Basel III puts forward an idea of overnight, 7 day, 14 day, 1, 2, 3, 6 and 9 month, and 1, 2, 3, 5 and beyond 5 year periods. Open maturity instruments will be reported separately and without any assumptions, and off-balance sheet items will also be included.

   The contractual maturity mismatch report should be used within the risk management framework for more purposes than just being a regulatory return due to its understanding of the overall maturity transformation risk the bank is undertaking. The amount of maturity transformation risk is a key risk figure, which both Board and senior management should be aware of. Not all banks look at the contractual cash flows separately but go straight into the full cash flow statement, missing the information it provides. The contractual mismatch report can be used as the calculation board for an overall risk limit or tolerance.

2. *Funding concentration.* This is one of the Sources of Liquidity Risk in the first step of the '6 Step Framework'. The way Basel approaches it is to limit their observations to the wholesale funding sources that are of significance. The concentration is calculated separately on a counterparty and product basis, which makes the reading more interesting and useful. The two ratios are defined as:

   A. Funding liabilities sourced from each significant counterparty as a percentage of total liabilities.

   B. Funding liabilities sourced from each significant product/instrument as a percentage of total liabilities.

   The definition of a significant counterparty is a single counterparty or a group of connected counterparties accounting in aggregate for more than 1% of the bank's total balance sheet. The same 1% rule is used to define significant products.

As part of this measurement, banks are required to provide a list (by time buckets) of the amount of assets and liabilities in each significant currency, where a currency is considered significant if the aggregate liabilities denominated in that currency amount to at least 5% of the bank's total liabilities.

Funding concentration is a useful metric but not a perfect one, as was further discussed in Section 8.5 on funding strategy. The funding concentration risk is most evident for banks that are reliant on wholesale funding, especially if it is short dated. The problem is that the counterparties for wholesale funding are unknown as the instruments are for public issuance and are traded freely. This considerably limits the reasonableness of this measure. Furthermore, this measurement does not capture the herd mentality of investors, which can be considerable for some products.

3. *Available unencumbered assets.* This metric is of use to supervisors to gauge the quantity and characteristics of the assets that could be used as HQLA or collateral for secured funding. The report should include available unencumbered assets that are marketable as collateral in secondary markets as well as available unencumbered assets that are eligible for central banks' standing facilities. One would expect a bank to already be using these numbers in its liquidity risk overview, but the definition of the template can provide the necessary discipline to the bank's internal reporting. As an example banks are required to report the location of the collateral, which is something not all banks frequently look into but is of importance should it be needed with a short notice under market-wide stresses. Additional information such as estimated haircuts and a separate report for each significant currency are of value to the bank as well as the regulator and should not be neglected.

4. *Market-related monitoring tools.* The last requirement is one of setting appropriate early warning indicators (EWIs), which is discussed separately in Chapter 10 on contingency funding planning. The regulator recognizes how high-frequency market data with a short time lag can provide reliable early signs of emerging risk. This measurement is aimed at the local regulators and how they should approach setting an adequate EWI, which is further broken down into market-wide information, information on the financial sector and bank-specific information. To provide market-wide information Basel III suggests indicators like equity prices for the overall market and subindices, debt market spreads for the short-term and long-term markets, credit default swaps and government bond prices. They also expand into monitoring foreign exchange market conditions, commodity markets and even markets for specialized securitized products. Both the absolute level and the directional trends should be monitored. As mentioned in the Chapter 10, the EWIs are a vital feature in the risk management framework, which is now widely understood. Basel III draws attention to the special market EWI, which especially banks in niche markets should pay attention to. Indicators like commodity prices or real estate prices can give a very early indication of problems that with a lagging time effect can be a risk to the bank. Some of the indicators can also provide some insight into the possible behaviour of clients that the bank has provided credit or liquidity lines to and who could emerge as an off-balance sheet risk.

The information on the financial sector is for the benefit of the supervisor but will be interesting reading for individual banks to assess their possible market funding and appetite for some of the contingency funding plans. This can become important as the contingency plans do tend to be similar from bank to bank, but most banks do not make the plans under the assumption that many banks will be seeking the same arrangement as they are.

Possible vulnerabilities and sources of risk

Possible metrics and measurements	Retail deposit outflow	Wholesale liability outflow	Rapid loan growth	Funding concentration	Increased cost of funding	Inability to raise term funding	Reliance on unstable deposits	Drop in HQLA value or quantum	Intra-day liquidity risk	Increase in off-balance sheet commitments	Currency mismatch
Cash-flow projections (mismatch buckets)	✓										
Stress testing	✓	✓	✓	✓	✓	✓	✓	✓	✓	✓	✓
Loan/deposit ratio	✓	✓	✓					✓			
Stable deposits/loans ratio	✓	✓	✓								
Stable deposits/total deposits ratio	✓	✓									
Deposit profiling (size, channel, type)	✓	✓	✓	✓	✓	✓	✓		✓	✓	✓
Repo haircuts								✓			
Liquid asset coverage (net liquid assets/total volatile liabilities)	✓	✓					✓				
Excess liquidity ratio	✓	✓	✓			✓		✓			
Off-balance sheet/stable deposit ratio	✓	✓	✓							✓	
Stable deposits/illiquid asset ratio	✓	✓	✓							✓	
Survival horizon (days)	✓	✓	✓			✓	✓		✓		
Top 10 depositors/funding providers	✓		✓	✓				✓			
Amount of repoable collateral								✓			
Amount raised with management actions				✓	✓	✓					✓
Liquid assets ratio	✓			✓	✓		✓				
Short-term liq. assets/short-term liq. liabilites	✓		✓	✓	✓						
Wholesale funding/total assets	✓	✓		✓		✓	✓		✓	✓	✓
HQLA-short-term liabilities	✓	✓						✓	✓	✓	✓
Net funding requirement (6m)/HQLA	✓	✓					✓	✓	✓	✓	✓

Figure 9.3 Metrics and measurements for Bank A

The bank-specific information should already be included in the internal EWI table and will provide the bank and the regulator with an idea of whether the market is losing confidence in a particular institution or even types of institutions. These metrics include equity prices, CDS spreads, money market yields, rollover propensity and prices for various bond instruments, all for a specific bank.

Setting the Measurements Needed

So far, a wide set of metrics and measurements have been introduced. The next step is to choose the ones needed to provide a specific risk profile for the firm. Rather than going out and simply picking ratios other banks are using it is useful to perform gap analyses on the identified Sources of Liquidity Risk and vulnerabilities versus possible metrics. Figure 9.3 is an example of such an assessment done for a fictional bank, Bank A.[6]

The gap analysis is performed by listing all the possible vulnerabilities or Sources of Liquidity Risk against a list of metrics to get an idea of how well the bank's risk is being 'covered' by the metrics. The more 'ticks' each measurement has, the more useful it is to the bank.

Something Old, Something New

Like other features of the liquidity management framework, the art of measuring liquidity is constantly under review and best practice needs to include the lesson learnt from financial crises. The *Risk Management Lessons from the Global Banking Crisis of 2008* report points out that, before the crisis, most banks relied worryingly on a 'months of [contractual]

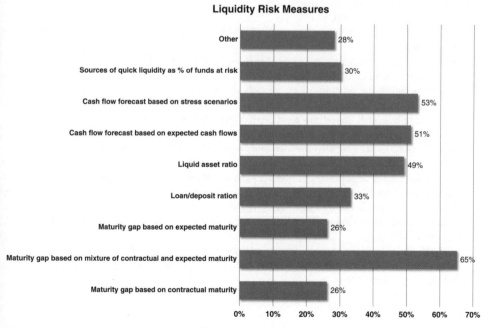

Figure 9.4   The use of liquidity measures[8]

coverage' metric that did not sufficiently reflect the contractual and behavioural demands triggered under stressed market conditions. The report points out as an example that the coverage metrics did not capture many of the stresses that developed and occurred during the crises.[7] This echoes the words of warning set out at the beginning of this chapter about the static liquid asset approach or that the balance sheet ratios alone are not sufficient measurements.

A survey conducted by PWC on the status of balance sheet management practices amongst international banks performed in 2009 gives a good indication of what is the standard approach. Figure 9.4 is derived from the results from that survey and shows that the majority of banks use the maturity gap cash flow analysis, including contractual and expected maturities. One third of the banks surveyed, however, do not use this approach, which is surprising as the institutions surveyed are both large and complex banks. Only a quarter of the banks surveyed perform the cash flows separately for a contractual transaction, which makes the Basel III requirement for contractual cash flow reports a timely and relevant request.

Not surprisingly, many banks use the liquid asset ratio but one wonders how adequate the measuring framework is at banks that neither look at their liquid asset ratios nor at cash flow projections. The survey's results are a clear indication that banks in general still have a long way to go in improving how they measure their liquidity risk properly and without the necessary quantitative measurement the liquidity framework cannot be effective. As the banks included in the survey are most likely to be the more sophisticated part of the banking community, the question remains what the status is amongst the multiple smaller organizations, which when aggregated account for the larger part of the banking system.

Endnotes

1. Basel Committee on Banking Supervision, *Principles for Sound Liquidity Risk Management and Supervision,* September 2008, p. 10.
2. Australian Prudential Regulation Authority (APRA), Draft Prudential Practice Guide, APG 210 – Liquidity, May 2013.
3. See, further, Fitch, *Managing Cash Capital in Banks*, London, July 2010.
4. See any public rating report from Standard & Poor's. The rating methodology takes various factors into account where the liquidity ratios are only one factor of many and are an instrument for the agencies to compare banks.
5. See, for example, L.D. Raffis on how KeyCorp has expanded on the cash capital metric and applied this within its own framework. Raffis, L.D. (2007),The net cash capital tool in bank liquidity management, Chapter 11 in *Liquidity Risk Measurement and Management*, John Wiley & Sons, Singapore.
6. For ideas of possible useful ratios see, for example, Montes-Negret, F. (2009), *The Heavenly Liquidity Twin, The Increasing Importance of Liquidity Risk*, The World Bank Europe and Central Asia Region Finance and Private Sector Department, Section 46, November 2009, and *Comptroller's Handbook*, Office of the Comptroller of the Currency, June 2012.
7. See Senior Supervisors Group, *Risk Management Lessons from the Global Banking Crisis of 2008*, 21 October 2009, p. 3.
8. See PWC, *Balance Sheet Management Benchmark Survey, Status of Balance Sheet Management Practices among International Banks – 2009*, and PWC, *Liquidity Risk Management, Staying Afloat in Choppy Seas*, April 2010.

10

Step V: Stress Testing and the Contingency Funding Plan

In the penultimate step of the '6 Step Framework', the framework has moved beyond the stages of defining and measuring and is now set to produce more detailed results and guidance of the management of liquidity.

If someone is asked to name the reason for doing liquidity management, they would most likely answer that it is the necessity to be able to conduct liquidity stress testing and have a rescue plan ready should a liquidity storm break out. This chapter is focused solely on these two concepts but as everything else in the latter parts of the '6 Step Framework', it draws upon results and findings from the earlier steps. If the groundwork has been properly constructed and the base built on sound assumptions, then the stress testing and contingency funding planning should not be a giant leap into the unknown.

10.1 STRESS TESTING – THE HEART OF THE LIQUIDITY FRAMEWORK

Stress testing is undoubtedly one of the cornerstones of a liquidity management framework and probably the most tangible part it deals with. It is also the part of the regime that needs the most maintenance as assumptions and risk levels change constantly. Due to the uncertain nature of liquidity risk, stress testing is vital to be able to quantify what the bank is up against. For the same reasons, the stress methodology and assumptions need to be regularly challenged for their relevance. For many other risk types, banks have built a generally accepted approach and models that, if applied, should keep risk at bay. The discussion here is thus more about the outcome and less about the tool or method applied. Liquidity risk is to that end materially different and picking the appropriate method for testing is and should be debated. By the same token, liquidity stress test results cannot be read or applied in the same way as the outcome of some models, especially the stochastic ones.

Stress scenarios measure the amount the bank needs to maintain in liquid assets and provide the ground upon which to base the CFP. They are aimed at identifying potential weaknesses or vulnerabilities in the bank's liquidity profile, which enables the bank to react and put in place measurements to decrease the risk. If the risk cannot be reasonably mitigated at the outset by, for example, amending the funding profile or decreasing the off-balance sheet exposure, then the bank needs to take the precaution of holding liquid assets against the risk. Stress testing is especially important for liquidity risk as it enables the practitioner to overcome the limitations of models and historical data. It is also vital to support the internal and external communication on the bank's health as well as having input into capital planning and assessments.

The banking sector seems to quickly forget the past. One of the reasons why the financial crises had such a forceful impact was that there had not been any material events for a long period of time. Benign conditions can shift the focus to more 'actual' and pressing challenges, which makes stress testing an even more important concept to have as an on-going systemic approach to risk quantification both in good times and bad.

10.1.1   How Banks Perform Their Stress Tests

Before going into stress testing methodology it can be useful to take a look at how banks have been conducting their stress tests. In 2005, the CGFS (Committee on the Global Financial System) published the outcome of a survey on stress test practices, *Stress Testing at Major Financial Institutions: Survey Results and Practice*.[1] Though predominately focused on credit risk it still gives an idea of how banks test their liquidity. The results showed how segregated the ALM function can be from other risk functions, as at first it appeared that only a third of the banks performed a scenario analysis. When banks were probed and interviewed it was discovered that scenario stress testing was actually performed but outside the risk division and in most cases by the ALM and was therefore not included in the first response! The scenarios generally included the impact of a rating downgrade, increased funding costs, a sharp increase in drawdown of commitments and a change in the composition of deposits. Most of these scenarios were based around a firm-specific event. Some banks linked their liquidity risk stress tests closely to operational risk events and even the impact of trapped liquidity to the overall liquidity positions of the bank.

10.1.2   Where Stress Tests Failed during the Financial Crises

The studies done after the financial crises revealed that in many cases stress testing failed to serve its purpose in making the banks better prepared to meet stressed conditions. Even though there is always an element of 20/20 hindsight after such a devastating storm, the number of observations show that the stress test did not sufficiently prepare the banking sector for the nature, magnitude or duration of the shock, so much so that in some instances a fundamental review of the stress testing approach was needed. It is worth assessing the liquidity stress model against the list of observed shortcomings in liquidity risk models during the crises:[2]

- Stress testing had focused too much on idiosyncratic or firm-specific shocks. Although of value against independent name-specific events the crises demonstrated that stress tests needed to capture better the implications of wider disruptions (e.g. market-wide events) where the behaviour of affected banks had an impact on other banking organizations.
- The stress tests failed to incorporate the contingent liquidity exposures sufficiently, both contractual and noncontractual. This problem was a direct consequence of the highly leveraged system, which had been curtailed. However, there are several other contingent liabilities in a bank's balance sheet and with greater banking activity this is an area to watch out for.
- Secured borrowing is another recollection from the financial crises. Too much emphasis was placed on a single type of funding, almost to the point where the funding channel became the key to the business model. The stress tests failed to properly capture the funding concentration risk.
- The risk horizon and the overlap between firm-specific and market-wide stresses were misunderstood. The view was that stress tests failed to consider the overlap between firm-specific and market-wide stresses. For some banks the market-wide stress became a firm-specific problem due to their business model. It is also pointed out that in many cases the models did not expect the deteriorating conditions to last as long as they did.

- Banks did not properly understand the behavioural characteristics of their deposit base to find out which deposits were more likely to leave. The call was for more granular analysis to evaluate deposits and their vulnerabilities by size, type of customer, type of market and the impact of the deposit insurance scheme.
- There were gaps in the ability to conduct firm-wide stress tests to understand the overall impact. The chain is not stronger than the weakest link and banks in multiple jurisdictions and entities did not have the necessary oversight.

It should be noted that the review does not necessarily point out all the weaknesses of the stress test methodologies applied but focused on the shortcomings of dealing with the scenarios of the last financial crisis. As mentioned earlier, the next episode will surely be different. Therefore, rather than using the list of failures too literally it is more useful to look at the underlying sources and see if they are captured. As noted above, many stress test models did not capture the overreliance on secured funding. This failure should be used as a general warning not to be overexposed to any single type of funding, rather than focus the attention on the shortcomings of secured funding. There is always a tendency to try to avoid the last mistake repeating itself, but that does not stop other events from happening.

10.1.3   The Principles of Stress Testing

After reading what is the usual practice of stress testing and learning about the shortcomings of the models during the crises we should be well equipped to set out what a sound stress testing methodology should be like. It is also useful to pay attention to what global regulators have emphasized in their search for comprehensive risk principles and how they have responded to the shortcomings of the stress tests previously mentioned. The *Principles for Sound Liquidity Risk Management and Supervision Guidance* provides the groundwork for what we could term the 10 commandments of stress testing, all of which need to be honoured when building a stress test regime:[3]

1. Stress testing needs to include idiosyncratic, market-wide scenarios and a combination of both.
2. Focus on identifying and quantifying the risk.
3. Pay the greatest attention to the major liquidity risk factors the bank is exposed to.
4. The stress test assumptions should be challenged and reviewed for severity and nature and are expected to evolve over time.
5. Give consideration to scenarios through different time periods.
6. Should be performed regularly in proportion to the size and complexity of the bank.
7. Conducted at the appropriate level, realizing the risk of trapped liquidity and the possible interconnection of liquidity within a banking group (subsidiaries and branches).
8. The stress test should include sensitivity analysis to the major key assumptions.
9. Realize that history is at best only a good guide and benchmark but cannot predict what will or can happen in the future.
10. The outcome should be used to adjust the overall liquidity framework, policies and strategies, and the outcome should play a key role in shaping the CFP.

Needless to say, the outcome of the stress tests and the assumptions need to be discussed at the correct level of the firm, including the Board of Directors.

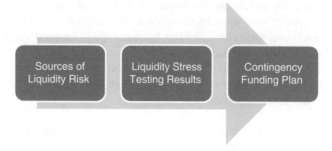

Figure 10.1   The link between the Sources of Liquidity Risk, stress testing and the CFP

10.1.4   Stress Testing within the '6 Step Framework'

Stress testing is a key factor in the '6 Step Framework' methodology as it provides the necessary link between the Sources of Liquidity Risk identified early in the process and the contingency funding plan (CFP). Both of these two steps would only fulfil a part of their purpose if they did not have the stress test results to connect them (see Figure 10.1). The first step, Sources of Liquidity Risk, identifies the most relevant channels of liquidity risk to the bank. The outcome is used as a blueprint for a stress testing model (or at least one of them). If done properly this should ensure all the relevant factors are being stress tested.

The contingency funding plan, which acts like a safety net for the bank, is used to set out a firm's strategies for dealing with stress scenarios. The CFP becomes increasingly relevant if it is based around and supported by the results of the stress tests. The plan does not necessarily need to be aligned only to the stress test results but the stress test results give a data point, which the overall contingency planning needs to work from, either by maintaining HQLAs or having alternative sources planned. In short, there is a good reason for following the chain from the Sources of Liquidity Risk through stress testing into the CFP and a deviation from the plan needs to be justified only when it leads to more robust results.

Stress testing also serves as the function to assess the bank's risk profile against the approved risk appetite. Some of the exposures can only be quantified through stress testing and hence the outcome will provide the bank with the necessary confirmation that not too much is at risk.

A bank should have documented stress test policies and procedures where the assumptions are laid out. The governance of the policy should be such that changes of assumptions can be easily tracked and justified. The risk specialist should not be able to change the official scenarios without proper approval. The stress test framework and assumptions should be assessed independently from time to time.

10.1.5   Picking the Model

The next step is to find an appropriate model or a methodology that enables the principles to be transformed into a useful regime. It is imperative to keep an eye on the main principles and not run with the model until some confirmation is reached on whether it is fit for purpose. The main thing we want from the methodology is for it to deliver an outcome on which to base the liquidity holding. Only then is it possible to conclude that the bank has sufficient and adequate liquidity.

The term stress testing has been used as a generic term to describe how banks test their ability to sustain the impact of exceptional but severe events. For clarification, the stress tests in this book are either *scenario stress* tests or *sensitivity stress* tests. This should not be confused with the terminology coming from the credit risk worlds, where the term stress tests is usually only applied to stochastic tests and not deterministic ones.

The sensitivity test is the stressing of a single risk factor or assumption in order to assess the sensitivity of the institution to changes in that factor alone. They are usually for shorter periods of time. The more important stress tests are the scenario stress tests which, according to the name, describe an integrated future view under a scenario that consists of multiple variables or assumptions. The scenario can either be historical or hypothetical.

Overall, there are two main ways to approach the stress testing. There are methodologies that are based on probabilities, like the VaR model, and there are deterministic models, which include the scenario analysis mentioned above.

10.1.6 The Limitation of VaR for Liquidity Risk Stress Testing

Every risk management method needs to include some modelling of risk to estimate its properties and the generally accepted standardized methods are generally the tool of choice. The value at risk (VaR) is a popular and useful statistical method to apply to link probability and severity together into an understandable outcome. The outcome is easy to interpret, where statements like '*the maximum loss that is likely to be experienced over a period of one week with a 99% level of confidence is $10m*' capture the risk profile quite well. This is, however, not a great indicator of liquidity risk as liquidity risk is not really probability based and the VaR does not capture what happens in exceptional circumstances. By definition, exceptional circumstances happen rarely and without sufficient observations the VaR model does not provide a reliable outcome. Luckily most banks do not have sufficient experience of liquidity problems to build the necessary data for good VaR calculations. The number of stories from the financial crises about events that according to the VaR models should only have happened once every 1000 years shows that this model (like all others) cannot be solely relied on, or rather its assumptions are not adequate. The use of Monte Carlo simulations, such as the VaR method, is generally of questionable use as the necessary parameters such as volatility are not easily available or are of questionable value.

Not all risk specialists will agree with the assessment of the VaR method and the Monte Carlo simulations, but for the purpose of the '6 Step Framework', which is also meant to increase the understanding of the risk involved, the VaR model is less useful than the scenario stress testing discussed next.

10.1.7 The Deterministic 'What If' Approach

We have learnt that in most cases the past cannot be used to predict the future and future liquidity shocks are unlikely to be similar to the ones experienced so far. The past will not provide the likelihood (probability) of a liquidity event happening and neither will it give a good indication of its severity. Here one might stop and assume that nothing can be done as these two major yardsticks in risk modelling are missing. Not quite. The deterministic approach or the 'what if' scenario do have merits when it comes to liquidity stress testing. However, they do not help us to determine the probability of an event and neither will they predict what will happen. Again, one might ask, so why bother with them then? The short answer is that, even though they have many shortcomings, they are still the best tools available. If executed properly they can help assess the nature of the risk, its potential severity and timing. If the deterministic models can provide some answers to those questions, they are worth doing.

There are risk managers who prefer the probabilistic models over the 'what if' scenarios for various reasons and this can sometimes be a hot topic. This book's preference for the latter is based on the fact that they give greater understanding of the limitations of risk models and place importance on the nature of the risk and assumptions. By going through a 'what if' scenario and reviewing the impact of each variable and assumption, the risk specialist will learn a great deal about the bank's vulnerabilities. It is true that deterministic models are far less sophisticated than the other ones, but they reflect the uncertainty of the risk field. Having the best hammer in the world in your hand is not of much use if you do not know where the nail should go.

10.1.8   Setting of the Deterministic Scenario

The liquidity risk literature emphasizes the usage of scenario-based stress testing and the regulatory world is also a supporter of the approach. Some of the criticism directed against the scenario analysis is due to the confusion that they are some sort of predictive exercise, which they are not.

The objective with analysing the nature of the risk, its severity and timing is not to try to forecast what can happen but to prepare for different scenarios. In his book, Leonard Matz quotes President Eisenhower to labour this point: '*Plans are worthless but planning is everything.*'[4] The misconception that the deterministic tests are trying to predict the future is something every risk analyst needs to deal with as the results can be dismissed by those not familiar with the methodology as a 'this will never happen' verdict. As explained earlier, the 'what if' scenarios are for the risk specialist and management to spot the vulnerabilities and major risk driver and have more benefits than just providing raw numerical results. To be able to discuss the outcome, it is good to explain the main concepts of the methodology to the audience.

When setting the 'what if' scenarios they should provide answers to the following four questions:

1. What can go wrong? (Nature)
2. What are the implications? (Severity)
3. How quickly can it happen? (Timing)
4. How long will it last? (Timing)

Of the four, the first one is the most important to get right and that is where the Sources of Liquidity Risk yet again become handy in building scenarios around the relevant risk factors.

The reason for assessing the Sources of Liquidity Risk regularly is to verify whether the nature of the risk has changed. The severity can more easily be adjusted and in most cases only scales the risk. What we are looking for in the first step is to analyse if there have been any structural changes to the bank's risk. Failing to spot a change in the structure can have dire consequences as the model outcome becomes useless and we have to hope that some other scenarios have captured a similar severity so that the bank is sufficiently prepared.

As the past does not predict the future, the stress tests need to be based on hypothetical assumptions. For most banks the lack of data on extreme events also forces them to think hypothetically. Some 'blue-sky' thinking is necessary to think of shocks that can be simulated and could be useful, but they could be supported or drawn from historical experiences without trying to replicate the history. This is a subjective exercise, which can cause a problem when explaining the outcome to an audience that thinks the models should be able to predict the future, as mentioned earlier. Therefore, spend time on the structure (nature) of the risk.

The scenarios need to incorporate multiple risk factors and to feed back their effects through sensitivity analyses for the largest factors. We have discussed how interlinked many of Sources of Liquidity Risk are and therefore the scenarios need to have multiple dimensions.

10.1.9   Choice of Severity

Severity cannot replace a comprehensive understanding of the risk factors explained above. It is, however, vital to quantify the stress outcome, so the choice of severity needs to be as adequate as possible. It is useful to create a few scenarios that each describe a certain level of business conditions. Frequently they are given the colour codes of green, yellow and red with some specialists having the amber status in between yellow and red. How many distinct levels are chosen is not a crucial factor, but they do need to be clearly defined.

The green status is the business-as-usual status and the base case. The adverse conditions called yellow show a mild to medium adverse business environment. The medium risk status of yellow should capture the conditions where the bank has started to experience funding challenges but not difficulties. The orange or amber is the severe stage where funding becomes difficult and deposits are decreasing materially. The highest risk status is red, where the bank is experiencing major funding difficulties, with only secured funding channels still open, deposits are being withdrawn within all categories and market liquidity has started to dry up, etc.

The four basic scenarios shown in Figure 10.2 should be multidimensional and ought not to be confused with sensitivity analysis. Each scenario is built up on various assumptions and

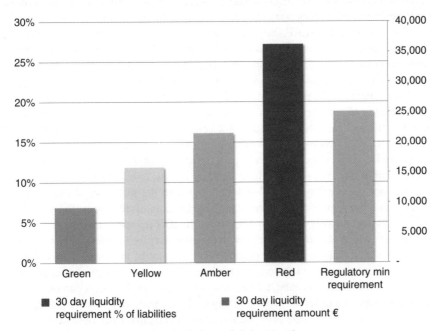

Figure 10.2   Stress test results for four basic deterministic scenarios

consideration should be given to the connection and correlation between different sources. If one moves, then the chances are that the others will be impacted, and a robust scenario should include as realistic a picture as possible where one thing leads to another. The 10 principles will give guidance on what needs to be included, but it is more common to forget a variable rather than being too severe on the scaling. Keep in mind the fact that interactions between firm-specific and market-wide factors and the scenario results should reflect not one or the other but both. The outcome of the red scenario in the graph shows that it is considerably more severe than the others, which it should be. The red scenario needs to reflect the worst nightmare and not get diluted when times are good. I guess that far too many treasurers agree that their red test was not severe enough to capture the financial crises that happened. Expect the unexpected.

So far the picture drawn has been painted with rather broad strokes and literally few colours. One man's yellow world might be another's worst red nightmare so it is relevant to consider the stress the regulators apply and call severe.

PRA's Scenarios in the ILG

In 2010 the UK regulator set out the stress assumptions they use to determine the appropriate liquidity holdings, which are a useful method to understand. The model is standardized but the PRA sets the severity individually to each financial institution, called the ILG (Individual Liquidity Guidance). The ILG is a result of the ILAA (Individual Liquidity Adequacy Assessment) which banks are expected to conduct at least annually (see Section 5.2, The Heightened Regulatory Focus on Liquidity, for further details). An ILAA is a bank's review of its overall liquidity regime, where the stress test results play the most important part but all aspects of the liquidity framework should be looked at. The assessment is discussed at the Board level and is verification that the Board both understands and accepts the liquidity risk within the bank and how it is being managed. After reviewing and discussing the ILAA results with the institution, through what is called the SLRP (Supervisory Liquidity Review Process), the PRA issues the ILG, which is the set of assumptions the PRA feel are adequate to that bank's individual risk profile. This includes setting the run-off factors for each liability class, which have been categorized according to their nature and stability. This also includes setting the appropriate coverage for off-balance sheet items, derivatives and intraday risk. The outcome is the total regulatory liquidity requirement. When the regime came into effect in 2010 it was understood that the UK banking sector was generally not able to fulfil the full requirement. The PRA therefore established a 'glide-path', allowing banks only to fulfil a certain percentage of the full outcome of the stress tests. This 'glide-path' ratio was also set individually for each bank. Over time the objective was for the whole banking system to adapt to the full requirement. This goal has not yet been formally abandoned, but with the inclusion of the PRA into the Bank of England, the regulatory requirements have been assessed against the overall aim of the bank to stimulate the real economy. Therefore, the ILG regime is now more linked to the economic policy, which now is to foster growth through increased lending of banks. The Bank of England has stated that the liquidity requirements will not be increased at this stage and to stimulate growth it has softened the criteria for banks to use the liquidity buffer from time to time. The Bank of England has even defined what proportion of the buffer can be used for this purpose, which signals a different understanding to the meaning of a reserve buffer.

The scenario applied in the ILG is explained below and incorporates both firm-specific and market-wide stresses. The test is broken up into two horizons, a 2 week firm-specific test and a 3 month market-wide test. The roll-off assumptions are more severe in the first test, where the severity is most felt in the treatment of less stable wholesale funding, where the model assumes that they cannot be rolled over in the first two weeks. The closure of the F/X market is also a great hurdle for larger banks, particularly as the PRA has assumed a tougher stance than many other regulators in smaller currency systems. The liquidity requirement is set according to the outcome of the 3 month test. The assumptions are:[5]

First 2 weeks

- Inability to roll over credit-sensitive wholesale secured and unsecured funding.
- Sizeable retail outflow.
- Reduction in the amount of intraday credit provided to a customer by its settlement bank.
- Increase in payments withheld to a direct participant by its counterparties.
- Increase in need for all firms to make payments.
- Closure of F/X markets.
- Intragroup deposits repaid at maturity, with intragroup loans treated as evergreen.
- Multiple downgrade of long-term rating with proportionate impact of all other downgrade triggers.

3 month duration

- Uncertainty as to the accuracy of the valuation of a firm's assets and those of its counterparties.
- Inability to realize or the ability to realize only at excessive cost of particular classes of assets.
- Risk of aversion among participants in the markets on which the firm relies for funding.
- Uncertainty as to the ability of a significant number of firms to ensure that they can meet their liabilities.

The ILG assumption can be adapted into an amber scenario and should address all the factors included in the ILG. It is not, however, granular enough to use as the only scenario. There are those who are of the opinion that the PRA has been overly cautious and the regime is tougher than the new LCR. The stress assumptions were set by the PRA at the end of the financial crises when the PRA had been under criticism for not being able to spot or prevent the crisis from happening. Therefore, the PRA adopted a firm stance on all assumptions.

The LCR Scenario

The new LCR is another played-out 'what if' scenario that can be useful to take into consideration. The timeframe is 30 days and in most cases the assumptions are less severe than in the ILG. Note that the LCR is very concerned about noncontractual obligations, such as the need to maintain and even step up buy-backs. The main characteristics of the LCR scenario are:

- Run-off of the proportion of retail deposits (determined by their stability, which is largely determined by whether they are insured or not). Run-off rates are between 5% and 10%.
- Loss of some wholesale unsecured funding (greater run-off rates than for retail funding). Run-off rates are 25% for operational deposits and others 40%.
- A partial loss of secured, short-term funding.

- Up to a three-notch downgrade, impacting collateral requirements and other additional contractual outflows.
- Increased market volatility resulting in greater collateral haircuts and additional collateral needs.
- Unscheduled drawdowns on committed but unused credit and liquidity facilities the bank has provided.
- A potential need for the bank to participate in contractual buy-backs to mitigate reputational risk.

Chapter 12, on Basel III, discusses the methodology and classification of liabilities used in the Basel III regime, which places great emphasis on the comfort that established deposit guarantee systems provide to the retail customer. This is something the risk specialist needs to assess for the bank funding profile.

10.1.10   Choice of Time Horizon

Earlier it was established that liquidity risk has two elements, quantum and time. The firm-specific risk is usually event driven and therefore can happen suddenly. However, under most scenarios the situation gradually becomes worse as the organization loses credibility from more and more funding channels. Think about what can go wrong in the first round and then how the problem could escalate and become prolonged.

Commercial banks should use relatively short time horizons. Since these firms tend to be more reliant on rolling over short-term unsecured funding, surviving a disruption in this funding source needs to be emphasized. Short-term funding sources for investment banks are in many cases supported with securities that can be sold or repoed, effectively ensuring that short-term, unsecured obligations can be funded with secured sources. This industry standard needs to be reflected in the assumptions and choice of time horizon.

Firm-specific risk can also derive from the market place. I started working for Lehman Brothers in London in the month the Russian crises happened. Lehman Brothers had been rumoured to be badly affected by Russian default and immediately experienced difficulties in securing funding. When I showed up to the office for the first morning, the first thing my new boss did was to assure me that Lehman had sufficient money and I should not worry about my job! Not exactly the challenge I expected from my first day on a new job, but I quickly learnt how fragile the funding franchise of investment banks can be and how relationship driven the channels are. The clients I was assigned to, which included the German Landesbanks, provided a great deal of funding at these times of need and hence for the coming years were treated like royalty.

As the outcome of the liquidity stress is used to determine the survival period the tests time horizon needs to be aligned to the survival period. A bank should have a survival period of at least one month and within that period a shorter time horizon should also be considered to reflect the need for a higher degree of confidence over a very short time.[6] The BCBS is of a similar view, recommending that banks reliant on short-term funding should concentrate on a very short-term period (out to 5 days), which requires banks to be able to calculate their liquidity position on a day-to-day basis.[7]

The reason for having two time periods is not only to be able to apply different run-off factors but also to recognize the time it takes to realize part of the liquidity buffer and utilize the bank's other counterbalancing capacity (CBC).[8] Breaking up the test into two tiers does

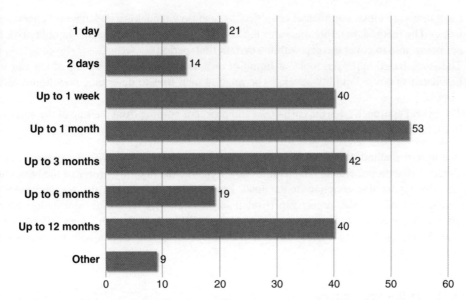

Figure 10.3   Liquidity stress test time horizons[10]

not influence the overall liquidity requirement, which is set by the risk appetite as the survival horizon, as stated above. The requirement may, however, only include the shorter period covered by HQLA whereas the longer requirements may take mitigating action into account as well as the CBC.

A survey by the European Central Bank performed in late 2008 shows a variety of practices amongst European banks when it comes to the time horizon. Overall the most commonly used time horizons were 4 weeks and 12 months respectively, but the longer market stress scenarios were from 1 week to 4 weeks.[9] The cash flow mismatch method introduced below will also give a good indication of the risk profile of the bank, that is whether the mismatches are in the short end or longer out on the horizon. A bank with most of its risk in the first week (most likely a commercial bank) will need to adjust the time horizon accordingly. Another survey done by PWC in 2009 shows the 1 month horizon being the most common amongst the 43 banks surveyed, but a growing number of banks are introducing a longer time period out to 1 year (see Figure 10.3).

10.1.11   Scenario Stress Testing, Step by Step

We are now ready to go through the scenario stress testing method step by step. The method we use to quantify the bank's liquidity position is a hybrid between the cash flow approach and the stock-based approach. The three different approaches can be described as follows:

- The cash flow approach is defined as the difference between daily cash inflows and daily cash outflows over the defined time horizon, where the inflows and outflows have been grouped into homogeneous categories. This tells us the amount of inflows/outflows and their timing.

Cash flows are either contractual or subject to cash flow modelling (behavioural characteristics). The method therefore measures the liquidity gap (remember that the liquidity risk is not being able to cover the gap within a certain time period).

- The stock-based approach looks at liquidity as a stock of financial assets, which can be liquidated to cover liquidity shocks. The method then tries to determine how liquid each asset is.
- The hybrid approach adds the cash flows and proceeds coming from the sale of the stock of financial assets to actual and expected cash flows.

The hybrid method allows us to link together the liquidity buffer with the expected and contractual cash flows, which demonstrates how dynamic the liquidity profile of the bank can be, and the impact of assumptions to the flows. From the template we can also see where along the maturity ladder is the largest gap (risk) is, which can give us useful information when constructing the adequate liquidity buffer and other CBCs. A bank with a very front-loaded mismatch (within 2 weeks) needs to have a different CBC than banks with the mismatch further out in the future.

10.1.12   Define the Scenarios

The first step is to define the scenarios that will be included in the universe of stress testing. In addition to the four 'colour' scenarios set out earlier, the bank should have at least four others and a bank reliant on short-term market funding would benefit from various scenarios being played out (10+).

Most scenarios are hypothetical but plausible scenarios, which if possible should be backed up with historical information to decrease the subjectivity. As the hypothetical scenarios are built around expert judgement and are subjective it is useful to have them set by more than one individual. It is important to obtain the management buy-in on the assumption for them to later respect the results.

To build up the scenario a cash flow template needs to be created where each category of assets and liabilities is listed and grouped by similarity. The more granular data can be provided the better, as it is always possible to aggregate the results if needed, but the reverse is not possible. Information on the most important products, client types and channels should be compiled separately and if possible these categories should be broken down further into size categories or into insured/uninsured ones. Then the data will allow for more varied kinds of assumption to be used. Again, the suite of scenarios needs to include firm-specific, market-wide and a combination of the two factors. Figure 10.4 shows a hypothetical example of a suite of scenarios for a mid-sized bank.

As the scenarios are simply a bundle of assumptions, sensitivity to the setting of assumptions needs to be outlined. Therefore, most scenarios should be backed up by a sensitivity analysis for all material variables.

Hypothetical assumptions are only an expert judgement and can easily (and most likely) be flawed. It is vital that the stress testing quantifies what 'being wrong' means. An example would be a traditional retail bank with a large amount of on-demand retail deposits. The overall liquidity requirement can be very sensitive to the setting of the expected retail run-off rates during stressed conditions. The expert judgement might conclude that a factor as low as 3% could be applied whereas a slightly increased rate of 5% (not a material change) could result in the liquidity buffer being well under the minimum requirement.

Bank A: Liquidity Stress Test Scenarios

The following tests are conducted monthly and reported to ALCO and senior management

No	Firm-specific/ market-wide/ combination	Working title	Short description
1	C	GREEN	Business as usual
2	F	Creditworthiness I	Sudden event leading to a drop in market confidence
3	F	Creditworthiness II	Prolonged lack of market confidence
4	F	Operational failure	IT failure leading to client payment failures
5	C	YELLOW	All major stress factors started to become visible
6	F	Northern Rock	Adapted Northern Rock style scenario
7	C	AMBER	All stress factor materially affected, incl. collateral
8	M	EuroZone	Wide interbank disruption due to Eurozone problems or break-up
9	M	Market trouble	On-going dysfunction of the interbank markets
10	F	Creditworthiness III	Sudden event leading to progressively deteriorating situation. Contingency actions included
11	M	9/11	Global market-wide disruption across markets and products
12	C	RED	Severe outflow of deposits, interbank market in crisis mode, market for collateral disrupted, increased haircuts

- Liquidity holding requirement set according to AMBER results
- For stress assumptions see '*Liquidity Stress Testing – Assumptions and Methods*' in *2014 ILAA*
- In addition to the 12 scenarios ALM has monitored the outcome of 4 other models
- The scenarios include sensitivity analyses for the major variables
- Approved by ALCO, reviewed annually

Figure 10.4   Suite of deterministic stress scenarios for a mid-sized bank

10.1.13   Playing Out the Scenario

To understand the mismatch risk we need to differentiate between contractual cash flows and those that are subject to uncertainty and allow us to set the severity. To play out the scenarios we can set up a cash flow table for three main categories:

PART I	Contractual cash flows
PART II	Noncontractual cash flows
PART III	Counterbalancing capacity and management action

Figure 10.5 is an example of PART I, the contractual cash flow statement. The category headings are simplified and for illustrative purposes only. Each bank needs to use the categories applicable to its business model and balance sheet items. In PART I only contractual cash flows are illustrated so on-demand deposits or overdrafts are excluded. The outcome of this table,

	First Period						Second Period		
	Day 1	Day 2	Day 3	Day 4	Day 5	Week 2	Week 3	Week 4	Month 2	etc.

PART I Contractual Cashflows
  1.1 Customer contractual cashflow
    1.1.1 Assets
      1.1.1.1 Retail lending, contractual
        a) Mortgage repayments
        b) Personal loans repayments
      1.1.1.2 Corporate lending, contractual
        a) Corporate lending, repayments
        b) Committed pipeline
    1.1.2 Liabilities
      1.1.2.1 Retail deposits, term
        a) Stability I
        b) Stability II
        c) Stability III
        d) Online accounts, Stability II
        e) Online accounts, Stability II
      1.1.2.2 Corporate deposits, term
        a) Stability I, operational
        b) Stability II, nonoperational
      1.1.2.3 Other financial instituitions
  1.2 Noncustomer contractual cashflow
    1.2.1 Bond issuance
      1.2.1.1 Long-term borrowing
      1.2.1.2 Short-term borrowing
    1.2.2 Treasury activity (nondiscretionary)
      1.2.2.1 Treasury portfolio proceeds
      1.2.2.2 Central bank borrowing
      1.2.2.3 Repos
      1.2.2.4 QLA's maturity proceeds
Total contractual cashflows

Figure 10.5 Cash flow projections, PART I, contractual cash flows

which is the mismatch in each bucket, should be the cash flows that are certain to happen and not subject to any assumptions. In the example the deposits are categorized by their stability but the classification method is not of importance and is only done to match the categories in PART II.

The stability is not the focus in PART I as the obligations are contractual. In the sample the first period is for the first 2 weeks and the second from week 3 up to 6 months. It is possible to get the contractual obligations for a longer period of time, but for the table to match the noncontractual analysis the maximum is 6 months, as forecasting behaviour for a longer period of time can be too subjective to be of relevant use.

The next part, PART II, contains all the noncontractual or discretionary cash flows, both from the asset and liability sides (see Figure 10.6). As these cash flows are subject to assumptions it is important to break them down as granularly as possible. Part II contains all the on-demand liabilities that are subject to outflow assumptions. Notice needs to be given if term deposits are allowed to be broken and withdrawn prior to their maturity and if that is a standard practice within the bank. The question should also be asked whether the bank would yield to pressure and allow depositors to break deposits that are nonbreakable under standard terms and conditions, rather than facing the negative publicity. Basel III has strong opinions on how deposits that can be withdrawn early should be reported, requiring them to be stated as on-demand.

Possible asset sales or additional borrowing should not be included in PART II, even though they are discretionary. They belong to PART III, which contains the counterbalancing capacity (see Figure 10.7). An identical table to PART II should be created, containing the stress test assumptions for each category.

The European Central Bank's survey shows that the most common assumption on loss of retail deposits was that 10% of retail deposits would be withdrawn whereas the assumptions for interbank deposits ranged from 0% to 90%. This wide range might reflect the different conditions and strengths of the banks surveyed, but it is important to give notice to as many banks as possible as interbank funding is the most important funding source. The survey was done in 2008 and since then retail depositors might be more aware of their local deposit guarantee schemes and the protection they provide to the consumer. The run-off rates in the LCR reflect this. Matz suggests 3–6% for the most sticky funds and 25–30% for the most volatile funds as an indication for a severe stress.[11] The European Banking Authority's (EBA) *Consultation Paper on Draft Guidelines on Retail Deposits Subject to Different Outflows for Purposes of Liquidity Reporting under Regulation (EU) No. 575/2013 (Capital Requirements Regulation – CRR)* provides a good overview of things to consider when setting the appropriate run-off rates.[12] In addition to the minima rates (5% and 10%) there is a separate category for retail deposits with 'high risk' and 'very high risk', where banks are expected to apply higher run-off rates for deposits that fall under these definitions. 'High risk' comprise the following risk factors:

   I. The currency of deposits, that is deposits in foreign currency
  II. Product-linked deposits
 III. Products that are rate driven or have preferential conditions
 IV. High-risk distribution channels, including internet only access and brokered deposits
  V. High value deposits, which EBA defines as between €100,000 and €500,000[13]
 VI. Other characteristics that the institution considers as high.

	First Period						Second Period		
	Day 1	Day 2	Day 3	Day 4	Day 5	Week 2	Week 3	Week 4	Month 2	etc.

PART II Noncontractual Cashflows
2.1 Customer noncontractual cashflow
  2.1.1 Assets
    2.1.1.1 Retail lending, noncontractual
      a) Mortgage pre-payments
      b) Personal loans repayments (est.)
      c) Personal overdrafts
      d) Personal loans repayments
      e) New personal lending, incl. mortages (est.)
    2.1.1.2 Corporate lending, noncontractual
      a) Corporate lending, prepayments (est.)
      b) Expected drawdowns
      c) New corporate lending (est.)
      d) Corporate overdrafts
    2.1.1.3 Off-balance sheet commitments
      a) Retail customers drawdown (est.)
      b) Corporate customers drawdown (est.)
      c) Liquidity backup lines (est.)
      d) Derivatives collateral (est.)
  2.1.2 Liabilities
    2.1.2.1 Retail deposits
      a) Stability I, on-demand
      b) Stability II, on-demand
      c) Stability III, on-demand
      d) Online accounts, Stability II, on-demand
      e) Online accounts, Stability II, on-demand
      f) Roll-over of term deposit in PART I
    2.1.2.2 Corporate deposits
      a) Stability I, operational
      b) Stability II, nonoperational
      c) Roll-over of term deposit in PART I
    2.1.2.3 Other financial institutions
      a) Nonoperational
      b) Roll-over of term deposit in PART I
2.2 Noncustomer noncontractual cashflow
  2.2.1 Treasury activity (discretionary)
    2.2.1.1 On-demand repayments
    2.2.1.2 Roll-over of short-term borrowings
    2.2.1.3 Roll-over of central bank borrowing
Total noncontractual cashflows

	First Period						Second Period		
	Day 1	Day 2	Day 3	Day 4	Day 5	Week 2	Week 3	Week 4	Month 2	etc.

PART III Counter Balancing Capacity
3.1 High Quality Liquid Assets
   a) Level I assets
   b) Level II assets
3.2 Other AFS assets
3.3 Sell of nonmarketable assets
3.4 Stand-by facilities
3.5 Management actions
   3.5.1 Curtailing of new lending
   3.5.2 Packaging and repoing of loans
Total CBC

Figure 10.7 Cash flow projections, PART III, counterbalancing capacity (CBC)

'Very high risk' comprise the following risk factors:

   I. Maturing fixed-term or notice period deposits
  II. Nonresident deposits
 III. Very high value of the deposit, which EBA defines as larger than €500,000.

The approach EBA recommends is a scorecard methodology. Deposits that meet two or more of the above factors are subject to higher outflows and not the minima run-off rates of 5% and 10%. Banks are then expected to build three-tiered buckets based on the number of the above risk factors that each deposit has. This scorecard method can be good in ranking deposits and assigning increasing run-off rates.

The first step of the '6 Step Framework', the Sources of Liquidity Risk, should contain a good analysis on how the bank defines which deposits are sticky and which are not. That approach is, however, a static one whereas the stress testing is dynamic in nature and subject to wider factors. Interest rate changes are an example of an exogenous variable that can not only shift the severity or scaling of the stress testing results but also change the nature of the risk. Part of the deposit book might be gathered through on-line channels, which can be very sensitive to the rate offered. Hence, a change in rate might create a binary scenario, where either all of the deposits will be renewed or none. This needs to be taken into account as well as the role interest rate levels have on pre-payment and other parts of the asset side of the balance sheet. The impact the rate has on the outflow might not be a sudden one but becomes more apparent when a longer scenario is chosen.

The off-balance sheet items need to be broken down into subsegments according to their nature. The traditional letter of credit only results in an outflow for the bank if the counterparty defaults, so it is unlikely that the bank will be hit by many simultaneous drawdowns, whereas lines to provide working capital are easier to trigger and hence should be stressed higher. It is also useful to split the off-balance sheet items between retail and corporate and by the type of risk they contain, being either a liquidity back-up or a credit line. The LCR requirement assumes 5% utilization of the undrawn portion of committed credit and liquidity lines to retail and SMEs (liquidity and credit lines are here grouped together). For credit facilities to nonfinancial corporates, the stress factor is 10% of the outstanding line and 30% if the line is for liquidity purposes. Liquidity and credit lines to other regulated banks are stressed by 40% and liquidity lines to any other financial institution need to be fully stressed. Other contingent liabilities such as guarantees or letters of credit are subject to national discretion, but some guidance can be taken from the 0–5% stress factor applied to trade finance contingent liabilities. The PRA assessment on off-balance items is similar; unsecured facilities provided to credit institutions need to be fully stressed (this is a 3 month horizon versus 30 days in the LCR). For unsecured facilities provided to entities other than credit institutions the PRA would apply a factor of between 5% and 10% depending on the bank and a similar factor to overdraft and credit facilities provided to retail customers.

In PART III the CBC and management actions are introduced. There we start with the HQLA and assign to each time bucket the amount we could easily raise by liquidating the HQLA. Consequently the market liquidity is of importance. This is usually measured by looking at the average daily trading volume over a period of time. The bank then assumes that it can liquidate at a maximum an amount equal to a certain proportion of the total daily traded volume. This will give a good indication of how many days it will take to convert the HQLA to cash. The daily volume should be included in the PART III table. The same method is applied to all qualities of the assets within the HQLA portfolio and other assets classified as available for sale. Mindful of how difficult it is for banks to curtail new lending and to give out credit without facing reputational issues, the pipeline commitments are stressed higher in the eyes of the PRA (60–80%).

The scenarios will contain various assumptions about market liquidity, including the haircuts for the assets sold and how long it will take to liquidate them, etc. Again the LCR provides some simple haircuts to apply to the larger HQLA classes. Understandably, some CBCs are not available in all scenarios, such as using committed loan lines; rating agencies and regulators also do not give much credence to these as an available source under stress.

This part will also reflect the schedule of liquidation, that is which assets will be sold first. Some assets cannot easily be sold without a material impact on the bank's profitability so the liquidity problem might lead to a solvency issue. The order of sale also depends on the severity of the liquidity problem. Attention should be given to the impact rate changes might have on the proceeds when assets are liquidated. The tendency is to have a buffer quite long dated in order to get better returns, which makes it more rate sensitive.

10.1.14   Analysing the Outcome

By stacking up the cash flows in PARTs I and II, it is possible to look at the cash flow mismatch with different levels of certainty. Figure 10.8 shows a hypothetical output for a stress scenario. For each time bucket the table shows the respective inflows and outflows for contractual items (from PART I) and noncontractual (from PART II) only. Each time period therefore contains four legs of cash flows (some might be zero though). By segregating the contractual cash flows from the discretionary it is possible to identify which time buckets are most sensitive to the assumptions.

Figure 10.8 displays the cash flow cushion or deficit for each time bucket, which is sometimes represented as a ratio (inflows over outflows). This maximum gap can be used in setting risk tolerance (see Section 7.1, The Risk Appetite Statement) or the recommended minimum. The method can therefore be used to verify the compliance with risk limits. A decision needs to be taken as to whether expected new lending should be included in the ratio or not.

Finally, by adding the impact of the asset sale and other management actions (PART III) we have the full picture and the outcome of the stress scenario. The final table in Figure 10.9 pulls all the previous steps together including the impact of the CBC and management actions. These are the full results of the hypothetical stress scenario.

There are various ways to express the stress test results but Figure 10.10 is a common method and gives a detailed outcome of a hypothetical stress scenario for each time period, broken down into contractual and noncontractual cash flows, which gives an indication to what extent the outcome is determined by risk assumption. By analysing the total net inflows/outflows we can understand when the bank's resources run out under different scenarios, both with and without management actions. The figure shows clearly how much of the outflows or inflows are subject to assumptions versus the other cash flows, which are contractual. This is a good indication for the overall sensitivity to setting of assumptions. The most important figure is the net positions for each period both with and without CBC and management action. The aggregated surplus/deficit is often also shown on an illustration like this. The cumulative position over time should also be calculated as it shows the net surplus or deficit going forward.

The time measurement is a much more useful tool than showing the results as an amount. '*$1450m of excess cash after 3 months*' does not give any indication of what is going to happen after 3 months. If the 91st day has larger outflows than $1450 then the statement above hides

Scenario 1. Contractual and noncontractual cash flows

		Day 1	Day 2	Day 3	Day 4	Day 5	Week 2	Week 3	Week 4	Month 2	Month 3
PART I	Total contractual inflows	100	20	20	15	2	200	185	150	400	350
	Total contractual outflows	290	40	40	5	6	150	150	60	600	500
PART II	Total noncontractual inflows	50	10	10	10	10	50	60	70	40	40
	Total noncontractual outflows	100	90	80	70	40	100	50	50	170	120
	Surplus/Deficit before CBC and Management Action	−240	−100	−90	−50	−34	0	45	110	−330	−230

Figure 10.8 Cash flow projections, PART I and PART II combined

Scenario 1 Cash flow outcome

		Day 1	Day 2	Day 3	Day 4	Day 5	Week 2	Week 3	Week 4	Month 2	Month 3
PART I	Total contractual inflows	100	20	20	15	2	200	185	150	400	350
	Total contractual outflows	290	40	40	5	6	150	150	60	600	500
PART II	Total noncontractual inflows	50	10	10	10	10	50	60	70	40	40
	Total noncontractual outflows	100	90	80	70	40	100	50	50	170	120
PART III	Surplus/Deficit before CBC and Management Action	−240	−100	−90	−50	−34	0	45	110	−330	−230
	Total CBC net inflows	400	50	50	50	40	50	50	30	200	100
	Net position after CBC and Management Action	160	−50	−40	0	6	50	95	140	−130	−130

Figure 10.9   Stress test results including the CBC

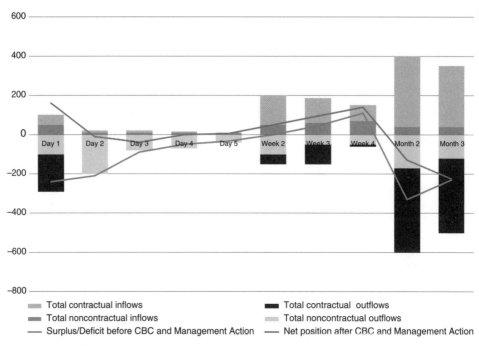

Figure 10.10   Cash flow projections under stressed scenarios

the actual truth of the liquidity risk. The cumulative net outflows are also the survival period discussed in the limit setting and risk appetite in Chapter 7. The survival period is where the cumulative net outflows exceed the liquidity buffer.

The overall outcome of the various stress tests should be expressed in survival days, which gives a good comparison between the severity of each scenario. Figure 10.11 illustrates the different survival horizons for a few of the scenarios. As they have various kinds of assumptions they do not move parallel to each other but the number of survival days is a good indication of the severity of each of them.

The survival days can also be calculated for each scenario (especially the most important one) after checking for sensitivity to the material variables. In the example in Figure 10.12 the sensitivity of the survival horizon to the stable retail run-off rate is calculated by recalculating the survival days with the stable retail run-off rates ranging from 3% to 15%.

10.2 FINAL NOTE ON SCENARIO STRESS TESTING

The examples above are a simplified version of an actual scenario stress testing, which will have more data and factors built into it. Moreover, there are additional requirements that need to be honoured and taken into account.

If the assumptions accept a closure in the F/X markets then a buffer might be required to be held in each currency and hence the scenarios need to be run separately for each currency. Even though we assume that F/X markets are open, there is still a risk at large if there is a currency mismatch between the buffer and liabilities. This should not go unnoticed.

Intraday liquidity risk has been in the spotlight and can be a large factor for clearing banks and other banks undertaking transactional business. The collateral posted with the payment

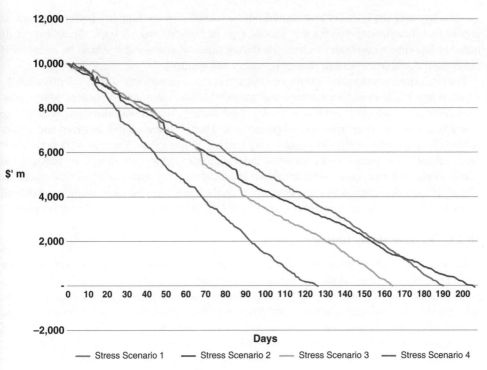

Figure 10.11   Survival horizon for various stress test scenarios

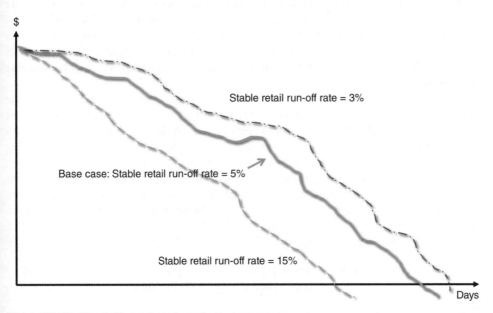

Figure 10.12   Sensitivity analysis for a single stress test scenario

systems to cover the intraday risk should not be included in the liquidity buffer as it can be argued that it is encumbered for this special type of liquidity risk. A bank should expect its intraday liquidity requirement to increase during times of stress and needs to be aware of if the collateral requirements can change (quantity and quality).

The sixth stress testing principle requests that stress tests be performed at an 'adequate level', which is applicable to financial groups and banks with operations across borders. Many jurisdictions require each entity to be viewed on a stand-alone basis and only allow groups to utilize liquidity across the group after special permission. There is always a risk involved and a bank should check its vulnerability to possible ring fencing of operations. This can work both ways; the regulator of the parent might not allow the bank to support its subsidiary with funds or the parent might no longer be allowed to include the local liquidity buffer in its own calculations. Simply put, borders require an extra assessment on the connection between entities and overall reliance, which can span more fields that just the HQLA, such as system and staff reliance.

10.2.1   Reverse Stress Testing

Some countries require banks to undertake 'reverse stress testing'. Reverse stress tests are stress tests requiring banks to assess scenarios and circumstances that would render its business model unviable, thereby identifying possible business vulnerabilities. They are firm specific in nature and have similar benefits as event-driven scenarios where the focus is primarily on the firm-specific liquidity sources. As the name indicates, the starting point is a known stressed outcome such as the bank no longer being viable as it has breached its regulatory thresholds. The test requires the bank to come up with events or scenarios that could lead to such an outcome. At the best of times reverse stress tests are difficult to undertake as the possibilities are many and it is problematic to pinpoint which of the very remote possibilities is the one to analyse. It is, however, good for senior management and the Board to understand that there are liquidity events and circumstances that would make the banks cease to exist. They are designed to encourage banks to understand better their vulnerabilities, which is the same objective as that of the Sources of Liquidity Risk exercise, so a bank that has spent a good amount of time on the first step in the '6 Step Framework' should have a good overview of the possible circumstances.

'What if' scenario analyses are not the only way to stress test a balance sheet and some banks have come up with an additional model to support the scenario assumptions. Behaviour models have been applied to balance sheet items such as on-demand deposits in order to try to predict their propensity to outflow and mortgage institutions have put effort into modelling the possible pre-payments in their mortgage book. These models can help scenario planning, which should rely on expert judgement and models of other divisions within the bank. There are also banks that swear by predictive models for their overall liquidity stress testing. There is no one solution or method that suits all, but every banking organization will benefit from undertaking scenario stress testing and it is very difficult to argue why they should not be conducted. Therefore they have been the weapon of choice in this book.

10.3   CONTINGENCY FUNDING PLAN (CFP) – THE SPADE OF THE LIQUIDITY FRAMEWORK

If liquidity stress testing is the heart of the liquidity framework, then the Contingency Funding Plan (CFP) is the spade (SPADE is an acronym for Spot the risk, Assessment, Decision, Execution of liquidity plans). Banks' liquidity contingency planning has been given this rather

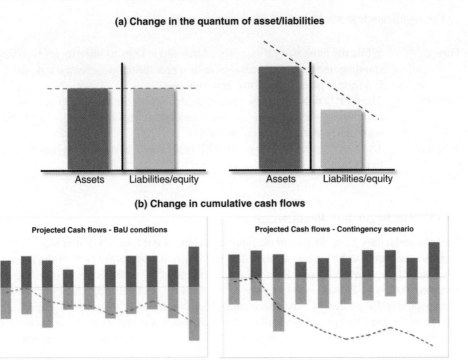

(a) Change in the quantum of asset/liabilities

Assets   Liabilities/equity   Assets   Liabilities/equity

(b) Change in cumulative cash flows

Projected Cash flows - BaU conditions   Projected Cash flows - Contingency scenario

Figure 10.13   Reasons for a contingency scenario

imprecise name, the Contingency Funding Plan (CFP), which does not do it justice as a sound CFP should entail much more than a funding plan. The Liquidity Contingency Plan is a more descriptive name as the plan is not solely to increase funding but to mitigate and respond to risk. However, as the acronym CFP is becoming a market standard, this book will honour the tradition.

As the name is not very helpful, CFP needs to be further defined. Contingency liquidity risk can be defined as *the risk of future, unlikely but plausibly, severe events requiring significantly larger amounts of liquidity than the bank's plans or projections allow for.* This event is called a contingency scenario (scenario of low probability, high severity). Figure 4.5 in Section 4.3, The Timing Factor of Liquidity Risk: Tactical, Structural and Contingent, gives an idea of how a contingency scenario might happen.

The usual suspects of liquidity risk are again at large: timing and quantum of cash flows. More precisely, the contingency risk has generally two causes, as demonstrated in Figure 10.13: a large change in *timing* of cash flows (cash flow mismatch) or unexpected shifts in the *quantum* of assets or liabilities. The latter can happen if the assets increase suddenly, usually due to unexpected drawdowns on committed credit or liquidity facilities, and a sudden decrease in deposits can happen due to large deposit outflows or the sudden failure to roll over maturing debt.

A CFP is therefore a plan against contingency liquidity risk and can be defined thus:

A Contingency Funding Plan is a formal plan of procedures and actions to detect and respond to unlikely but plausible events requiring a significantly larger amount of liquidity than the bank's plans or projections allow for (The Contingency Scenario).

The significant features from the CFP definition are:

Formal: While the bank has various procedures and actions to improve its liquidity
             standing under stress conditions or as a precaution to increased risk, the CFP
             is a formal plan, with formal governance.
Detect: The CFP is not only a rescue plan. It also serves the purpose of formally
             identifying whether liquidity risk is emerging. This is accomplished through a
             set of early warning indicators (EWI).
Respond: The most central feature of the CFP is the menu of options on how to respond
             to crises.

10.3.1   The Regulatory Requirement

Unfortunately, the CFP is the part of the liquidity management framework that most frequently becomes the victim to be viewed as regulatory compliance. Most other parts of the framework are a part of the frequently used liquidity management so their meaning and significance are accepted. As the CFP deals with low probability events it can fall off the radar of importance. Moreover, as CFP addresses very uncertain and hypothetical events, it might seem vague in the eye of the practitioner and not looked at as being such a useful tool. However, if the CFP is correctly and adequately constructed this criticism is not justifiable. A CFP that is treated like a compliance burden, is a clear indication of it being wrongly constructed and not fit for purpose.

There are requirements from regulators for banks to have an effective CFP, which needs to be taken into consideration when the plan is being constructed. One of the principles in *BCBS Principles for Sound Liquidity Risk Management and Supervision* addresses the need for CFP and states that '*a bank should have a formal contingency funding plan (CFP) that clearly sets out the strategies for addressing liquidity shortfalls in emergency situations. A CFP should outline policies to manage a range of stress environments, establish clear lines of responsibility, include clear invocation and escalation procedures and be regularly tested and updated to ensure that it is operationally robust.*'[14] All the regulatory regimes I have come across include CFP requirements, which mirror the above Basel principle. The UK regime especially points out the necessity for the CFP to take into account the outcome of the formal stress scenarios and the Australian regime requires the plan to contain a rescue plan for certain defined events, such as a retail deposit run. From the supervisory point of view minimizing negative externalities to other market participants is important.

10.3.2   Why Banks Need a CFP

If it were not for the regulatory requirements, would banks still need to have and maintain a CFP? There are many other types of risk within a banking system, such as interest rate risk, credit risk and capital risk, so why should liquidity risk be treated differently by having a rescue plan?

- The first reason is that liquidity risk cannot be hedged and mitigated and offset like interest rate risk and credit risk. The bank has to bear the liquidity risk. To some extent it can be argued that underwriting liquidity risk (providing maturity transformation) is the service banks provide to the real economy and the core of their business model, so it should not be (fully) mitigated.

- The only way to mitigate liquidity risk is to maintain a liquidity buffer sufficient to cover all liquidity risk. Realistically, no bank can be a viable business if it does that. Moreover, it is impossible to have sufficient HQLAs to sustain all levels of liquidity events.[15]

Therefore, the only way to prudently undertake the liquidity risk is to have a rescue plan in case the liquidity risk gets beyond the levels where it can be managed as business as usual.

10.3.3 The CFP Process

There are number of items that all sound CFPs have in common. It is, however, not advisable to write the CFP like a 'tick-the-box' exercise as once again there is no such thing as a 'one-size-fits-all' CFP and, as with the building of liquidity stress test, the value is in going through the process. Therefore, before listing the things an adequate CFP needs to include, it is worthwhile to go through the mechanics of the CFP.

In order to build a dynamic and useful CFP there needs to be an established understanding of its merits to the business. The CFP should be the SPADE of the liquidity framework and this acronym could assist in understanding its usefulness (see Figure 10.14).

The SPADE process is the functional framework of the CFP.[16] The first step is to create a mechanism to *SPot* the build-up of liquidity risk or heightened risk environment. As the CFP is a formal plan the indicators for increased risk need to be documented. These are the

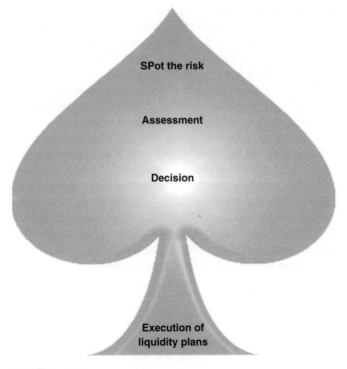

SPot the risk

Assessment

Decision

Execution of liquidity plans

Figure 10.14   The CFP process

early warning indicators (EWIs). Moreover, the CFP will include what the outcome (reading) from these metrics should be under normal conditions and which outcome shows signs of elevated risk.

The next step is to *Assess* the EWI outcome to determine if any actions are needed or if the situation should continue to be monitored. Some metrics and EWIs automatically require certain direct actions or *Decisions* to be undertaken, such as to heighten the risk status, activate the rescue part of the plan, etc. Management judgement can also be the ground for moving to the next phase of the plan and starting to decide on a plan of action. The final part of the CFP process is the *Execution*, which contains all the various plans to preserve liquidity and raise new funds. If each of these four steps is well defined, the CFP will become a useful tool for the risk manager.

10.3.4   Spotting the Risk – Triggers and Early Warning Indicators

Identifying triggers for alerting the bank to potential problems is the first task in the process. The CFP is supposed to address how to deal with extreme conditions, the contingency scenarios. Though these scenarios can be as many as there are banks, they do tend to have certain features in common. Luckily catastrophic events are rare and the most common feature of liquidity events is that they do not happen in a vacuum and the risk can be identified before it crystalizes in its full severity. This is one of the main reasons for the construction of the CFP. As funding crises progress in stages, the CFP needs to have a similar structure.

Time is not only a key factor in the cash flows risk but also plays a major role in a powerful CFP. Contingency scenarios can be compared to some human diseases; if spotted early there is a better chance to avert them than at later stages. Early on in the progress, the bank has more open funding channels and tools to amend the problem and recognizing the trouble early on gives the bank more time to respond and put the necessary actions in place. At later stages it is almost impossible to enhance the liquidity. More specifically, the unsecured funding channels are the first to go and if a bank has limited other options to raise funds, it needs to be able to reach them quickly. The unsecured funding options are generally of benefit for the bank's reputation and strength and can therefore be executed without much impact. Some of the secured funding options, such as asset sales, can come at a large cost and require the bank to be in dire straits to be executed. Therefore, they can take time to get approved and accepted. Therefore, knowing early allows the bank to react early with minimum consequences.

Under business-as-usual conditions there is a tendency to underestimate the signs that the EWIs are showing and to provide a reasonable explanation to the problem that does not require further actions. To eliminate uncertainty, some of the EWIs are also triggers that automatically call for certain plans to be put in place. This can be to convene a meeting of the ALCO or risk committee to address the issue or heighten the risk status. Breaching of regulatory or internal risk limits is another example of triggers that demand certain actions and cannot be ignored. When setting the EWI the following should be kept in mind:

- Use both firm-specific and market-wide metrics. This reflects the fact that Sources of Liquidity Risk are both firm specific and market wide and the indicators should alert the bank to recognize not only the liquidity risks coming from within but also the market.
- Use a wide range of indicators. This is especially important for the market EWIs. As we do not expect the next crisis to be like the last one, the wider the range of indicators the better. Therefore, not knowing what we are looking for, the more indicators there are the

better, within reason. If the bank has significant operations within certain markets, type of business or geographic area, then they need to be covered by an EWI.

- Each indicator should be as independent from the others as possible. True to the concept above that more is better, there is a tendency to have many EWIs measuring the same thing. Assess what kind of increased risk the EDI is intended to capture and if other indicators are fulfilling the same duty.
- Do not throw away the stable EWI. Expect some indicators to be stable most of the time. An EWI that always shows the same reading does not have to be useless and should not be excluded without good justification.
- Not all EWIs are numeric. Bankers prefer the clear world of numbers but not all EWIs can be expressed on a speedometer. When constructing a list, the most obvious things to look for is something that can be measured by numbers, which can lead to other important indicators being omitted. A mixture of quantitative and qualitative indicators is needed.

Needless to say, the EWIs need to be set in advance and not ad hoc; even when this is done the most comprehensive set of EWIs cannot replace the judgement of an experienced manager, but are rather intended to support them by highlighting areas for possible concern. The qualitative indicators give scope for the risk specialists to exercise expert judgement and should therefore not be neglected. The expert's judgement may and should vary but the qualitative EWIs are there to focus the assessment on certain threats rather than taking too wide an approach. This should not be interpreted as being appropriate to ignore signs or trends that are not to be found on the EWI and limit the conversation solely to the list. The list is there to facilitate the assessment and avoid falling into the trap of arguing from the particular to the general.

To ensure that the EWIs serve their purpose to evaluate and escalate risk concerns, their outcome is assigned a stress level that will be discussed in the next section, Assessing the Risk Level and Alert Level. When picking the appropriate EWIs it is good to keep in mind the two main reasons why a contingency scenario arises (Figure 10.13).

The EWI monitoring sheet should consist of triggers and the daily/weekly/monthly monitoring metrics, which are discussed further in Chapter 9, Step IV: The Quantitative Framework. Generally, the difference between the two is that the triggers are used for important variables that could have a major and a sudden impact on the bank's viability and justify an elevated risk status. An example could be a large drop in the bank's stock price. The monitoring part is to alert the risk specialists of the build-up of trends, which often are linked to the structural funding profile of the bank. These could be measures like the reliance on on-demand deposits or the average cost of short-term funding over a longer period of time:

Triggers:	Single variable of importance to the bank's viability.
	Formal threshold defined.
	Need a formal response if the threshold is breached.
Monitoring metrics:	Variables that either stand alone or as part of a cluster reflect medium or long-term changes in the bank's balance sheet composition, cash flow projections or market condition.
	No formal threshold (unless defined in the risk tolerance statement).
	Do not necessarily require a formal response.

Figure 10.15 is an example of the 'trigger' part of the EWI monitoring sheet, where the numbers are for illustrative purposes only. The choice of triggers should strike the right balance

Approved triggers by ALCO

	Green	Yellow	Amber	Red
Market (external) EWI				
3rd party repo haircuts, collateral A		3%	7%	10%
4th party repo haircuts, collateral B		5%	8%	15%
5 Y CDS spread, Bank vs. Five Peers (weekly)		10 bp	30 bp	50 bp
CD/CP spreads, Bank vs. Five Peers (<30d total)		5 bp	15 bp	30 bp
Stock price (3 day movement)		−5%	-8%	-12%
Internal EWI				
Liabilities				
Daily outflows (% of total)		1%	5%	10%
Weekly outflows (% of total)		5%	8%	15%
Monthly outflows (% of total)		5%	8%	15%
Daily ATM withdrawals		$3m	$5m	$10m
Term deposit roll-over percentage (weekly)		75%	50%	30%
Frequent buy-back requests (incl. no quote)		Y	Y	Y
Branch negative sentiment reported		Y	Y	Y
Assets				
HQLA daily value decrease (NPV) - haircut		−2%	−5%	−10%
HQLA weekly value decrease (NPV) - haircut		−4%	−10%	−20%
HQLA monthly value decrease (NPV) - haircut		−10%	−15%	−25%
Utilisation of credit overdrafts (w-o-w)		−5%	−8%	−15%
Utilisation of liquidity overdrafts (w-o-w)		−5%	−8%	−15%
Other				
Call centre volumes (daily)		250%	500%	750%
BACS daily volume (m)		110	180	250
CHAPS daily volume (m)		110	180	250
Rating downgrade short term			below A1/P1 below A1/P2	
Rating downgrade long term		1 notch	2 notch	>2 notches
Profit warning issued		Y	Y	N
Quarterly/annual losses reported		Y	N	N

Figure 10.15   Example of EWIs

between spotting a risk coming from the market (more precisely the bank's market access) and changes coming from within of the bank. There also have to be triggers for both sides of the balance sheets. As operational risk can create liquidity risk, the trigger monitoring sheet needs to include a set of operational triggers. This requires the EWI to have input from other divisions and link into the overall risk framework.

The outcome of the triggers will (amongst other things) set the risk alert status for the bank. If a trigger is breached the status becomes elevated to the corresponding level. As the trigger thresholds for every risk level can never be very precise, the bank can apply a scorecard approach. An example would be for the risk level to be raised from green to yellow, with at least two trigger EWIs needing to be breached. This is useful for the lower alert statuses, where the CFP corresponding action is to monitor the situation more closely and frequently rather than executing a formal contingency plan. Not all triggers are created equal and there are some that should be taken more seriously than others, meaning an unusual outcome is usually a sign of increased threat that needs to be dealt with and not shrugged off. Relative changes in the stock price and CDS levels are market indicators that are difficult to ignore. In the past, they have more often than not shown signs of things to come, even though the problems could not yet be seen from reading financial statements or company announcements.

When choosing the EWIs it is essential to include 'slow moving' metrics and not solely focus on the simple binary metrics. Ratings downgrade is an example of the latter, but, as discussed further, it is not a good predictive measure but rather a lagging indicator. The main reason for picking indicators like rating downgrade is how easy it is to interpret their readings, that is either a downgrade has happened or not. Unfortunately, the world of threat is not this simple, which is where the slow-moving indicators provide assistance.

An example of such EWIs would be:

- Increase in currency mismatch.
- Decrease in the rate of term deposit rollover or increase in unexpected deposit loss.
- Shortening of the intrabank funding and increase in the average spread paid.
- Decrease in the weighted average maturity of deposits and liabilities as a whole.
- Increase in negative news flow, adverse publicity and increased concerns raised by customers.
- Increased concentration (in terms of products) on both sides of the balance sheet.
- Swift asset growth.
- Higher reliance on unstable funding in relation to illiquid assets.
- Increase of requests for withdrawing deposits prior to their contractual maturity.
- Unwillingness of counterparties to renew credit limits or decrease in lines.
- Frequent requests for additional collateral to cover counterparty exposure.

10.3.5 Assessing the Risk and Alert Level – The Boy Who Cried Wolf

This is the tricky part of the CFP but should not be ignored. The liquidity risk status is set by expert judgement and reading from the early warning indicators (EWIs).

The EWI monitoring sheet will help the risk manager to spot and identify liquidity risk. Moreover, history shows us that most liquidity events, both firm specific and market wide, could have been spotted and would have been caught through a wide set of EWIs. So, why did they go unnoticed? The difficult part is to assess correctly which are signs of real threats and which are not. Here is where all the modelling in the world will not help but expert judgement, preferably from various backgrounds and perspectives, is the only solution. One might argue that this is an imperfect approach, but this is more widely practised than model specialists like to think. As flawed as it may be, there is no substitute for expert judgement. There is an inherit bias in most of us to provide a plausible explanation for the abnormal readings from the EWI metrics. The markets are constantly moving and volatility is something that can be taken as a given. The bank's balance sheet and cash flows are in nature also dynamic. Therefore, apart from the 'fire-alarm' triggers, most indicators are variables that are supposed to move and shift under general conditions. The difficult part is to spot the movements that signify a looming accumulation of risk. It is the task of the ALCO, which should consist of members from various backgrounds and areas of expertise, to assess the situation.

The Four Alert Levels

The CFP has four levels of stress, which are the same as illustrated in the stress testing section, namely green, yellow, amber and red. The difference is that within the stress testing framework, the four levels represented four liquidity outflow scenarios. Under the CFP the four stages are risk alert levels, which do not always mean funds are leaving but rather that there is a risk that they do (yellow alert level).

Box 10.1   The four levels of stress in the CFP

Green	Business-as-usual conditions, characterized by: Benign operating environment Stable deposit trends Stable market conditions, e.g. market liquidity, haircuts, etc. Stable liability pricing
Yellow	No liquidity issues, but (perceived) heightened level of risk characterized by: Unsatisfactory business results (increased loan losses, decreased profitability) Stable deposit trends Adverse market conditions, e.g. widening of bid/offer and credit spreads, increased haircuts, less market liquidity Increased cost of funding
Amber	Adverse funding situation, characterized by: Deterioration in business results Abnormal increase in deposit outflows Access to unsecured funding channels difficult Challenging or eroding market conditions Increased cost of funding
Red	Deteriorating funding situation, severe funding problems, characterized by: Material deterioration in business results Material deposit outflows Access to unsecured funding channels lost Access to secured funding channels difficult or lost Eroding market conditions Increased cost of funding

---

Each alert level needs to be clearly defined and its meaning understood by those impacted. Green, the lowest risk level, represents the normal business environment. The next alert stage, which is the first alert status (yellow), is an alert status of increased possible but not realized threat, that is the bank is not experiencing any liquidity problems. The amber alert status is crucial as this is where most of the mitigation action happens. By the same token, this status captures mild stress conditions up to rather severe outflow scenarios. It can be argued that different levels of threats require different responses and actions but the menu of actions should be built so that the appropriate mitigation action is being applied. This is so that the risk managers have more flexibility in their work and are not being constrained by the CFP. There is, however, nothing wrong in splitting the amber alert stage in two, one for low impact and the other for increased risk. Here again, it is the risk manager's and senior management's responsibility to find the adequate balance, keeping in mind that the CFP is advance planning, so if a threat or a possible threat should arise, the bank has already prepared itself and done part of the assessment beforehand and can therefore be quicker to apply the most appropriate remedy. Being hit with crises without a sound CFP will mean that time will be lost assessing and debating the seriousness; such an assessment could easily be inadequate, leading to the wrong response. As can be derived from the EWI, the bank can elevate the risk status to amber alert as a precaution due to an incident or a seriously adverse reading from the EWIs without experiencing funding problems.

Contingency Stress Scenarios within the CFP

A part of the risk assessment phase is to have an idea of the possible risk impact, which is where the liquidity stress scenarios come in. The CFP needs to identify severe but reasonably plausible stress events, which may turn into a stress scenario. This allows the bank to analyse liquidity risks based on the performance of different risk drivers and variables under distressed circumstances. As a result stress testing gives the bank the opportunity to define in its CFP the liquidity needs that it may face under the contingency scenarios. It can thereby test the adequacy of the level of the HQLA and design the appropriate mitigation actions.

This is not an easy task and is likely to be the reason why some put little faith in CFPs. The challenge is to come up with relevant scenarios for the bank. When designing the scenario guidance on building the liquidity stress scenario provided in the liquidity stress testing section is fully valid. The scenario should include cash flow projections, which estimate funding needs under different defined adverse conditions. Some of the most severe scenarios from the stress testing section can be used as the CFP scenarios, keeping in mind that CFP is focused around low probability but high severity (contingency scenarios) only. As the CFP scenarios should be very severe it might be that the suite of scenarios in the liquidity stress model is not sufficient and others need to be built. The scenarios should be commensurate with the bank's complexity, risk exposure, activities, products and organizational structure and need to simulate idiosyncratic problems and systemic problems that affect the banking system as a whole, or a combination of the two. As shown in Figure 10.13, the contingency scenarios need both to address liquidity risk as a timing issue (cash flows) as well as a change in quantum both on the liability and asset sides. The contingency scenarios are the base for the action plans; hence it is vital that they reflect various origins of liquidity risk. As a part of the overall liquidity framework, the stress tests within the CFP need to be reviewed at least annually and also if business market conditions or the major composition of the funding structure change.

10.3.6 Decisions and Action Plans

At this stage the bank has identified and assessed its possible liquidity risk and measured its impact via various liquidity stress tests. The next step is to determine the output of the CFP, which many believe to be the main objective of a sound contingency funding plan. The key parameters are to:

- Coordinate and plan the bank's response to funding difficulties.
- Set out actions and possible funding sources under stressed conditions.
- Set the external and internal communication policies.

The starting point is the defined contingency scenarios in the assessment section, all of which should be matched to appropriate actions. In reality the bank is hardly going to experience an event that is completely the same as described in one of the scenarios. Therefore the set of actions needs to be up to a point specific but at the same time applicable to mitigate various Sources of Liquidity Risk. This might read like a contradiction but it is difficult to accurately predict the exact actions that will be required for each scenario. Thus it is useful to list the possible actions by the level of risk they apply to.

It is essential to bear in mind that the list of possible actions should not be viewed as a list of inflexible instructions but rather as a menu of possible mitigating actions applicable to that specific level of risk. The risk manager and ALCO can decide which of the plans from the menu they think are most appropriate and which are not. Note that a certain plan of action might only be suited to a particular alert status and ill-suited to another.

Possible Actions for Yellow Risk Status

As the lowest risk level, yellow is a stage where there is only a possible threat of liquidity risk. The corresponding actions can be described as preventing measures where the bank tries, without creating much cost, to immunize itself from the impact should the risk progress further. These measurements include:

- Enhancing monitoring and reporting. Increased risk on the horizon requires the bank to be more alert to any further adverse developments. This is done via a formalized increase in monitoring and reporting frequency and details. The metrics can be calculated more frequently and the management should be kept closely abreast of the situation.
- If the bank has some liquidity risk monitoring forums, they should convene under the yellow alert level.
- The ALM and treasury will start to look at whether any inexpensive enhancements of the HQLA are possible, both in terms of quantity and quality. This could include:
  - Optimizing repo lines, so the best collateral is not used up in repo contracts that have wider eligibility criteria.
  - The tenor of the repos should be reviewed and the demand for extended maturities should be quantified.
  - Centralizing free cash from pockets where it could get trapped or is of less use.
  - Reviewing collateral allocation in branches and divisions and centralized unused collateral.
- Decrease, where possible, the use/reliance on less stable sources of liquidity.
- Investigate whether the bank can increase its deposit gathering or issuance with enhanced pricing.
- If the threat is crystallizing in increased funding cost, the funding plan needs to be reviewed, assuming that the market conditions will prevail over a period of time. Higher prices might render some funding options no longer economically viable for the bank.
- Verify if the assumptions in cash flow forecasts are still fully applicable and realistic. If the bank is not experiencing any unusual outflows, they should still hold valid.
- Review the details of the action plans corresponding to the higher alert stages to verify whether they still hold valid in quantity and timing.
- Review the scenario stress test assumptions with the objective to verify their adequacy under the current threat.
- Refresh the role and responsibilities of crises management teams and make sure that all relevant staff are aware of their duties. Update contact details and membership lists of relevant committees.

In short, the move from green to yellow should be a wake-up call for the ALM and ALCO to take a fresh look at the plans within the CFP. Even though the CFP should be updated annually, there could be assumptions within it, especially around the details of the remedial plans, which have not fully been played out and need updating. This is especially relevant for any of the secured funding options that have been identified, where the assets in question might have decreased in value or are no longer eligible for the funding mechanism. Chances are that other banks are also doing the same review and might have changed their terms for providing funding (haircuts, eligibility, etc.). Most likely the bank has not been in yellow conditions recently so the roles and responsibilities might not be clear to newcomers.

Notice that the most obvious action against increased threat, to increase the HQLA, is not on the menu at this stage. This does not mean that increasing the liquidity buffer is out of the question but as it always comes at a cost, the justification needs to be clear. To decide to increase the buffer might indicate that the ALCO does not believe the risk level is only at the yellow level but is higher. Keep in mind the fact that the overall objective of the exercise is to preserve the bank's viability as an on-going concern, something that is largely dependent on the bank's credibility and reputation. The plans put in place need therefore to be carefully executed so as not to be seen as an indication of liquidity problems, which could exacerbate the problem.

Possible Actions for Amber Risk Status

If the risk alert status has been raised to amber, it has already been through the yellow stage and we can assume that the relevant counteracting action has taken place. The bank is now in an abnormal funding situation where it is experiencing funding problems that, if continued, could create a material risk to the bank. At the same time the market for selling off assets might have become less liquid.

The menu of possible remedies for the amber risk status should contain various 'dishes' as this alert status captures mild to medium severe scenarios, for which different mitigating action can apply. Some of the items that should be on the menu for amber are:

- Increased frequency of scenario liquidity risk testing. If the current scenarios do not encompass the adverse scenario the bank is experiencing, it needs to be created with immediate and increased severity.
- Review of cash flow forecasts and recalculation of the survival horizon, assuming that the funding troubles will continue and escalate. This should provide an overview of the problem at hand and make the choice of appropriate actions easier.
- Increase the level of HQLA. If the bank has possibilities to increase its liquidity buffer it should do so now. Keep in mind that usually it is only possible to increase the funding or level of cash at the early stages of liquidity events.
- Increase unsecured funding of tenors greater than 90 days. The increased funding plans set out under yellow should be reviewed and executed where applicable.
- Set out a plan for deposit retention through price and communication. The 'action team' described below will communicate the strategy to the deposit gatherers, which will now become the 'price to win'.
- Reassess the value of assets that are available for sale, especially the ones that form a part of the liquidity buffer. The assets need to be regularly valued while operating under amber alert status.
- Draw on unsecured standby back-up lines as needed. Experience shows that even committed back-up facilities can be difficult to execute under stressed conditions as the providers

become reluctant to honour their obligations. If a bank has external back-up lines as part of its contingency plans, it needs to draw on them from time to time to avoid the drawdown being seen as a sign of liquidity shortfall.

- Revalue the expected loan outflows with management. If possible, the bank should review larger lending projects with the aim of delaying the payments where possible without facing negative consequences or loss of trust.
- Many of the liquidity-generating actions through securitization take time to implement and execute. Using the information from the updated cash flow forecasts, decide which ones should be implemented and review the time table. As this usually requires an input from various divisions, the bank should assign this to a project team.
- Under the amber status the bank needs to proactively address and manage the situation instead of just monitoring its progress. Information that was only relevant to the ALM and the liquidity experts can now play a major role in the bank's operations, so an appropriate platform needs to be created. A team, the liquidity management team (LMT), should be put together to manage and coordinate actions under the stressed conditions. The team, which needs to have representatives from the businesses, marketing, operations and the ALM, should have a defined mandate or terms of reference to work from. This needs to set out the role of the team, authority, etc.
- Under more severe conditions, the bank should start to increase its efforts in centralizing its cash and asset positions. The plan needs to consider the fact that national regulators are particularly worried about liquidity being transferred in times of crisis and the F/X risk can also be of additional concern. Yet again, the timing of the mitigating actions is of importance.

The overall difference between the plans for mild and more severe problems is usually how much emphasis is given to the cost and impact on profitability. A higher liquidity threat will mean that solving a liquidity problem takes precedence over profitability. With the amber status, the liquidity risk stops being an issue for the ALM and treasury only and becomes a risk level that the bank as a whole needs to address. The liquidity management team (LMT) serves that function and its role and responsibilities as a central body need to be set out in the CFP. The LMT is not a crisis team and its gathering should not be looked on as a sign of desperate measures. It is there first and foremost to coordinate responses. With members from the businesses, treasury, the ALM and investor relations the team should have sufficient information and authority to manage the situation. The terms of reference for the LMT should include:

- A list of divisions represented.
- A set agenda for its meetings, the meeting structure and the information it needs to consider.
- A definition of the authority it has been delegated and its management responsibilities.

The LMT will be the centralized body to enable the bank to respond to increased liquidity risk. Apart from coordinating the action plan to increase funding it also has a function to provide internal and external information, both formal an informal. The terms of reference will split out individual tasks to each member but the communication message is one which the team will decide upon jointly. This should include how to manage the relationship with large counterparties and providers of funds, how queries from depositors should be responded to, etc. There are two major areas the LMT should pay notice to. It should try to be proactive in communication to drive behaviour rather than being reactive to yesterday's news. This is of course not always possible, but the LMT can prepare their response to escalating events. If the LMT is constantly putting out fires and responding to events, it is more likely to make mistakes and take the wrong actions. It should, where possible, try to have prepared answers to events that are likely to happen. Secondly, the LMT needs to be especially aware of the flow of communication upwards and downwards. Communication is usually the first thing that goes wrong in crises, especially if the committee has started its work too late. The LMT needs to have a formal and open communication channel to management, to know quickly and precisely of any developments that only management might be aware of. By the same token it needs to communicate to the management and other stakeholders in a concise and frequent manner.

Possible Actions for Red Risk Status

Under the red risk status the bank is facing very adverse conditions, access to unsecured funding markets is closed, material amounts of deposits are flowing out and the only access to funding is through secured funding channels. If red conditions are reached, the CFP becomes formally and unconditionally activated and the crisis management team comes together. The actions under red put liquidity as the priority over profitability and the focus becomes one of maintaining the longest survival horizon possible. In most cases the bank has very limited possibilities to increase its liquidity at this stage (apart from central bank funding) and the plan is how to weather the storm and avoid further escalation. The red alert status will see the following taking place:

- Establishing of a formal Crises Management Committee (CMC), consisting of senior management and risk experts. The CMC will direct the implementation of the CFP and needs to be empowered with the authority to make and execute decisions.
- The LMT will act as a subcommittee of the CMC and execute its decisions. The two committees should not work as an additional layer of management, which can slow down the process, but as a way to keep tasks and people organized. Other subcommittees or working groups may be assigned certain tasks.
- The CMC works according to preassigned duties covering areas like internal communication, communication with regulators and media, etc. Each member should have a designated substitute.
- The action plan for red includes the items mentioned in yellow and amber but with a greater emphasis on retaining all funding and intensifying the efforts of turning assets into cash.
- The CMC needs to revalue its commitment to buy-backs and other liquidity support. There is no clear rule to work by but the bank should try to minimize its support where possible without triggering confidence crises.
- The frequency of reporting and monitoring needs to be increased from previous risk levels and communicated to the CMC.

The CFP should contain the functions of the Crisis Management Committee, which is not only responsible for making clear, defined decisions in a timely manner but also being in charge of communications, both internal and external. In order to facilitate a timely response, the plan needs to set out a clear decision-making process on what actions are to be taken at what time, who can take them and what issues need to be escalated to more senior levels within the bank. Do not forget to define who can activate the CFP.

10.3.7   Execution

The final part of the CFP is to provide a list of sources for additional funding. The previous parts of assessing, managing and deciding on what to do all lead to the execution part. The menu of available actions, on which the 'decision' part is heavily focused, needs to be backed up by a concrete list and assessment of available additional funding.

Sources of Contingency Funding

The CFP should contain a range of alternative additional funding that can be used in a crisis. The bank should define the volume and quality each instrument can provide under each scenario. As mentioned previously, the amount of funding the bank can expect from each funding source is determined by the risk status and the will of the bank. Under yellow conditions the bank might only want to access some of the available sources for a small amount, whereas under red it might take all it can. The sources of contingency funding can be grouped into four categories:

- Unsecured borrowing
- Secured borrowing
- Asset sale
- Other.

1. *Unsecured borrowing.* For less stressful scenarios the bank can include unsecured borrowings. This action could include deposit growth efforts, the lengthening of liability maturities and issuance of new short- or/and long-term instruments. Drawing on committee back-up lines also falls under this category. Banks have been criticized for putting too much emphasis on unsecured funding options in the CFPs. This is true now more than ever, after banks had incurred counterparty losses during the financial crises. Therefore, banks should not include any unsecured funding as a possible source under more severe stress conditions. This includes committed back-up facilities as providers are likely to renege on their commitments and face the consequences rather than provide funding, which has a high chance of getting lost. This rather pessimistic view on the quality of committed credit lines is a sign of the times. Prior to the financial crises banks took comfort from these types of facilities, which in many instances were set up with the main objective to be contingency funding. Both regulators and rating agencies were in acceptance of this view but all market participants have changed their opinions.
2. *Secured borrowing.* Almost all banks rely on some type of secured borrowing in their CFP. Borrowing against collateral is less risky than unsecured borrowing even though the counterparties might not be as many. The secured borrowing is either through a private sector repurchase agreement with a variety of collateral or with the central bank with its eligible assets. The private secured borrowing market can be included in less to medium severe liquidity risk scenarios, but can be expected to follow a 'flight to quality' behaviour under stress. The bank needs to decide upon its reliance on this market and primarily on the quality of the collateral the bank intends to use for funding. As haircuts increase under stress conditions and can be followed up with margin calls, the bank needs to be sure that this funding source does not become the reserve and start to soak up liquidity. This will surely happen at the time the bank is in the worst position to meet additional collateral calls. Consideration needs also to be given to the number of private parties providing the service

and their own liquidity standing under adverse market conditions. Increased levels of stress will also make those counterparties select their clients more carefully and decrease the overall amount of liquidity they are willing to provide. They might also take other factors into account when assessing the continuation of the business, such as the jurisdiction of the borrower and the risk of ring fencing.

3. *Asset sale*. Sale of assets is a feature in most CFPs and nearly all firms expect they can raise funds if needed with asset sales. This is true for some asset classes but less so with others. Firms may expect to sell down their trading portfolio or government securities in most scenarios, but even then the past has taught us that most liquid markets can come to a halt under severe conditions.

   The 'flight to quality' is not the only trap on the way to realize cash from assets. The margin/haircut spiral, which can happen when participants start to deleverage, can lead to much less value for assets than expected.[17]

   This should make banks take a different view on the cash that an asset sale can generate, depending on whether the stress is firm specific or market wide. It is not uncommon to see banks being overconfident in their capabilities to sell off illiquid assets or even parts of businesses. This provides another reason for splitting up this category depending on the source of liquidity event, making the proceeds from asset sales less prominent as a viable action plan under market stresses.

   Another favourite dish on the menu is securitization of assets, which many believe can provide funds under stress. If the bank has not done any securitizations before and is unknown to the market or does not have the necessary process in place, then securitization is at best a strategic business goal but not a source for contingency funds. Even if all necessary conditions are satisfied the bank should expect execution to take much longer than under normal conditions.

4. *Other*. Banks might have some additional businesses or setups that enable them to source contingency funds from other means than stated earlier. An example would be additional intragroup borrowings. A banking group will do its utmost to preserve the group's overall liquidity health and a part of that plan is to support all subsidiaries and branches. Even though this support might not be contractual or in any other way committed there are various reputational and legal reasons for parent companies to look at the subsidiaries as their own liquidity requirement. Therefore, subsidiaries can for mild and medium stress scenarios allow the group to provide some contingency funding. However, national regulators are fully aware of the problems this can create and can without warning put cash flow restrictions in place. This is a relevant risk and not a hypothetical one and hence banks should not over rely on group funding in times of need.

Some banks incorporate in their CFP steps to take if clearing and settlement systems do not work properly. This could be in the form of having access to more than one settlement system, an alternate provider and in other instances the reliance on the central bank. This was a risk element that took the Icelandic banking system by surprise in the crisis, as the banks had unexpected problems of even making outward payments, which fuelled the risk. In the end the payments had to be done via the central bank, but the banking system had not expected that the payments systems might be a source of liquidity risk. Each bank needs to assess whether their reliance on payments systems is such that a formal back-up solution is needed. At least the bank should have the capabilities to identify critical payments and be able to sequence or rank payments based on their priority.

The CFP will include provisions for the sources of contingency funding to be tested and key assumptions to be reviewed. In general the CFP should be reviewed and tested regularly to assess its operational feasibility. This is usually done via an annual CFP test and simulation, where the main focus is on the operational aspects of the CFP. The test will ensure that roles and responsibilities are understood and clear, that contact information is up to date, etc. It is also a great opportunity to gain more understanding of the general function of the CFP. The practice of simulating contingency plans seems to be better practised in US banks compared to their European counterparts. A monthly or quarterly simulation seems to be widely practised in the United States, where they are tested, something which is needed in Europe.[18]

The Role of Communication

The CFP is not only a funding plan but rather a guide that help the bank's management to tackle severe liquidity events. Effective communication needs to be a part of that plan. This is where many banks have fallen short and it is difficult to find a bank that has been through crises without any criticism of the way things were communicated and how different parts of the bank were kept abreast of the situation and what was being done at each stage. The role of the crisis committee has been set out above. In order to avoid mishaps and facilitate swift decisions the CMC needs to have a rough communication plan to support general confidence in the bank. The plan should set out who is responsible for communicating to each of the following groups of stakeholders: market participants, clients (including custodians), employees, shareholders, supervisors/central banks, rating agencies and media. It also needs to state when each group should be contacted.

Putting It All Together

Figure 10.16 demonstrates how an effective CFP framework should work within an institution. It should provide the management with a high degree of flexibility to address each liquidity event in the most efficient way and as quickly as possible.

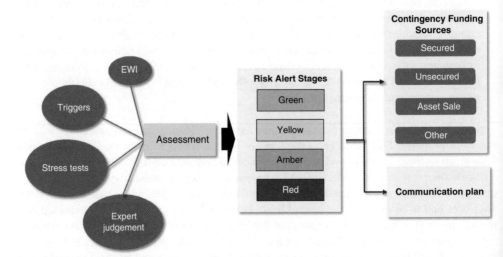

Figure 10.16   Procedures of a Contingency Funding Plan

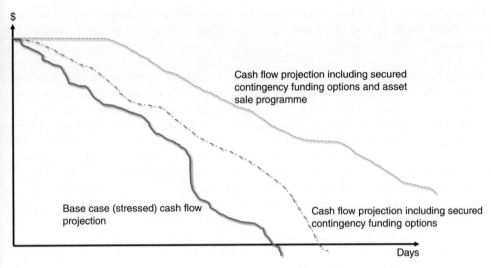

$

Cash flow projection including secured
contingency funding options and asset
sale programme

Base case (stressed) cash flow
projection

Cash flow projection including secured
contingency funding options

Days

Figure 10.17   Cash flow projection (shown as survival days) for a CFP stress scenario

The assessment of the risk is the first and an on-going feature of the CFP, where four different features, EWI, stress testing, formal triggers and expert judgement, provide the ingredients for the evaluation. The conclusion of the assessment is determined in the four risk stages, green, yellow, amber and red. The final stage is to act out the plan, both its contingency funding as well as the communication agenda.

Part of the risk assessment is to have a good overview of the expected cash flows. This is of critical value for the risk management as the bank can clearly see the impact the contingency funding sources provide and the additional time they offer to the bank. An example of such a cash flow projection can be found in Figure 10.17. The first scenario is the base case stressed outflows, which gives the shortest survival time horizon. Then two further scenarios are included, firstly by adding the secured contingency funding options and secondly by adding the impact of a possible asset sale.

Lessons Learnt

It might be difficult to see the silver linings in the most recent financial crises. However, one can say it has helped in improving and building appropriate contingency plans. Economics and finance are unlike some other fields of science, which enjoy the luxury of being able to experiment and test their proposals in a laboratory. Consequently, some specific risk mitigation actions or plans are left untested for years and assumed to be effective until proven otherwise (take the committed back-up lines as an example). This puts greater emphasis on the risk specialists to be able to draw parallels from the limited historical experience and in short apply the 'expect the unexpected' approach in risk management.

Very few banks had sufficiently strong CFPs to meet the epidemic crises and most have revisited their assumptions and plans since then. Even though banks have a wide range of liquidity profiles and funding structures, the shortfalls of the CFPs were perhaps more universally uniform than expected. It is therefore useful to analyse the factors that went wrong but at the same time to keep in mind the fact that the financial crises were just one wave in an ocean of risk and, as we have discussed earlier, it is not likely that history will repeat itself. The lesson drawn by both firms and supervisors in the aftermath of the crises revealed the following:

- One of the key points was that complex corporate structures hindered contingency funding. Corporate structures are becoming increasingly complex across different jurisdictions and groups of companies. This holds especially true for financial institutions, which can be much more flexible in terms of their setup than, for example, a manufacturing company. The crises revealed that the CFP had not fully captured the complexity of the organizations and the company structures imposed significant constraints on the flow of funds between entities. The reason for the shortcoming can be that the CFP is in many cases written within the ALM or treasury without the full knowledge and understanding of the overall banking structure. Many banks only write their CFP on consolidated bases, which does not help each individual legal entity. This problem was even pointed out prior to the crises by a BCBS study done on liquidity management practices.[19]
- The CFPs had in many cases become too focused on firm-specific risk events and neglected the stress coming from the markets.
- Within a firm-specific event the banks were overly reliant on ineffective early warning indicators. The most common answer to the question of how to spot an emerging threat is a rating downgrade. This answer implies that the rating agencies know more about the company than the management itself, which does not hold true, if only for the reason that the rating agencies base their assessment mostly on public data.
- Noncontractual contingencies not fully incorporated in the CFP. Supervisors are now putting more emphasis on the fact that banks estimate the noncontractual support they need to exercise, even under times of stress. When constructing the CFPs banks have been overly confident in their capabilities to stop doing 'unnecessary' business and have failed to recognize the reputational aspect of that action. These are various activities, such as being a market maker on the secondary market, providing bids for your own bonds when needed and even providing liquidity support to funding. The reason for this gap in CFPs is the standpoint their authors have taken, assuming that the CFP is only used during severe times, under an 'every man for himself' scenario that excludes noncontractual obligations. The CFP should become effective earlier in the process and hence needs to take a wider approach so as not to escalate the problem.
- Lack of sufficient stress scenario cash flow projections. Banks were criticized for not playing out various assumptions through their cash flow projections. The outcome was that the cash flows were not a useful tool to predict what could happen, which could have enabled the bank to implement further mitigating actions. Others have pointed out that stress tests and contingency funding plans were often not sufficiently integrated.
- Communication breakdown and confusion. Banks are usually willing to communicate but the approach under stress has been criticized. Some CFPs do not specify the individuals responsible for communicating with various stakeholders, which is essential when crises hit and time is of the essence.
- Failure to take proactive measures after a trigger breach or a risk alert coming from an EWI. It is the ALCO's and risk specialist's role to assess the EWI readings and determine whether to escalate or whether there is a reasonable explanation that does not constitute a threat factor. After a long period of benign market conditions there can be a built-in reluctance or hesitancy to read the signs correctly. The CFP relies on judgement, which will always be

biased one way or the other. The only way to improve is to apply the four eyes principle (i.e. more than one person reviews the metrics) and secondly to add 'hard triggers' that will escalate the concerns.

- Overreliance on market liquidity. This became obvious during the crises where liquidity evaporated even in markets that were assumed to be safe. The CFP plans had made assumptions about the continuous market liquidity for too wide a range of products, including structured products, mortgage securities and ABCP. The halt of the interbank market and the ABS secondary market proved these assumptions wrong and consequently the CFP have had to adjust their assumptions on market liquidity in general.
- The CFP and stress tests underestimated the risks of the off-balance sheet and contingent commitments. The CFP is built on assumptions with the stress test models, which include the estimated drawdown on off-balance sheet commitments. If the stress tests do not recognize the risk appropriately the consequence is that the CFP does not provide sufficient support for that risk, with dire consequences.

It is essential to approach this list of deficiencies with the right attitude about learning from the past. The 20/20 hindsight is tough to avoid and one can easily dismiss these past failures and view them as management failures, something that will not happen again, now that the pitfalls have been discovered. This might not be the case. Assumptions that we might fully believe to hold true today might look unreasonable when revisited a few years from now. An example was the overreliance on market liquidity. Before the crises some 60% of ABCP was AAA rated versus only 1% of the corporate bonds in the United States.[20] It could have been argued in the early days of 2007 that the ABCP market was both strong and solid and the last market to dry up if banks needed funding. We know that assumption turned out to be entirely wrong.

Dos and Don'ts in Making the Contingency Funding Plan

In a nutshell, the objective of an effective CFP is to spot the threat, measure the threat, have a clear predefined line of action and contingency funding sources. The framework provided in this chapter should give good guidance on how to approach the work of building a sound CFP. It is useful to keep the following list in mind when embarking on the project. By doing that you will capture the 'best practices' and at the same time learn of the mistakes of others.

- Compose the CFP at the right level within the firm. Only the one sitting on the highest branch of the tallest tree has a good overview of the forest. Ask someone sitting on the lower branches and you will not get a CFP that incorporates the consolidated bank. Build a group of people from various divisions to incorporate all the knowledge needed. From the consolidated CFP, work towards creating a CFP (or separate chapter) for subsidiaries or operations in other jurisdictions. The ALM usually does not have all the answers even though it controls cash flow centrally within a group under business-as-usual conditions.
- Be flexible yet firm and specific. It is a tricky balancing act that must be accomplished. Imagine that the CFP will be used as a fire rescue guide under times of severe acute events and think what kind of instructions you need to have. Be as specific and clear as possible – spell out who does what and when. Assign the responsibility and accountability without forcing an action to be done. It is good to write the instructions and menu items separately.

- Use the experience of others and do not take market liquidity for granted.
  - ○ Assume a flight to a quality situation and be conservative when assessing which assets can be relied upon for liquidity. Central banks provide some guidance on what is useful and what is not.
  - ○ Bilateral lines, even though committed, will not provide funding under severe scenarios.
  - ○ Paying more for funding is not going to solve any severe problems.
  - ○ Assume haircuts will increase at the worst time for the bank and through all various means (asset discount, collateral calls, etc.).
- Be careful of assuming that the F/X market will help when needed.
- Funding crises (usually) happen in stages but not overnight. Think hard about all the EWIs that can save the bank and wake you up early enough to get to your weapons. Assume (rightly or wrongly) that the ratings agencies will not hear the alarm bell ring and their ratings are a lagging indicator.
- Avoid the 'boy who cried wolf' scenario by having the EWIs reviewed by various people or invent a scorecard that will automatically escalate concerns.
- Avoid operating in a vacuum. If a storm breaks you need to know how it will impact on the bank. Therefore, spend time on various stress scenarios and update the cash flow projections. They will tell you where you are and you will be better able to see what the bank is up against.
- Take a second look at your off-balance sheet commitments, especially the liquidity ones. There is a reason for Basel III treating them severely. The CFP is the plan to get you safely out of the problem, minimize reputational risk and restore confidence. To do that you will need to honour noncontractual commitments for as long as you can.

To preserve flexibility, some banks prefer to have the CFP set out in two layers. The first layer is the official CFP, which is approved by the Board. That document sets out the responsibilities and duties but does not go into specific details. The second document is the implementation guide, which contains the up-to-date stresses and their outcome, the latest contingency funding arrangement, etc. By splitting the CFP like this, the management can prevent a situation where the Board-approved plan restricts them from certain actions. The second part can also more easily become a living document, which can easily be updated.

Endnotes

1. See Committee on the Global Financial System, *Stress Testing at Major Financial Institutions: Survey Results and Practice*, January 2005.
2. See, for example, Senior Supervisors Group, *Risk Management Lessons from the Global Banking Crisis of 2008*, 21 October 2009, and Final Report of the IIF Committee on *Market Best Practices: Principles of Conduct and Best Practice Recommendations, Financial Services Industry Response to the Market Turmoil of 2007–2008*, IIF, July 2008.
3. Adapted from Basel Committee on Banking Supervision, *Principles for Sound Liquidity Risk Management and Supervision*, September 2008.
4. See Matz, L. (2011), *Liquidity Risk Measurement and Management, Basel III and Beyond*, Xlibris, p. 183.
5. See Prudential Regulation Authority (PRA), *Prudential Sourcebook for Banks, Building Societies and Investment Firm (BIPRU)*, Chapter 12.5. Available at: www.fsa.gov.uk.
6. See Guideline 3 in Committee of European Banking Supervisors (CEBS), *Guidelines on Liquidity Buffers and Survival Periods*, December 2009.

7. Basel Committee on Banking Supervision, *Sound Practices for Managing Liquidity in Banking Organisations*, February 2000, p. 7.
8. CBC is the term used for the funds and management actions the bank has to take to meet liquidity needs in stress scenarios.
9. See European Central Bank, *EU Bank's Liquidity Stress Testing and Contingency Funding Plans*, November 2008.
10. PWC, *Balance Sheet Management Benchmark Survey, Status of Balance Sheet Management Practices among International Banks – 2009*, 2009.
11. Matz, L. (2011), *Liquidity Risk Measurement and Management, Basel III and Beyond*, Xlibris 2011, p. 233.
12. European Banking Authority (EBA), *Consultation paper on Draft Guidelines on Retail Deposits Subject to Different Outflows for Purposes of Liquidity Reporting under Regulation (EU) No. 575/2013 (Capital Requirements Regulation – CRR)*, August 2013.
13. When this was written the EBA technical standard had not been formally set, so the amount can change in the final requirement.
14. Basel Committee on Banking Supervision, *Principles for Sound Liquidity Risk Management and Supervision*, September 2008, Principle 11.
15. Adapted from Matz, L. and Neu, P. (editors) (2007), *Liquidity Risk Measures and Management, A Practitioner's Guide to Global Best Practises*, John Wiley & Sons, Ltd.
16. After hearing about the acronym, my colleague reckoned the more appropriate acronym was SAD, applicable both to the process and the author.
17. See Brunnermeier, M. (2009), Deciphering the Liquidity and Credit Crunch 2007–2008, *Journal of Economic Perspectives*, **23** (1), Winter 2009, 94.
18. PWC, *The Journal, Liquidity Risk Management Staying Afloat in Choppy Seas*, April 2010. Available at: www.pwc.com.
19. See Basel Committee on Banking Supervision, *The Management of Liquidity Risk in Financial Groups*, May 2006.
20. See Rajan, R. (2010), Fault Lines, in *How Hidden Fractures Still Threaten the World Economy*, Princeton University Press, p. 134.

11

Step VI: Reporting and Management Information

Liquidity management and reporting are inseparable. Through the '6 Step Framework' we have looked at various types of reports and most if not all the individual steps conclude their findings in some sort of a report. This should not come as a surprise; one of the key objectives of the liquidity management framework is to provide information on the risk status to enable the correct and timely decisions. Without the information and reports we would be taking a shot in the dark.

The sixth and final step is, however, not so much about writing reports but rather the point in time where we look over the various outputs of the other steps, sort and evaluate them and compile them into digestible reports for the different audience. There are a few high-level principles we should try to honour:

- Tailor the information to the needs of the audience. Ask yourself:
  - What role does that specific audience play in the liquidity governance framework?
  - What information do they need to fulfil their duties?
  - What are the settings and frequency of the meetings (is a meeting only to discuss liquidity risk or is it only one topic out of ten)?

  Keeping this in mind will help to avoid information overload, which is the tendency of most risk professionals. The result is that the information packages for the Board or management could become the size of a phone book and lose their purpose. From time to time, it can be useful to give more background to the information, but that should not be the rule. I generally think that most banks are guilty of providing too much information (of relatively little value) rather than too little. Providing the audience with the information they need will also mean that the information package to the Risk Committee and ALCO should be very different from the Board package. A 'copy and paste' exercise will not do.
- Not all numbers are created equal. Highlight the key outcomes so the reader knows what is expected of him/her. A spreadsheet with 300 numbers is not very useful unless the information is discussion material for the risk specialists. For most purposes, highlight what is needed and have supplementary appendices ready (or ready to be provided if asked for). This will give the appropriate level of information for the decisions at hand and at the same time satisfy the curiosity of someone who wants to dig deeper behind the numbers.
- Expect different levels of 'financial literacy' and bridge the information gap. I have seen Board packages that read more like pages from *The Journal of Mathematical Economics*. That approach does not help anyone. Neither is the approach that provides only a very limited amount of data without describing how they were derived and simply pointing to the models. The risk specialists will need to provide the missing pieces in between to make the information useful.
- Have an 'information agenda'. The information package should follow an agenda and tell a story instead of simply being a collection of scattered bits of information. Think: Where

do we come from? What are we? Where are we going?[1] The report will show the history or the position we are in, the impact of our actions and activities and last but not least forecast numbers and projections.

- The right balance should be achieved between history and projections depending on the purpose. There are reports that are made to show compliance with risk limits and triggers, but they are not sufficient and not the appropriate material for high-level discussions. As pointed out in the chapter on the role of the ALCO in liquidity risk management, the tendency is to focus too much on what has been done and avoid the difficult discussions about the future. As the future is the only thing we can change, the appropriate forum needs to be equipped with the necessary tools. The Board and Exco meeting should not be spent making sure that the CRO and CFO have performed their role of signing off compliance with ratios.
- Keep a balance between absolute numbers and trends. Changes over time can tell a very important story and snapshot quantity numbers do not always serve their purpose. The Board will be unlikely to understand the meaning of, for example, the amount of unencumbered HQLA if it is provided in isolation from everything else, whereas for the risk committee and those working more frequently with liquidity risk this is a key figure.
- Do not shy away from using graphs and charts. They can prove to be very useful, not only to convey a trend but also to explain methodologies.

It can be useful to build up a hierarchy of reports, starting with the lowest, most frequent and detailed level and building up to the high-level Board pack. The two key points to keep in mind to build up the appropriate level of information are level of detail and frequency. The day-to-day risk manager's report is the most frequent and detailed, etc., but should still follow the 'Gauguin principle'. The reports to the Risk Committee and ALCO should be less granular but necessarily forward looking to enable the ALCO to fulfil its duty as a strategic committee. Finally, with the Board pack, the information becomes more high level and aggregated and we change the approach from providing details to highly summarized information presented more in graphs and illustrations, where appropriate. This should by no means lead to the Board being kept away from critical data or breaches of triggers.

The various levels of reports should include the following elements from the risk management framework. The level of detail and aggregation depends on who the information package is being produced for.

- Cash flow projections and funding mismatch gaps over different horizons. The number of scenarios and detail depend on the audience and do not forget to include the vital assumptions used in the projections. The compliance with a survival time horizon is shown with the outcome of cash flow scenarios and should be reported and compared to previous results (forecasted versus limits).
- EWI.
- Collateral levels and usage (both historical and projected) including haircuts and market values.
- Asset and funding concentrations.
- Availability of funding and the status of funding sources.
- Status of contingent funding sources.
- Expectations in the volume and pricing of assets and liabilities that may significantly affect the bank's liquidity.
- Trends in cost of funding and net interest income.

As with other elements of sound liquidity risk management, the sophistication of management reporting should be consistent with the size and liquidity profile of the institution. The above list is not the only information that needs to be provided, but as a standard set for the regular overview, it should give good guidance. There are a number of other reports that will need to be discussed, such as a new product report, stress test results, CFP, market conditions, etc. Moreover, some of the reports above need to be carried out at various levels of the organization to provide the necessary information.

There is a reason for the cash flow projections to be at the top of the list. We have assessed and discussed the various ways of understanding the liquidity threat in the bank, from EWI to monitoring. The cash flow projections are, however, a fundamental measure of the bank's liquidity prospective under various scenarios. These measurements should not only be undertaken and reported but also given the appropriate attention for them to serve their full purpose. As the assumptions play a critical role in the constructions, the use of the cash flow forecast demands that the audience play a role in the assessment and agree that the assumptions are both reasonable and appropriate. It is not good standard conduct to simply read the output from the cash flows, such as reading a trigger indicator, without having a discussion on the assumptions. Too much focus on consensus can devalue the meaning of the cash flow projections and the help they provide. As inadequate assumptions are a big risk factor that cannot easily be mitigated, the reports need to bring attention to this downside and establish sufficient material for the reader to have a view on their appropriateness. This makes the cash flow forecasts a slightly complicated thing to present but under no circumstances should they be excluded for that reason.

11.1 INTERNAL CONTROLS AND INTERNAL AUDIT PROCESSES

Liquidity risk management needs to be included in the bank's overall set of internal controls. There is no doubt about the importance of internal controls but to define and develop effective internal controls and review process for the management of liquidity risk can be tricky. A good starting point can be the first publication of the sound liquidity principle by the BCBS, which captures the objective of effective internal controls well. The principle reads: '*Each bank must have an adequate system of internal controls over its liquidity risk management process. A fundamental component of the internal control system involves regular independent reviews and evaluations of the effectiveness of the system and, where necessary, ensuring that appropriate revisions or enhancements to internal controls are made. The results of such reviews should be available to supervisory authorities.*'[2]

The first thing to note is the importance of having liquidity processes reviewed by an independent third party to ensure that policies and procedures are being followed. To formalize the approach, banks can set up few lines of defences where the first line is the execution, the next monitoring and the third the independent review (risk). This works well, but the key point is to have the last line of defence sufficiently strong in their capabilities. The know-how tends to build up in the front and middle layers between the treasury and ALM, thus 'living' the risk, or the internal control is not fully equipped or knowledgeable enough to perform their duties and provide the comfort one expects and takes from the process. There is no one solution to the problem, but it works well to have the ALM or risk management spend actual time with the controllers, rather than submitting only their output and treating the relationship like Chinese walls. Internal control still has the duty to maintain its full independence. The top-down approach to internal control requires the following to be considered:

- The internal control function needs to reflect the bank's focus and priorities. If controlling is not given the status it needs, the outcome and effectiveness will be inadequate.
- Internal control should assess the adequacy of the bank's risk identification and assessment process.
- Policies and reporting process. The control should be twofold, firstly to review compliance with the policies and procedures and secondly to independently review the policies.
- Internal control should validate risk assumptions and the adequacy of the measurement systems. Risk control is the area where the ALM should expect to get the most appropriate feedback from their assumptions as the controlling function should be well equipped and have sufficient subject matter expertise.
- To avoid risk metrics being changed after being breached or prior to a foreseen breach, the internal controls need, amongst other things, to keep track of the historic limit setting and all changes thereof.

Endnotes

1. This is the name of a painting by the French artist Paul Gauguin. If nothing else, it should help you to remember the approach. Interestingly, Gauguin was a banker before becoming a painter.
2. Basel Committee on Banking Supervision, *Principles for Sound Liquidity Risk Management and Supervision*, September 2008, Principle 12, p. 18.

Basel III: The New Global Framework

The banking sector should by now be used to receiving orders from the centralized regulatory unit in Basel, Switzerland. For a credit risk specialist this is nothing new, as the Basel frameworks have for a long time been the cornerstone of credit and capital risk calculations and requirements. For some reason liquidity risk has not had many supporters in Basel and until Basel III came out the contribution has been limited, with the frequently mentioned 'Sound Principles' paper being the most significant exception. However, this has now changed and going forward one can expect Basel to shape liquidity management in the same way it has done with other risk factors. Basel III is therefore only the beginning.

12.1 BASEL III – BEYOND THE BUZZWORDS

Banks have been trying to get to grips with the impact of orders from Basel and Basel III is no exception. Its content around liquidity risk measurement might by now not be that alien to risk managers and they should know in broad terms what they are up against. Its overall impact on liquidity risk monitoring and the reporting framework is less clear, as well as how the new regulatory framework will filter into each jurisdiction and shape global best practice. Without going into much history, the following is useful to know.

12.1.1 The Basel Committee on Banking Supervision (BCBS)

The Basel Committee on Banking Supervision (BCBS) or the Basel Committee develops and sets the international minimum standards for prudential regulation of banks. With the overall purpose of enhancing financial stability the Basel Committee works towards strengthening practices of both banks and supervisors. It is based at the headquarters of the Bank for International Settlements (BIS) in Basel, Switzerland, and has 27 member countries. Its recommendations are not only applicable to banks in Europe but to all of its member states. Until 2013, when the single rulebook was introduced to implement Basel III, it was up to each of the countries to adopt its directives into their own legal framework.

12.1.2 Short Summary of the Regulatory Framework Leading up to Basel III

The minimum standards developed by the BCBS have been named after the place of origin and called Basel I, Basel II and now Basel III. They can be viewed as a work in progress as the standards continue to develop over time and, more often than one would like, as a response to the most recent risk outbreak.

Basel I: The first Basel accord, *The International Convergence of Capital Measurements and Capital Standards*, came out in 1988 and published a set of minimum capital requirements for banks, which was adopted into local legislation by the G-10 countries in 1992 and has since been adopted in principle in various

Table 12.1   The Basel II model

Pillar I, Regulatory Capital Requirement	Pillar II, Supervisory Review	Pillar III, Market Disclosure
Pillar I sets out a capital requirement for three major types of risk: – Credit Risk – Operational Risk – Market Risk	Pillar II introduced the Internal Capital Adequacy Assessment Process (ICAAP), which is a method of taking risk factors like systemic risk, pension risk, concentration risk, strategic risk, reputational risk and liquidity risk into account when assessing the capital needs	To support Pillars I and II, Basel II includes a disclosure requirement for market participants to be able to review the capital adequacy of a bank

                countries. Its primary focus was on credit risk and risk weighting of assets, being able to create an approach for a minimum capital requirement.

Basel II: Basel II, which first came out in 2004, is the model banks have applied and was set to revise the capital adequacy standards and further enhance and converge the risk approach introduced in Basel I. It is based on a three pillar concept: minimum capital requirements (based on risk), supervisory review and market discipline (see Table 12.1).

Basel II has been enhanced over the years, with the latest version requiring banks to hold greater capital against the market risks they run in their trading operations, which is called Basel 2.5.

12.1.3   Basel III

The financial crises revealed the shortcomings of the regulatory framework in various countries and triggered a major shift in emphasis towards liquidity risk. The fact that crises arising in one market within one country managed to cripple banking systems in various other countries, leaving almost no one untouched, demonstrated that there were underlying systemic problems at play that needed regulatory attention. Almost immediately regulatory bodies started working on improved requirements, as can be seen in the examples in Figure 12.1.

Needless to say, most of the pressure was on the BCBS, where Basel II did not address properly the quantity and quality of capital and liquidity in periods of stress. Following a review, the BCBS responded in December 2010, with *Basel III: A Global Regulatory Framework for More Resilient Banks and Banking Systems* and *Basel III: International Framework for Liquidity Risk Measurement, Standards and Monitoring,* which presented the liquidity portion of the reforms. After amendments and consultation the latter became the final document called *Basel III: The Liquidity Coverage Ratio and Liquidity Monitoring Tools,* issued in January 2013.

The following are the new risk measurements proposed in Basel III:

- Capital reforms. Both the quality and level of capital are raised with a much greater focus on common equity to absorb losses.
- Increased risk coverage by amending requirements for counterparty credit risk, securitizations and trading book.

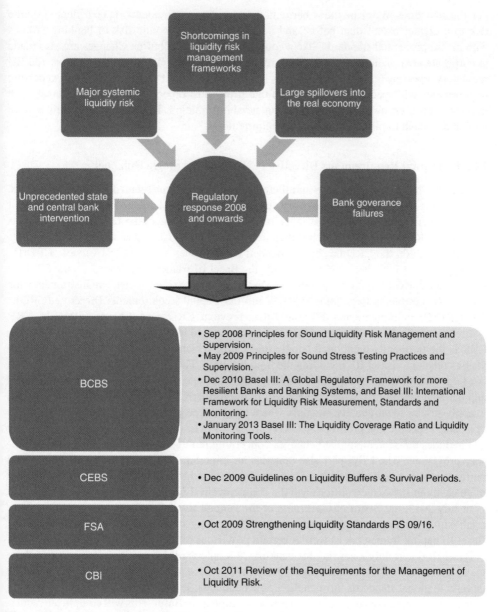

Figure 12.1   Recent enhancement of regulatory frameworks

- Introduction of two new liquidity ratios (i.e. the liquidity coverage ratio and the net stable funding ratio).
- Reducing pro-cyclical incidents by introducing both a conservation and countercyclical capital buffer.
- Supplementing the risk-based capital requirements with a leverage ratio.

For the first time, Basel includes harmonized liquidity requirements. It considers systemic risk to a greater extent than before and addresses macroeconomic risk of banking failures with macro prudential standards, like a countercyclical capital buffer. Changes are also made to corporate governance rules, including remuneration, and a much needed standardized EU regulatory reporting is introduced – usually referred to as COREP and FINREP. These reporting requirements will specify the information that firms must report to supervisors in areas such as large exposures, own funds and other financial information. This signals in general a more unified approach to minimum regulatory requirements.

12.1.4 Capital Requirements Directive (CRD) and the Single Rulebook

The Basel directives are not laws and therefore need to be implemented by local legislators. The way for the European supervisory framework to be implemented within the states of the European Union is via the issuance of a legislative package, the Capital Requirements Directive (CRD) by the EU, which is then transposed into legislation at a local level. Since its inception in 2006 the CRD has been amended several times and the latest version, CRD IV, was approved in June 2013 and implements the Basel III framework. From 1 January 2014 it replaces the current Capital Requirements Directives with two new legislative instruments: the Capital Requirements Regulation (CRR)[1] and the Capital Requirements Directive (CRD).[2] The CRD IV is implemented differently than previous CRDs and the part within the CRR is directly applicable in Europe without being transposed into local legislations or rules. The CRR is the frequently mentioned 'single rule' book, which contains the majority of the provisions related to Basel III, including the liquidity ratio. This uniform application of Basel III is a large change in the competitive banking landscape and should close regulatory loopholes and national discretions, which were a part of the former CRD. It only allows member states to apply stricter requirements, and only where these can be justified by national circumstances or a bank's specific risk profile. The CRD part must still be implemented through national law and includes the aforementioned changes concerning remuneration, governance and supervisory provisions. The CRD part also contains an important addition in Basel III, the capital buffer requirements, both the capital conservation buffer that will enable firms to absorb losses more easily in stressed conditions and the countercyclical capital buffer.

In July 2013, the Board of Governors of the Federal Reserve System approved final rules establishing the new capital framework for US banking organizations that implements the Basel III capital framework as well as certain provisions of the Dodd–Frank act.

Basel III is certainly a new era for banking. Not only are there new requirements to adhere to, which can always cause challenges, but firms also have to become accustomed to adhering directly to global standards through the single handbook. It is therefore not enough to comply with the local regulators but also the directives coming from Basel. This will complicate regulatory compliance issues as local reporting and risk frameworks are in many cases quite different from the Basel III ones and banks need to satisfy both. The single rulebook can also be a challenge for countries with less developed banking systems and regulations, which have relied heavily on the national discretions. The implementation phase of some of the requirements reflects the reality that the banking systems are not all as strong or as tightly regulated.

This single rulebook is also creating some unexpected challenges. The details of the new liquidity ratios have become clearer over time and banks have had a considerable time to adjust themselves to the main concepts. However, the final details (for the LCR) were only known in January 2013 and approved six months prior to the effective date (January 2014). Furthermore, the technical standards and templates will continue to be worked on until Basel III goes live.

What banks have been realizing is how different the Basel definitions can be to their local and internal regime. The single rulebook has, for example, its own definition of what 'stable' deposits are, which might be very different to what banks and even jurisdictions have been applying. Banks therefore need to decide if they want to preserve their own methodology and have a different set of definitions for Basel III reporting, or if they want to adopt the definitions from Switzerland and change their internal regime. This is not only a liquidity management question but is also one in which system constraints play a big part in finding the appropriate solution.

12.2   THE BASEL III LIQUIDITY RATIOS

Basel III introduces two liquidity ratios, the liquidity coverage ratio (LCR) and the net stable funding ratio (NSFR). It also brings in new liquidity buffer concepts. The ratios reflect the sentiments and main regulatory concerns from the period when they were invented. The ratios were first published in 2010 in the *Basel III: International Framework for Liquidity Risk Measurement, Standards and Monitoring* in an attempt to come up with requirements that could prevent the crises from repeating themselves.[3] Consequently, the overarching aim is to reduce the reliance on short-term wholesale market funding, thus increasing the focus on relationship-based retail deposit funding.

The ratios need to be given the credit they deserve. If followed, they will develop a more 'resilient banking sector', which is their stated purpose. The liquidity coverage ratio is a very useful tool, requiring the bank to maintain enough liquidity to survive 30 days of stress. That is certainly something very appropriate for a bank to maintain and is difficult to contradict. By the same token, the concept of a requirement to maintain a stable funding profile cannot be easily rejected.

However, like any other single dimension measurement, they do not fix everything and even though they are the only standardized requirement available, they should not become the only tool in the box. The people at the BCBS are mere mortals and the outcome of the ratios is highly determined on the outflow assumptions, which are also set by the BCBS. Do not assume that just by complying to the ratios the bank's liquidity affairs are in good order.

Banks will generally have a greater problem complying with the NSFR than the LCR, should the former go ahead in its proposed form. The delays in defining the LCR and in setting out the implementation schedule show that already the sentiment is changing and liquidity is no longer the only measurement prevailing. The decision to delay the NSFR's implementation shows that not all member countries are willing to go so far in standardizing liquidity measurements. Therefore, judging from the changes the LCR took during its consultation stage and the long time it took to implement, which was longer than expected, and furthermore taking into consideration how far many banks are from conforming to the NSFR criteria, it is certain that the NSFR will change considerably from the current proposal and implementation will be further delayed. Therefore the focus will be more on the LCR.

The major concerns and resistance from the banking community for the calculation of the LCR was around what assets were eligible as a buffer, but there are other pros and cons to consider for the ratios:

- The introduction of a global liquidity standard is a great step forward. This can benefit banks as well as increasing the overall systemic stability. We have gone through the period where idiosyncratic liquidity risk easily transposed itself into a market-wide crisis and harmonized transparent measurements, which when reported in a uniform way will decrease the asymmetric information in the market place, making contagion less likely.

- These are both specific parameters, one concerning the ability of the bank to survive 30 days and the other mainly giving credit to funding greater than 1 year. They are a one-size-fits-all measurement, with all its advantages and shortcomings and were not intended to be a sufficient measure of all aspects of the liquidity risk. They should therefore not be used to replace many other measurements or give the notion that certain other (especially qualitative) measurements are not needed.
- The specific nature of the ratios can encourage the wrong behaviour by banks in an attempt to fulfil their requirements. As an example, the stable funding ratio gives strong preference to funding greater than 1 year. This could lead to banks chasing longer-dated but very unstable deposits to meet the requirement. The same applies to the LCR, where the tendency could be to extend transactions only up to 31 days so as not to be included in the ratio.
- Retail deposits and especially insured retail deposits are favoured as they are stable. This will increase the demand and cost for those deposits.
- Wholesale deposits are not as well defined as retail deposits and generally considered of little quality, which might not always be the case and hence may encourage the wrong behaviour.
- In some instances, the ratios might be too severely set and by solving one problem (liquidity risk) they may create another problem, preventing banks from fulfilling their role providing sufficient lending for economic growth or adequate profitability. This has been partly dealt with by the phase-in schedule and extension of eligible criteria for the HQLA.

In addition to introducing the two ratios, Basel III sets out additional monitoring metrics (called monitoring tools), which are the minimum information banks need to report to their supervisor. These metrics are used to capture specific information on cash flows, balance sheet structure and other indicators and are covered in Chapter 9, The Quantitative Framework.

12.3   THE LIQUIDITY COVERAGE RATIO (LCR)

The rules for the LCR were announced in January 2013 and became a part of the single rulebook in June that year. All Basel member states will have to follow the definitions and honour the timeframe. The minimum ratio will be phased in from 2015, starting at 60% and increasing by 10 percentage points each year until reaching 100% in January 2018. These are minimum requirements and at least one local supervisor has indicated they will start off at a higher glide-path.

In short, the objective of the LCR is to enable 'short-term resilience of the liquidity risk profile of banks'. The standard does that by requiring banks to maintain an adequate level of unencumbered, high-quality liquid assets that can be converted into cash to meet liquidity needs for 30 calendar days under significantly severe liquidity stress scenarios.

The LCR has two components, the value of the HQLAs and the total net cash outflows:

$$LCR = \frac{\text{Stock of high} - \text{quality liquid assets}}{\text{Total net cash outflow over the next 30 calendar days}} \geq 100\%$$

The definitions and calculation methods for both components are standardized and set by the CRR, including the minimum run-off rates for the deposits. The ratio is therefore a simple calculation of the amount of coverage the liquidity buffer provides against net outflows. The only caveat in the calculation is that expected cash inflows used in the calculations are capped at 75% of the total expected cash outflows. This is expressed as

Total net cash outflows over the next 30 calendar days

= Total expected cash outflows

− Minimum (total expected cash inflows; 75% of total expected outflows)

Though the calculations are simple, the definition of what assets are eligible as the HQLA and their separation into Levels I and II is quite detailed and best followed directly from the CRR. The BCBS decision on what assets can and cannot be included and their appropriate haircuts can be debated and criticized and will surely change over time. For the risk experts the main concerns should be to maintain a liquidity buffer that can withstand all the impacts of a market-wide 'flight to quality'. The 'flight to quality' has many faces and it is very difficult to pick a permanent criterion for collateral that will weather a market storm. The simple answer used to be to buy government bonds, but we have recently seen that they were not proven to be the safe haven they were expected to be. Accepting the uncertainty of the market, the risk manager therefore looks for adequate diversification when building a buffer, paying attention to the correlation between the assets and the bank itself.

As the formula above demonstrates, the ratio is to ensure that sufficient liquid assets are available to meet outflows over a 30 day period of stress. It is useful to summarize what the 30 day scenario consists of in order to measure it against the bank's own severity assumption. Moreover, they specify many of the shocks experienced during the financial crises and as such are a useful minimum benchmark. The stress entails a combined idiosyncratic and market-wide shock which results in:

- Run-off of the proportion of retail deposits, determined by their stability, which in turn pays great attention to the deposit guarantee schemes (DGSs).
- Loss of some wholesale unsecured funding (greater run-off rates than for retail, see above).
- A partial loss of secured, short-term funding.
- Up to a three-notch downgrade, impacting collateral requirements and other additional contractual outflows.
- Increased market volatility resulting in greater collateral haircuts and additional collateral needs.
- Unscheduled drawdowns on committed but unused credit and liquidity facilities the bank has provided.
- A potential need for the bank to participate in contractual buy-backs to mitigate reputational risk.

The aim is therefore to have the buffer covering the predefined 30 days of net outflows. The tendency is to look at the LCR as some 'buckle your seatbelt' safety precaution. However, the LCR can be put to far better use. Rather than taking the level of risk as a given quantity and trying to mitigate it, the LCR should be used to review and even reduce the quantity of risk taken. The requirement (the denominator of the LCR) gives the risk quantum. It is useful to analyse the largest contributing factors, not only in isolation but also jointly as a gap mismatch, and question whether the risk can be reduced rather than increasing the buffer. The bank should go through the liabilities as there will likely be transactions (especially within the treasury) that fall within the 30 day horizon but could as easily be extended in duration so as not to impact the LCR. This has to be done, keeping the spirit of the regulation in mind and honouring its principles. Actions like extending short-dated liabilities out to day 31 are not an example of prudent liquidity management and in the spirit of the regulation.

12.3.1   Challenges the LCR will Bring to the Liquidity Framework

Basel III may have a bigger impact on the liquidity management framework than many expected, which has only become clear now that the reporting has been defined. The CRR and the consequent technical details and specifications set out by the EBA (European Banking Authority) show that the definitions of what to put into the LCR are both detailed and, more importantly, prescriptive. This might not come as a surprise as the LCR is supposed to be a standardized requirement. However, this will require banks to start thinking along the lines of Basel and either have a separate set of definitions for the Basel III reporting or adjust their own framework to match that of the Basel III framework.

Basel III, through the LCR, has its own definitions of what are 'stable' and 'less stable' deposits. These definitions are unlikely to match or mirror the current framework many banks have, even though many European countries have taken steps towards this standardization, but a bigger task awaits banks in other jurisdictions, if they agree at all to align themselves to Basel.

Liquidity risk is focused on the stability of deposits and hence the task for the risk manager is to assess if the descriptive Basel III framework can replace the bank's own definitions or if the two methods can be run simultaneously. Things to consider:

Adopting the Basel III definitions

+   It can be of benefit for a firm to state that it uses a standardized, globally recognized set of definitions that are known and easy to understand for all stakeholders.
−   The one-size-fits-all model and definitions might not be well suited to all banks and even misrepresent its liquidity risk profile.

Operating two parallel frameworks

+   There are strong arguments for using a tailor-made methodology and definitions, if they are the result of a suitable firm-specific assessment. An internally made model is made by those who best know the bank and is based around the specifics of the bank and even the country.
−   Confusion. It can become complicated and difficult to use and communicate to stakeholders if many definitions of the same thing are being used.
−   It is likely that the local regulators will change their reporting requirements (definitions) to match that of Basel III, increasing the influence and footprint of Basel III.
−   Cost issues.

So what should be done? The risk manager needs to perform a comparison or gap analysis between the internal definitions and the Basel III definitions. If there are not great contradictions between the two, an amendment to the internal model can be suggested so that it complies with Basel III. Banks that do not use categories like 'stable' in their own stress testing and liability analysis can build a mapping framework to link their categories with those of Basel III. It should be noted that in some instances banks cannot simply switch from one regime to another as local regulatory frameworks are still not in line with Basel III. A practical example would be how the HQLAs are defined. Basel III has its own definitions, now including covered bonds and a wider set of securities, whereas some regulators do not consider corporate bonds and covered bonds to be eligible.

12.3.2   The Basel III Definitions and Stress Assumptions

The Basel III reporting and definition methodology are set out in the CRR and supported by technical standards issued by the EBA. The CRR requires the EBA to develop Implementing Technical Standards (ITS) on the reporting of liquidity coverage and stable funding in addition to what is said in the actual text of the CRR law. The EBA has published a framework that will '*ensure that the CRD IV framework achieves its operational objective of developing an appropriately explicit and harmonised EU level regime for management of liquidity risk. The ITS will determine uniform templates and instructions on how to use them, the frequency of and dates for reporting as well as IT solutions for the purposes of liquidity reporting requirements.*'[4]

Figure 12.2 is an adaptation of the LCR common disclosure template, which is a summary of the more detailed EBA LCR reporting form. The perceived risk of the liabilities has been added to the table using the prescriptive run-off rates set out in the CRR. Note the clear distinction between retail and corporate liabilities.

The main features of the Basel III liquidity reporting methodology can be summarized as follows:

– The Basel III framework gives a lot of weight to the influence that the deposit guarantee schemes (DGSs) can have on deposit stability. Article 421 in the CRR states:

> *1. Institutions shall separately report the amount of retail deposits covered by a Deposit Guarantee Scheme in accordance with Directive 94/19/EC or an equivalent deposit guarantee scheme in a third country, and multiply by at least 5% where the deposit is either of the following:*
> *(a) part of an established relationship making withdrawal highly unlikely;*
> *(b) held in a transactional account, including accounts to which salaries are regularly credited.*
> *2. Institutions shall multiply other retail deposits not referred to in paragraph 1 by at least 10%.*

– Is this emphasis on the DGSs appropriate or not? In Europe, this is certainly the case; the DGSs have been widely discussed and their function and existence explained to the public. Banks also refer to the DGSs in the offers and communication with clients. It is, however, fair to say that prior to 2008, this statement was not as true. We will probably not witness queues again like the ones in front of Northern Rock in 2007. However, this is not universally true (which is recognized by Basel) and banks operating in countries where the DGS is weak or little known cannot build their risk framework around the deposit guarantee mechanism.

– Basel III does have its own definition of retail, which includes SME deposits below the threshold of €1m. The definition from the CRR is:

> *. . . 'retail deposit' means a liability to a natural person or to an SME, where the natural person or the SME would qualify for the retail exposure class under the Standardised or IRB approaches for credit risk, or a liability to a company which is eligible for the treatment set out in Article 153(4) and where the aggregate deposits by all such enterprises on a group basis do not exceed EUR 1 million.*[5]

	TOTAL UNWEIGHTED VALUE	TOTAL WEIGHTED VALUE	
	Average	Average	Perceived Risk
HIGH-QUALITY LIQUID ASSETS			
1 Total high-quality liquid assets			
CASH OUTFLOWS			
2 Retail deposits and deposits from small business customers, of which			
3 Stable deposits (insured)			**Very low**
4 Less stable deposits (un insured)			**Low**
5 Unsecured wholesale funding, of which			
6 Operational deposits (all counterparties) and deposits in institutional networks of cooperative banks			**MEDIUM**
7 Nonoperational deposits (all counterparties)			**MED/HIGH**
8 Unsecured debt			**HIGH**
9 Secured wholesale funding			
10 Additional requirements, of which			
11 Outflows related to derivatives exposures and other collateral requirements			
12 Outflows related to loss of funding on debt products			
13 Credit and liquidity facilities			
14 Other contractual funding obligations			
15 Other contingent funding obligations			
16 TOTAL CASH OUTFLOWS			
CASH INFLOWS			
17 Secured lending (e.g. reverse repos)			
18 Inflows from fully performing exposures			
19 Other cash inflows			
20 TOTAL CASH INFLOWS			
		TOTAL ADJUSTED VALUE	
21 TOTAL HQLA			
22 TOTAL NET CASH OUTFLOWS			
23 LIQUIDITY COVERAGE RATIO (%)			

Figure 12.2 LCR disclosure

- Banks that want to adapt the methodology for their internal purposes need to assess whether this is applicable to their groups of depositors or if it is still more appropriate to segregate retail into individuals and SMEs. The question is also whether the €1m threshold is the appropriate decision factor on the client's behaviour for their own best practice.
- The focus on the importance of the DGS also makes the Basel III framework view retail deposit as being far more stable than corporate deposits (i.e. corporates that are not SMEs). The 30 day minimum run-off rate for the standard retail is 5–10%, whereas wholesale deposits have either 25% or 40% run-off rates.
- There is a caveat to the prescriptive treatment of retail deposits. CCR 421(3) mandates the EBA to set prescriptive standards for retail deposits subject to different and higher outflows than the 5% and 10% categories. Into these categories fall deposits deemed to be 'high risk' and 'very high risk', where deposit sourcing channels and size are two of the determining factors. These categories are expected to receive run-off rates above those provided for the minima (5% and 10%). Banks can set the run-off rates but the criteria for what constitute a 'high risk' and 'very high risk' deposit are mostly prescriptive.[6]
- Apart from the SME's deposits, the framework categorizes corporate deposits on their attributes of being 'operational' or 'nonoperational'. This criterion for being operational is rather narrow, where a client must have a substantive dependency on the bank where deposits are required for certain activities (i.e. clearing, custody or cash management activities).

What the risk specialist should be reading from the template is the classification Basel III sets out for liabilities and the question as to whether they are appropriate for internal purposes. The absolute run-off rates need to be understood in relation to the time period to which they apply, i.e. 30 days. They do, however, give some guidance on the relative value the Basel Committee puts on each category. Over the period of 30 days operational corporate deposits are viewed as five times more likely to flow out than insured retail deposits.

To summarize:

- If the bank is using a 'stable/less stable' approach categorization in its risk methodology, it needs to assess whether a deposit protection is the most significant driver to determine the stability of deposits. This should encompass a view on the bank and the overall market.
- Consideration needs to be given to whether SMEs should be treated in the same way as retail enterprises.
- The bank needs to assess whether the classification into operational and nonoperational corporate deposits is applicable to the bank.
- The liquidity requirement coming from the 30 day outflows should be analysed to understand whether some of the mismatch factors are too large or can be easily amended, decreasing the overall liquidity requirement and liquidity risk.

12.3.3   LCR Common Disclosure Template

The BCBS has come out with a common disclosure template, which is intended to improve transparency and strengthen market discipline.[7] They are to be applied to all internationally active banks on a consolidated level and must be either included in banks' published financial reports or the financial reports must provide a link to where the LCR results can be found. The proposed template is a good way for all banks to express the LCR results (see Figure 12.3).

(local currency) (1)	TOTAL UNWEIGHTED VALUE Average (2)	TOTAL WEIGHTED VALUE Average (3)
HIGH-QUALITY LIQUID ASSETS		
1 **Total high-quality liquid assets**		
CASH OUTFLOWS		
2 **Retail deposits and deposits from small business customers, of which**		
3 Stable deposits		
4 Less stable deposits		
5 **Unsecured wholesale funding, of which**		
6 Operational deposits (all counterparties) and deposits in institutional networks of cooperative banks		
7 Nonoperational deposits (all counterparties)		
8 Unsecured debt		
9 **Secured wholesale funding**		
10 **Additional requirements, of which**		
11 Outflows related to derivatives exposures and other collateral requirements		
12 Outflows related to loss of funding on debt products		
13 Credit and liquidity facilities		
14 **Other contractual funding obligations**		
15 **Other contingent funding obligations**		
16 **TOTAL CASH OUTFLOWS**		
CASH INFLOWS		
17 **Secured lending (e.g. reverse repos)**		
18 **Inflows from fully performing exposures**		
19 **Other cash inflows**		
20 **TOTAL CASH INFLOWS**		
		TOTAL ADJUSTED VALUE
21 **TOTAL HQLA**		
22 **TOTAL NET CASH OUTFLOWS**		
23 **LIQUIDITY COVERAGE RATIO (%)**		

Figure 12.3 The proposed LCR template

This is a good template to use for all banks on reporting the LCR internally and will allow bankers to compare results to those of peers. Banks are required to report the LCR monthly and be able to provide weekly or even daily calculations if requested by the regulators.

12.4   THE NET STABLE FUNDING RATIO (NSFR)

The main objective of the NSFR is to promote resilience over a longer time horizon by requiring financial institutions to maintain a sound funding profile. This is to mitigate the risk of a large asset–liability mismatch, which, as discussed earlier, is the foundation of liquidity risk. This is done by requiring long-term assets to be funded with stable (or long-term) liabilities. Consequently, the reliance on short-term wholesale funding is mitigated. The difference between the LCR and NSFR should be clear. The LCR is a minimum liquidity buffer requirement whereas the NSFR is a requirement to operate and maintain a prudent funding structure and addresses the problem with the asset–liability gap.

The NSFR ratio was introduced in 2010 and was scheduled to move to a minimum standard by January 2018. In the CRR the NSFR general requirements were deferred until January 2016, which makes is unlikely they will manage to become a standard by 2018.

The NSFR is destined for a difficult childhood. On the face of it, requiring banks to maintain a sustainable maturity structure of assets and liabilities seems like a reasonable request, which will lead to an increased systemic stability. It is, however, difficult to apply. The ratio's objective, to curtail maturity transformation of the banking sector, can also have a negative impact on the real economy. The maturity transformation is the heart of the banking business model and a simple dimensional metric cannot capture all the underlying factors. Even though the idea is a good one, applying a single measurement to multidimensional and complicated operations can create outliers and strange outcomes that go against the ratio's objectives. Defining one set of rules might prevent banks from becoming too similar to each other but actually increase systemic risk when certain market instruments such as securitizations become less viable. A lot has been written about the details and pitfalls of the NSFR and how difficult it will become for many banks to comply with this overarching rule. We can therefore expect the final NSFR to be materially different from the current version and its timing of introduction depends on how well it is being received.

The NSFR ratio can be expressed as

$$\text{NSFR} = \frac{\text{Available stable funding}}{\text{Required stable funding}} \geq 100\%$$

The reporting frequency for the NSFR will be at least quarterly.

Even though the NSFR ratio is set to measure long-term liabilities versus long-term assets, both defined as being greater than 1 year, it realizes that maturity alone does not guarantee stability. It has therefore allowed short-dated liabilities to be included in the measurement as long as they can be deemed 'stable'. This underscores the fact that regulators are more concerned about the stability of deposits rather than their maturity. Banks can therefore include retail and SME deposits in the ratio as stable funding even though they are on-demand. The BCBS has issued rules on the weighting of these deposits, which are between 80% and 90% depending on their source and maturity. Figure 12.4 shows the largest components of the NSFR ratio and we can see that it has much in common with the balance sheet ratio discussed in Chapter 9, Step IV.

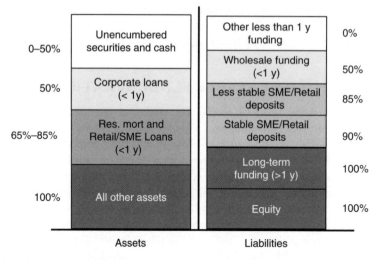

Figure 12.4   NSFR and the RSF and ASF

It terms of the asset side (the stable funding requirement), most assets require some stable funding. How much they require depends on their liquidity and maturity, where listed assets and shorter-dated assets only need to be partly covered with stable funding, but assets with greater than 1 year to maturity need to be fully covered. This requirement is called an RSF (required stable funding) requirement. Likewise, all liabilities are assigned an ASF (available stable funding) ratio depending on their stability and tenor.

The EBA has been mandated to recommend the methodologies for calculating the NSFR by December 2015 and has been asked to analyse the impact of stable sources of funding on the refinancing structures of different banking models. It is therefore not possible at this point to provide much guidance for banks on how to meet the requirements.

Endnotes

1. Regulation (EU) No. 575/2013 of the European Parliament and of the Council on prudential require-ments for credit institutions and investment firms. Available at: www.eur-lex.europa.eu.
2. Directive 2013/36/EU of the European Parliament and of the Council on the access to the activity of credit institutions and the prudential supervision of credit institutions and investment firms.
3. Basel Committee on Banking Supervision, *Basel III: International Framework for Liquidity Risk Measurement, Standards and Monitoring*, December 2010.
4. European Banking Authority (EBA), EBA FINAL draft Implementing Technical Standards on super-visory reporting under Regulation (EU) No. 575/2013, July 2013.
5. Regulation (EU) No. 575/2013 of the European Parliament and of the Council on prudential require-ments for credit institutions and investment firms, Article 411. Available at: www.eur-lex.europa.eu.
6. See European Banking Authority (EBA), *Consultation Paper on Draft Guidelines on Retail Deposits Subject to Different Outflows for Purposes of Liquidity Reporting under Regulation (EU) No. 575/2013 (Capital Requirements Regulation – CRR)*, p. 17, August 2013.
7. Basel Committee on Banking Supervision, *Consultative Document, Liquidity Coverage Ratio Dis-closure Standards*, July 2013.

Bibliography

Accenture (2012) *Basel III Handbook*, Accenture. Available at: www.accenture.com.

Acharya, V. (2009) A Theory of Systemic Risk and Design of Prudential Bank Regulation, *Journal of Financial Stability*, **5**, 224–255.

Adrian, T. and Shin, H. (2008) Liquidity and Financial Contagion, *Banque de France, Financial Stability Review – Special Issue on Liquidity*, No. 11, February 2008, pp. 1–7.

Adrian, T. and Shin, H. (2009) *Money, Liquidity, and Monetary Policy*, Federal Reserve Bank of New York, Staff Report No. 360, January 2009.

Adrian, T. and Shin, H. (2010) *Liquidity and Leverage*, Federal Reserve Bank of New York, Staff Report No. 328, December 2010.

Akerlof, G. (1970) The Market for 'Lemons': Quality Uncertainty and the Market Mechanism, *The Quarterly Journal of Economics*, **84** (3), August 1970, 488–500.

Allen, F. and Santomero, A. (1998) The Theory of Financial Intermediation, *Journal of Banking and Finance*, **21**, 1461–1485.

Allen, F. and Santomero, A. (2001) What Do Financial Intermediaries Do? *Journal of Banking and Finance*, **25**, 271–294.

Asian Development Bank, *Risk Management and Asset and Liability Management in Banks*, Technical Assistance Consultant's Report (date not disclosed).

Australian Prudential Regulation Authority (APRA) (2013) *Draft Prudential Practice Guide, APG 210 – Liquidity*, May 2013.

Australian Prudential Regulation Authority (APRA) (2013) *Implementing Basel III Liquidity Reforms in Australia*, May 2013.

Bagehot, W. (1873) *Lombard Street: A Description of the Money Market*, Henry S. King & Co., London. Available at: www.gutenberg.org.

Barclays PLC Annual Report 2012. Available at: www.group.barclays.com

Basel Committee for Banking Supervision (2000) *Sound Practices for Managing Liquidity in Banking Organisations*, February 2000.

Basel Committee on Banking Supervision (2001) *A Survey of Stress Tests and Current Practice at Major Financial Institutions*, April 2001.

Basel Committee on Banking Supervision (2004) *Principles for the Management and Supervision of Interest Rate Risk*, July 2004.

Basel Committee on Banking Supervision (2006) *The Management of Liquidity Risk in Financial Groups*, May 2006.

Basel Committee on Banking Supervision (2008) *Liquidity Risk: Management and Supervisory Challenges*, February 2008.

Basel Committee on Banking Supervision (2008) *Principles for Sound Liquidity Risk Management and Supervision*, September 2008.

Basel Committee on Banking Supervision (2009) *International Framework for Liquidity Risk Measurement, Standards and Monitoring*, Consultative Document, Bank for International Settlements, December 2009.

Basel Committee on Banking Supervision (2009) *Principles for Sound Stress Testing Practices and Supervision*, May 2009.

Basel Committee on Banking Supervision (2010) *Basel III: International Framework for Liquidity Risk Measurement, Standards and Monitoring*, December 2010.

Basel Committee on Banking Supervision (2012) *Monitoring Indicators for Intraday Liquidity Management*, Consultative Document, July 2012.

Basel Committee on Banking Supervision (2013) *Basel III: The Liquidity Coverage Ratio and Liquidity Risk Monitoring Tools*, January 2013.

Basel Committee on Banking Supervision (2013) *Instructions for Basel III Monitoring*, February 2013.

Basel Committee on Banking Supervision (2013) *Liquidity Coverage Ratio Disclosure Standards*, Consultative Document, July 2013.

Bessis, J. (2002) *Risk Management in Banking*, 2nd edition, John Wiley & Sons, Ltd.

Blundell-Wignall, A. and Atkinson, P. (2008) *The Sub-prime Crisis: Causal Distortions and Regulatory Reform*, July 2008. Available at: www.rba.gov.au.

Brunnermeier, M. (2009) Deciphering the Liquidity and Credit Crunch 2007–2008, *Journal of Economic Perspectives*, **23**(1), Winter 2009, 77–100.

Brunnermeier, M. (2009) *Financial Crises: Mechanisms, Prevention, and Management*, Draft 1. Available at: www.lse.ac.uk.

Brunnermeier, M. (2010) *Thoughts on a New Financial Architecture*, Princeton University. Available at: www.princeton.edu.

Brunnermeier, M. and Pedersen, L. (2007) *Market Liquidity and Funding Liquidity*, National Bureau of Economic Research, Working Paper Series, Working Paper 12939, February 2007.

Castagna, A. and Fede, F. (2013) *Measuring and Managing Liquidity Risk*, John Wiley & Sons, Ltd, June 2013.

Central Bank of Ireland (2010) *Review of the Requirements for the Management of Liquidity Risk*, October 2011.

Chen, W. (2012) *Funding Liquidity Risk: From Measurement to Management*, GARP Taipei Chapter Meeting, June 2012.

Chiodo, A. and Owyang, M. (2002) A Case Study of a Currency Crisis: The Russian Default of 1998, *Federal Reserve Bank of St Louis Review*, **84** (6), November 2002.

Choudhry, M. (2010) *Impact of the Financial Crisis on Bank ALM and Liquidity Risk Management*, PRMIA–Thomson Reuters Markets Academy, Singapore, 9 April 2010.

Choudhry, M. (2007) *Bank Asset and Liability Management: Strategy, Trading, Analysis*, John Wiley & Sons, Ltd.

Cœuré, B. (2012) Global Liquidity and Risk Appetite: A Re-interpretation of the Recent Crises, Speech by Benoît Cœuré, Member of the Executive Board of the ECB, at the BIS–ECB Workshop on *Global Liquidity and Its International Repercussions*, Frankfurt am Main, 6 February 2012.

Committee of European Banking Supervisors (CEBS) (2009) *Guidelines on Liquidity Buffers and Survival Periods*, December 2009.

Committee of European Banking Supervisors (CEBS) (2010) *Guidelines on Liquidity Cost Benefit Allocation*, October 2010.

Committee on the Global Financial System (CGFS) (2001) *A Survey of Stress Tests and Current Practice at Major Financial Institutions*, Bank for International Settlements, April 2001.

Committee on the Global Financial System (CGFS) (2005) *Stress Testing at Major Financial Institutions: Survey Results and Practice*, Bank for International Settlements, January 2005.

Committee on the Global Financial System (CGFS) (2010) *Funding Patterns and Liquidity Management of Internationally Active Banks*, CGFS Papers No. 39, Bank for International Settlements, May 2010.

Committee on the Global Financial System (CGFS) (2010) *CEBS Guidelines on Stress Testing (GL32)*, August 2010.

Comptroller's Handbook (2012) *Safety and Soundness*, Office of the Comptroller of the Currency, Washington, DC, June 2012.

Credit Risk Management Policy Group III: *Containing Systemic Risk: The Road to Reform*, August 2008.

Crockett, A. (2008) Market Liquidity and Financial Stability, *Banque de France, Financial Stability Review – Special Issue on Liquidity*, **11**, February 2008, 13–17.

Davies, H. and Green, D. (2010) *Banking on the Future, the Fall and Rise of Central Banking*, Princeton University Press.

Dermine, J. (2003) *ALM in Banking*, INSEAD, Fontainebleau, July 2003.

D'Haese, W. (2009) Liquidity Risk Management Comes in Three Loops, Presentation made at a Conference on *Liquidity Risk Management as Part of Centralized Asset and Liability Management*, Cairo, Egypt, 2009.

Diamond, D. and Dybvig, P. (1983) Bank Runs, Deposit Insurance, and Liquidity, *Journal of Political Economy*, **91** (3), 401–419.

Diamond, W. and Rajan, R. (1999) *Liquidity Risk, Liquidity Creation and Financial Fragility: A Theory of Banking*, NBER Working Paper No. 7430, December 1999.

Directive 2013/36/EU of the European Parliament and of the Council on the access to the activity of credit institutions and the prudential supervision of credit institutions and investment firms, July 2013.

Drehmann, M. and Nikolaou, K. (2009) *Funding Liquidity Risk, Definition and Measurement*, Working Paper Series No. 1024, European Central Bank, March 2009.

Eisenbeis, R. and Kaufman, G. (2009) Lessons from the Demise of the UK's Northern Rock and the US's Countrywide and Indymac, from *The Failure of Northern Rock, A Multi-dimensional Case Study*, SUERF – The European Money and Finance Forum, Vienna, 2009, pp. 73–94.

Ernst & Young, *Fund Transfer Pricing, Roadmap to Managing Pricing and Profitability for NBFCs* (undated).

Ernst & Young (2011) *Measuring and Managing Liquidity Risk, Ernst & Young's Liquidity Diagnostic Tool for Financial Services Institutions*.

European Banking Authority (EBA) (2013) *EBA Final Draft on Implementing Technical Standards on Supervisory Reporting under Regulation (EU) No. 575/2013*, July 2013.

European Banking Authority (EBA) (2013) *Draft Guidelines on Retail Deposits Subject to Different Outflows for Purposes of Liquidity Reporting under Regulation (EU) No. 575/2013 (Capital Requirements Regulation – CRR)*, Consultation Paper, August 2013.

European Central Bank (2007 and 2009) *EU Banking Sector Stability*, February 2003 and November 2007.

European Central Bank (2008) *EU Bank's Liquidity Stress Testing and Contingency Funding Plans*, November 2008.

Financial Services Authority (FSA) (2010) *Dear Treasurer: Funds Transfer Pricing*, FSA, 2010.

Financial Services Authority (FSA) (2011) *Dear CEO Letter – Asset and Liability Management*, FSA, January 2011.

Financial Services Authority (FSA) *Liquidity Reporting Workshop: Basic and Advanced Product* (undated). Available at: www.fsa.gov.uk.

Financial Stability Board (2012) *Resolution of Systemically Important Financial Institutions*, Progress Report, November 2012.

Financial Stability Forum (2008) *Report on the Financial Stability Forum on Enhancing Market and Institutional Resilience*, April 2008.

Financial Times, 10 July 2007.

Fitch (2010) *Managing Cash Capital in Banks*, London, July 2010.

Freixas, X. and Rochet, J.C. (2008) *Microeconomics of Banking*, The MIT Press, Cambridge, Mass.

Goodhart, C. (2008) Liquidity Risk Management, *Banque de France, Financial Stability Review – Special Issue on Liquidity*, **11**, February 2008, 39–44.

Goodhart, C. (2008) *The Regulatory Response to the Financial Crisis*, LSE Financial Markets Group Paper Series, Special Paper 177, February 2008.

Gorton, G. and Pennachi, G. (1990) Financial Intermediaries and Liquidity Creation, *Journal of Finance*, **45** (1), 49–72.

Grant, J. (2011) *Liquidity Transfer Pricing: A Guide to Better Practice*, Financial Stability Institute, Occasional Paper No. 10, Bank for International Settlement, December 2011.

Griffith-Jones, J. (1997) *Causes and Lessons of the Mexican Peso Crises*, Working Paper No. 132, The United Nations University, World Institute for Development Economics Research, May 1997.

Hanselman, O. (2009) Best Practices and Strategic Value of Funds Transfer Pricing, *Journal of Performance Management*, **22** (2), May 2009, 3–17.

Hervo, F. (2008) Recent Developments in Intraday Liquidity in Payment and Settlement Systems, *Banque de France, Financial Stability Review – Special Issue on Liquidity*, **11**, February 2008, 149–163.

Hornbeck, J. (2013) *Argentina's Defaulted Sovereign Debt: Dealing with the 'Holdouts'*, CRS Report for Congress, February 2013.

Institute of International Finance (IIF) (2007) *Principles of Liquidity Risk Management*, March 2007. Available at: www.iif.com.

Institute of International Finance (IIF) Committee (2008) *Market Best Practices: Principles of Conduct and Best Practice Recommendations Financial Services Industry Response to the Market Turmoil of 2007–2008*, Final Report, IIF, July 2008.

Jacobs, M. (2010) *Quantitative Measurement and Management of Liquidity Risk in a Banking Context*, Presentation to PRMIA/CIRANO Luncheon, Montreal, Quebec, November 2010.

Jensen, M. and Meckling, W. (1976) Theory of the Firm: Managerial Behaviour, Agency Costs and Ownership Structure, *Journal of Financial Economics*, **3** (4), October 1976, 305–360.

Knies, K. (1876) *Geld und Credit II, Abteilung Der Credit*, Leipzig.

KPMG (2010) *Basel 3 Pressure Is Building*, December 2010. Available at: www.kpmg.com.

Kyle, A. (1985) Continuous Auctions and Insider Trading, *Econometrica*, **53** (6), 1315–1335.

Lastra, R. (2009) Northern Rock and Banking Law Reform in the UK, in *The Failure of Northern Rock, A Multi-dimensional Case Study*, SUERF – The European Money and Finance Forum, Vienna, 2009.

Llewellyn, D. (2009) The Northern Rock Crises: A Multidimensional Problem, in *The Failure of Northern Rock: A Multi-dimensional Case Study*, SUERF – The European Money and Finance Forum, Vienna, 2009, pp. 13–34.

Lloyds Banking Group, *Annual Report and Accounts 2012*. Available at: www.lloydsbankinggroup.com.

Matz, L. (2009) *Anatomy of Liquidity Contingency Funding Plans*, ALM Summit 2009,Zürich, 11 May 2009.

Matz, L. (2011) *Liquidity Risk Measurement and Management, Basel III and Beyond*, Xlibris.

Matz, L. and Neu, P. (editors) (2007) *Liquidity Risk Measures and Management, A Practitioner's Guide to Global Best Practices*, John Wiley & Sons, Ltd.

Montes-Negret, F. (2009) *The Heavenly Liquidity Twin, The Increasing Importance of Liquidity Risk*, The World Bank Europe and Central Asia Region Finance and Private Sector Department, November 2009.

Moody's Analytics (2011) *Implementing High Value Funds Transfer Pricing Systems*, September 2011.

Moody's Investor Service (2001) *How Moody's Evaluates US Bank and Bank Holding Company Liquidity*, Global Credit Research, Moody's Investors Service, New York.

Moody's Investor Service (2011) *Banking Account and Ratio Definitions*, February 2011.

Moody's Investor Service (2012) *Moody's Consolidated Global Bank Rating Methodology*, June 2012.

Nikolaou, K. (2009) *Liquidity (Risk) Concepts, Definitions and Interactions*, European Central Bank, Working Paper Series No. 1008, February 2009.

Oesterreichische Nationalbank (2008) *Guidelines on Managing Interest Rate Risk in the Banking Book.*

Office of the Controller of the Currency (OCC) (2001) *The Challenges of Sound Liquidity Risk Management: OCC Expectations and Policy for Community Banks*, May 2001.

O'Hara, M. (1995) *Market Microstructure Theory*, Blackwell, Oxford.

Praet, P. and Herzberg, V. (2008) Market Liquidity and Banking Liquidity: Linkages, Vulnerabilities and the Role of Disclosure, *Banque de France, Financial Stability Review – Special Issue on Liquidity*, **11**, February 2008, 95–111.

Prudential Regulation Authority (PRA) *Prudential Sourcebook for Banks, Building Societies and Investment Firm (BIPRU)* (undated). Available at: www.fsa.gov.uk.

PWC (2009) *Balance Sheet Management Benchmark Survey, Status of Balance Sheet Management Practices among International Banks – 2009.*

PWC (2009) *Stress Testing Liquidity and the Contingency Funding Plan*, PRMIA Members' Meeting, February 2009. Available at: www.pwc.com.

PWC (2010) Liquidity Risk Management Staying Afloat in Choppy Seas, *The Journal*, April 2010. Available at: www.pwc.com.

PWC (2013) *Basel III Liquidity Regime – More Practical but Not Yet Workable*, FS Regulatory Brief, January 2013. Available at: www.pwcregulatory.com.

PWC, Risk Appetite – How Hungry Are You?, *The Journal*, Special Risk Management Edition (date not disclosed). Available at: www.pwc.com.

Raffis, L.D. (2007) The Net Cash Capital Tool in Bank Liquidity Management, in *Liquidity Risk Measurement and Management*, John Wiley & Sons, Singapore.

Rajan, R. (2010) *Fault Lines, How Hidden Fractures Still Threaten the World Economy*, Princeton University Press.

Regulation (EU) No. 575/2013 of the European Parliament and of the Council on prudential requirements for credit institutions and investment firms. Available at: www.eur-lex.europa.eu.

Rice, J. and Kocakulah, M. (2009) Funds Transfer Pricing: A Management Accounting Approach within the Banking Industry, *Journal of Performance Management*, **22** (2), May 2009, 17–26.

Rochet, J.C. (2008) Liquidity Regulation and the Lender of Last Resort, *Banque de France, Financial Stability Review – Special Issue on Liquidity*, **11**, February 2008, 45–52.

Senior Supervisors Group (2008) *Observation on Risk Management Practices during the Recent Market Turbulence*, March 2008.

Senior Supervisors Group (2009) *Risk Management Lessons from the Global Banking Crisis of 2008*, 21 October 2009.

Sinclair, M. (2013) *ALM Risk Management Observations*, Presentation at the ALMA 2013 Summer Conference. Available at: http://www.ukalma.org.uk/.

Slaughter and May (2010) *Basel III, Agreement at Last but Questions Remain*, September 2010.

Sungard (2008) *Liquidity Risk – New Lessons and Old Lessons*. Available at: www.sungard.com.

The Economist (2007) *When to Bail Out: The Case for More Regulation of Banks' Liquidity*, Print Edition, 4 October 2007.

UBS AG (2008) *Shareholder Report on UBS's Write-Downs*, April 2008.

UBS AG (2010) *Transparency Report to the Shareholders of UBS AG*, UBS, October 2010.

Vento, G. and Ganga, P. (2009) Bank Liquidity Risk Management and Supervision: Which Lessons from Recent Market Turmoil?, *Journal of Money, Investment and Banking*, **10**, 78–125.

Index

Page numbers in *italics* denote figures, those in **bold** denote tables.